Renascent Joyce

The Florida James Joyce Series

UNIVERSITY PRESS OF FLORIDA

Florida A&M University, Tallahassee
Florida Atlantic University, Boca Raton
Florida Gulf Coast University, Ft. Myers
Florida International University, Miami
Florida State University, Tallahassee
New College of Florida, Sarasota
University of Central Florida, Orlando
University of Florida, Gainesville
University of North Florida, Jacksonville
University of South Florida, Tampa
University of West Florida, Pensacola

RENASCENT JOYCE

Edited by Daniel Ferrer, Sam Slote, and André Topia

Foreword by Sebastian D. G. Knowles

University Press of Florida

Gainesville/Tallahassee/Tampa/Boca Raton

Pensacola/Orlando/Miami/Jacksonville/Ft. Myers/Sarasota

This book may be available in an electronic edition.

First cloth printing, 2013
First paperback printing, 2014

Library of Congress Cataloging-in-Publication Data
Renascent Joyce / edited by Daniel Ferrer, Sam Slote, and André Topia ;
foreword by Sebastian D. G. Knowles.
p. cm.
Includes bibliographical references and index.
ISBN 978-0-8130-4245-9 (cloth: alk. paper)
ISBN 978-0-8130-6091-0 (pbk.)
1. Joyce, James, 1882–1941—Criticism and interpretation. 2. Influence (Literary,
artistic, etc.)—History—20th century. I. Ferrer, Daniel. II. Slote, Sam.
III. Topia, André. IV. Knowles, Sebastian D. G. (Sebastian David Guy)
PR6019.O9Z78435 2013
823.'912—dc23   2012031966

The University Press of Florida is the scholarly publishing agency for the State
University System of Florida, comprising Florida A&M University, Florida
Atlantic University, Florida Gulf Coast University, Florida International
University, Florida State University, New College of Florida, University of
Central Florida, University of Florida, University of North Florida, University
of South Florida, and University of West Florida.

University Press of Florida
15 Northwest 15th Street
Gainesville, FL 32611-2079
http://www.upf.com

Contents

Foreword

In their admirable introduction to this volume, Messrs. Ferrer, Slote, and Topia lay out the broadest definition of Renaissance writing "immarginable" for the enterprise at hand. As the essays progress, the question becomes one of writing across periods: how the modern engages with the Renaissance, a period that was itself engaged with an early classical period, and how that engagement lends itself to dialectics and dynamism, to reflection and renewal. For many authors in this volume, the Renaissance returns as play, as farce, or even as hoax: neither Pantheon nor pantomime but "Pantheomime." Joyce's writing has its own periodicity, and the central question grows to include Joyce's revisions of his own work as well as the work of others, whether as *avant-texte* (for Saint-Amour and Froula) or as *après-texte* (for Rodriguez and Byrnes). From an engagement with Joyce's critical pasts, the book moves to an engagement with what Saint-Amour calls Joyce's "critical futurities": a Renaissance that is a looking forward as well as a looking back, both a reconciliation and a sundering. What the future holds—the "imprevidibility of the future"—is the crucial uncertainty in all of Joyce's work, and the only way to know that future is to return, again and again, to the past. *Renascent Joyce*, in retracing so many pathways to the lost worlds of Lucretius, Giordano Bruno, the missing *Hamlet* lectures, and what Christine Froula beautifully calls "these whimsical lost umbrellas and blossoming girls of Proyce and Joust," has opened limitless possibilities for future study. It is not for nothing that "Proteus" contains all the letters in "Proust" (to say nothing of all of the letters in "Stupor"): Froula shows, as Van Hulle has before her in this series, that Proust and Joyce share an eddying relation with their past writing. This volume establishes a link between the idea of Renaissance writing and genetic criticism, in the use of a writer's own past ("who will read these written words?"). Renaissance as release, as the expression of possibility. As Beckett said of *Finnegans Wake,* so too one could say of this book's approach to its subject: "it is not *about* something: *it is that something itself.*"

From Birgy's beginning, brimful with dagger definitions of the Renaissance, through Pollock's dynamic presentation of the idea of Renaissance as both *turba* (vortex, a state of turbulence) and *turbi* (turbine, a repeating cyclical process), terms that perfectly apply to *Finnegans Wake,* to the debates in Rodriguez and Byrnes on the inviolability of Joyce's authority, every essay in this collection is written with a verve and conviction that more than matches the Renaissance theme. One might even call them *Tours de force . . .*

Sebastian D. G. Knowles
Series Editor

Abbreviations

We have used the following abbreviations:

FW   plus page and line number. Joyce, James. *Finnegans Wake*. London: Faber and Faber, 1975.

GJ   Joyce, James. *Giacomo Joyce*. Ed. Richard Ellmann. New York: Viking Press, 1968; London: Faber and Faber, 1968.

JJ   Ellmann, Richard. *James Joyce*. New York: Oxford University Press, 1959.

JJA   plus volume and page number. *The James Joyce Archive*. Ed. Michael Groden et al. New York: Garland Publishing, 1978–79.

LI, LII, and *LIII*   Joyce, James. *Letters of James Joyce*. Vol. I, ed. Stuart Gilbert. New York: Viking Press, 1957; reissued with corrections 1966. Vols. II and III, ed. Richard Ellmann. New York: Viking Press, 1966.

OCPW   Joyce, James. *Occasional, Critical and Political Writing*. Ed. Kevin Barry. Trans. Conor Deane. Oxford: Oxford University Press, 2000.

P   Joyce, James. *"A Portrait of the Artist as a Young Man": Text, Criticism, and Notes*. Ed. Chester G. Anderson. New York: Viking Press, 1968.

SL   Joyce, James. *Selected Letters of James Joyce*. Ed. Richard Ellmann. New York: Viking Press, 1975.

U   plus episode and line number. Joyce, James. *Ulysses*. Ed. Hans Walter Gabler et al. New York: Garland, 1984, 1986. In paperback by Garland, Random House, Bodley Head, and Penguin.

Introduction

DANIEL FERRER, SAM SLOTE, AND ANDRÉ TOPIA

R eading Joyce through the lens of the Renaissance may appear to be a
paradox, considering his deep affinities with the medieval. Joyce himself often characterized his work as medieval, and in a discussion with Arthur
Power he championed the "emotional fecundity" of the Middle Ages (Power
110), adding: "in my opinion one of the most interesting things about Ireland
is that we are still fundamentally a mediaeval people, and that Dublin is still
a mediaeval city" (107). This association between Joyce and the Middle Ages
has been taken up and examined by a wide range of critics, such as Umberto
Eco (1982) and, more recently, Lucia Boldrini (2002). Joyce never denied his
affinities with Aquinas and Dante, as well as with the medieval Irish monks
who were "missionary to Europe after fiery Columbanus" (U 3.193).

On the other hand, his praise for the Renaissance, in his Padua essay, "The
Literary Influence of the Renaissance" (1912), is certainly double-edged.
His admiration for the great Renaissance thinkers and artists is tinged with
nostalgia for medieval thought, "that immense (and in many ways admirable) system of philosophy that has its fundamental origins in Aristotelian
thought" (OCPW 187). While recognizing that "the Renaissance arrived like
a hurricane in the midst of all this stagnation¹" (189), he sees in it the direct
origin of "present-day materialism": "Shakespeare and Lope de Vega are to a
certain extent responsible for modern cinematograph" (187–88). If modernism appears as a product of the Renaissance, it is with an ironical twist, as
"the Renaissance has placed the journalist in the monk's chair" (187).

Nevertheless, Joyce's indebtedness to some of the great Renaissance figures, in particular Shakespeare and Bruno, is clearly evident. Philosophically, it is Bruno's dualism ("all power, whether in nature or the spirit, must

create an opposing power without which man cannot fulfil himself" [*OCPW* 188]) that Joyce sees as the central discovery of the Renaissance, and psychologically it is Bruno's spirit of defiance against dogmatism that inspires him: Bruno is one of the most important linking threads for this volume.

It must be clear that the point of juxtaposing Joyce and a Renaissance work is not to document a source or to compare for comparison's sake but rather to suggest new ways of reading Joyce, a renascent Joyce through a Renaissance Joyce. This collection does not intend to deal exclusively with the relations between Joyce and various figures of the historical Renaissance—rather, it is a study of the Renaissance spirit in Joyce: the critical reexamination of tradition, the contextual reinterpretation of the classical heritage, the urge to translate and retranslate from one system of signs to another. Joyce is perhaps the author par excellence of perpetual recontextualization. No single perspective can do justice to such a multifaceted writer: next to the medieval Joyce, the modernist Joyce, the Irish Joyce, the European Joyce . . . we must learn to make room for a Renaissance Joyce.

The relation between Bottom's experience in *A Midsummer Night's Dream* and the beginning of Book III of *Finnegans Wake* is not a discovery,[2] but it is used by Jim LeBlanc to elucidate, so to speak, the question of obscurity in the *Wake* in relation to the Freudian notions of "nodal points" and "navels of dreams." On the other hand, it is not certain, perhaps not even likely, that Joyce ever read the *Hypnerotomachia Poliphili,* so it cannot be considered a direct source (at least until a reinterpreted inscription in the notebooks forces us to review the case); however, as described by Tracey Eve Winton, the similarities of the two projects, at an interval of four centuries and in very different literary environments, force us to revise our conception of the uniqueness of the *Wake.* Winton shows convincingly that both books are "cosmogonic dreams" with a metaphorical descent into the underworld and a corresponding movement toward resurrection. With its journey through classical ruins, rediscovering Latin, Greek, and Arabic inscriptions, this allegorical romance links Renaissance and renascence, while pointing to the babelian world of the *Wake.*

Beyond the particular relationship to some of the great figures of the age, it seems that Joyce's works have many of the characteristics that are generally associated with the spirit of the Renaissance: the refusal of dogmatic thinking, the drive toward universality, the belief that language is not a transparent medium and that form should reflect content, and a writing informed by sheer exuberance—even though the tension between a more medieval

Stephen, skeptical toward Mulligan's praise of a sensual neo-paganism and attached to Christian theological thinking, and a Bloom obsessed by an encyclopedic exploration more akin to the Renaissance spirit, would better reflect the ambiguities of Joyce's position toward these two periods. It is significant that to him, the culmination of Italian civilization was not humanism, Lorenzo the Magnificent, Leonardo, Tiziano, Michelangelo, or Galileo, but the "Roman church," an organization based on an admirable but stifling medieval system that found a way to divert enough of the energies of the Renaissance to produce the splendor and the corruption of Julius II, Leo X, Clement VII, and Alexander VI Borgia.[3]

One must not forget that the very concept of Renaissance is a cultural construct, a projection "by nineteenth-century historians on men of the fifteenth and sixteenth centuries," as Philippe Birgy reminds us in his essay. The past is reinterpreted in the light of the present, and the future is seen as a return of the past. From that perspective it is possible to consider that several Renaissances occurred during the Middle Ages, that the Irish monastic invasion marked a rebirth of culture in Europe, that the whole Renaissance spirit is already present in Dante (Francini Bruni 32), but also that the future must be a Mulliganesque neo-Hellenism. Although Joyce clearly distances himself from any parallel between the revival of classical culture during the Renaissance and the Celtic Revival, such a complex, nonlinear conception of time and history is the key to several aspects of his work. Behind the conflation of cultural trends at work in *Ulysses,* Birgy disentangles a complex cultural mesh of nineteenth-century influences.

Emphasizing the mutability of the category of the "Renaissance," François Laroque shows how Joyce's protean appropriation of Shakespeare in *Finnegans Wake* is a revolutionary reading of the playwright, following from but also expanding upon Renaissance traditions, associating orality, acoustics, songs, and music with the written word and the letter.

Federico Sabatini argues for the presence of another type of Renaissance influence on Joycean writing: Bruno's conception of an "intermedial" and interdisciplinary writing that traverses the styles of different arts. In this way, Joycean ambiguity and equivocation is imbued with the renascent character of the Renaissance. Bruno's philosophy of the coincidence of contraries produces a subversive cosmology where every word constitutes one of the possible and countless centers and where all knowledge stems in the first place from language, thus announcing the unbounded universal space of *Finnegans Wake.*

As both Laroque and Sabatini argue, the Renaissance was a crucible for the rebirth and re-gestation of earlier ideas, and in this light Jonathan Pollock looks at the redefinition of textual atomism, both in the Renaissance with Bruno and in the twentieth century with Joyce. He shows that Epicurean atomism not only provided Renaissance thinkers with a means of challenging the medieval world picture, largely inspired by Aristotle's physics and metaphysics, but has also been a major source of aesthetic and literary innovation from the sixteenth century to the present day. Bruno was at the center of this revival, and it is through Bruno, whose atomism, contrary to Lucretius's materialism, was an animism, that Joyce revisited the Lucretian tradition in *Finnegans Wake*.

The second grouping of texts in this volume is concerned with a more indirect definition of renascence and its relevance to Joyce. With Paul K. Saint-Amour the notion of renascence is ironically twisted through the notion of "backshadowing." Saint-Amour illustrates the importance of false prophecies in *Ulysses* as an embodiment of a pseudo-future that is framed by the past, in contrast with Bloom's open conception of futurity. Exploring the question of untimeliness, he sees in *Ulysses* "a reservoir of unfulfilled futures" that lie dormant, always ready for a renaissance in new contexts, but also an attempt to demystify prophecy and to expose past narratives about the future as historical artifacts.

The temporality of the genetic process is not a linear one either: far from being a sequence of unfolding intentions, it is a complex combination of anticipation and retroaction. Joyce was more aware of this than anyone else, and he made sure that the writing process would leave its mark on the published text and should be the basis of another, never-ending, renaissance taking place in the reading process. He once said to Arthur Power: "Though people may read more into *Ulysses* than I ever intended, who is to say that they are wrong: do any of us know what we are creating? . . . [T]he original genius of a man lies in his scribblings. . . . Later he may develop that talent until he produces a *Hamlet* or a 'Last Supper,' but if the minute scribblings which compose the big work are not significant, the big work goes for nothing no matter how grandly conceived" (Power 102–3). Christine Froula comments on this:

> By this logic, Stephen's "scribbled note" (*U* 3.438) stands in fractal relation to the aesthetic forms that surround it: the epiphanies, *Giacomo Joyce*, "Proteus," the vampire poem of "Aeolus," *Ulysses*, those late last

first scribblings "A way a lone a last a loved a long the" "riverrun"; all Joyce's works. And by this logic, the creator cannot foreknow the creation. Does the fictional Stephen who will write something "in ten years" know whether—or rather *that*—he is (already) scribbling *Ulysses*? Did Joyce know it as he scribbled this scribbler into the NLI draft, Stephen's writing hand a virtual extension of his own?

Incorporating genetic analysis, cultural translation, and narrative poetics in her approach, Froula explores early, generative moments in Joyce's Irish literary renascence. Emphasizing his brief Paris sojourns in 1902–3 and his awareness of contemporary avant-garde French writers and artists (Dujardin, Proust, Mallarmé, Rousseau, Nijinsky) as he drafted and revised the "Proteus" episode in 1917, the essay shows Joyce working to "hellenise" his native island and to render its "modern life" in a "living style"; to give Ireland's history, landscape, and people—and, not least, his own earlier writings—an aesthetic rebirth as, like Proust, his scribblings created from mundane time the "eternity" of the book.

Because of this projective and retrospective logic, the manuscripts, in spite of the wealth of material evidence that they provide, can never be interpreted univocally. The lost *Hamlet* lectures, discussed by Maria-Daniela Dick as an absent center of the genesis of "Scylla and Charybdis" and Stephen's Shakespeare theory, "imitating those lectures, *avant la lettre:* before the text because, within the economy of the text, eight years prior to the lectures of 1912, yet imitative because, in its genetic context, written five years after their delivery," can be taken as emblematic of the status of the genetic document.

Translation is a linguistic Renaissance, and individual translations are a special case of the continuous renascence of the text after its publication, an extreme form of the reinventions that it necessarily undergoes in the hands of its readers. Describing translation in this way is particularly appropriate when the writer himself played an active part in the translation process, which was the case, as Liliane Rodriguez demonstrates, for the French translation of *Ulysses*. She examines evidence of Joyce's role in the French translation of *Ulysses* and demonstrates that he stayed consistently involved all along, from 1921 to 1928, but also that he contributed directly to the French text and that his commitment was driven by his aesthetic program. The text of *Ulysses* is thus reborn for new readers, in a new language, to live a new life in a new cultural and literary context, but this new incarnation casts a new light back onto the English text: insofar as the translation is authorized, it may help us to solve some of the unsolved puzzles of the original (such as the enigmatic U.p.: up).

Robert Byrnes shows, however, that in many instances the recent translation is more faithful to the original than the one that was supervised by Joyce. He also demonstrates that examining a translation—or even better, two different translations of the same text—provides a renewed, *defamiliarizing* perspective on the original.

In all we hope that the essays collected here will occasion even further rebirths within the Joycean realm. One of the merits of this volume will be at least to show that one could apply to Joyce's writings what Panofsky said about Western art: there was one Renaissance but many renascences; and in Joyce's case there are probably as many as there are readers.

Notes

1. "Afa," literally "stifling heat."
2. It was noted a quarter of a century ago by Vincent Cheng (36).
3. According to Alessandro Francini Bruni, Joyce thought that the Italians were not proud enough of their greatest achievement: "L'Umanismo, il Magnifico, Leonardo, Tiziano, Michelangiolo, Galileo. Ma sì, tutta brava gente.... l'opera immortale creata dagli Italiani è la fondazione della chiesa romana.... Roma... papale mi piace di più perché mi fa pensare a quel maiale di Alessandro VI papa fra le braccia della sua amante Lucrezia Borgia; a Giulio II che si preparò la tomba da vivo; a Leone X e Clemente VII, due papi scollacciatissimi e grandi amiconi di Martin Lutero" (32).

Works Cited

Boldrini, Lucia, ed. *Medieval Joyce*. Amsterdam: Rodopi, 2002.

Cheng, Vincent. *Shakespeare and Joyce: A Study of "Finnegans Wake."* University Park: Pennsylvania State UP, 1984.

Eco, Umberto. *The Aesthetics of Chaosmos: The Middle Ages of James Joyce*. Tulsa: U of Tulsa, 1982.

Francini Bruni, Alessandro. *Joyce intimo spogliato in piazza*. Trieste: La editoriale libraria, 1922.

Panofsky, Erwin. *Renaissance and Renascences in Western Art*. 1960. London: Granada, 1970.

Power, Arthur. *Conversations with James Joyce*. 1974. Dublin: Lilliput, 1999.

1

"Another victory like that and we are done for"

Return and Repression of a Greek Spirit in Modernism

PHILIPPE BIRGY

The term "Renaissance" is commonly understood to mean the renaissance of Hellenism. But the possibility of bringing back the spirit of a period presupposes a preliminary work of periodization, a process of cutting up, of incision and extraction. And to achieve this end, it is necessary, in turn, to minimize, not to say altogether repress, the persistent influence of Greek and Roman sources throughout the Middle Ages. Nonetheless, for clarity's sake we propose to adopt as a working hypothesis this rather standard definition of the period, even if we have to deviate from it in the course of our demonstration. We will admit, then, that the term designates that particular construction projected by nineteenth-century historians on men of the fifteenth and sixteenth centuries, and that it refers to that cultural spirit or intention specifically belonging to the period and whose main characteristics would be:

—An affirmation of secular life and of the body meant as a reaction to
pure and exclusive religious spirituality
—A radical shift away from piety and toward secularism
—A return to the cultural model offered by ancient Greece

The reactionary or oppositional element is plainly visible in such a construction. The very concept of "civilization," the historical idea that civilizations succeed one another, rests on it (we shall have to come back to this point at a later stage).

The Renaissance implies a possibility of returning to an original state or to whatever has come and gone before, a cultural past, that of a civilization. But ultimately the term designates the possibility of recovering something much more elusive: a vitality, a density of felt and moral life. Parenthetically, let us notice that what goes by the name of "Modernism" has a lot do with that intensity of life. One finds it in Pound's and Woolf's criticism as well as in the avant-garde manifestos where it is opposed to the dead forms of art consigned to the museum, and one may well suppose that it has also something to do with Stephen's remarks in the *Portrait* about the "heaps of dead language" (*P* 179).

If one envisages the concept of Renaissance in this perspective, one immediately thinks of Mulligan's pseudo-Nietzschean project of a new Hellenism and its attendant rhetoric. But the historical perspective suggested here is equally conjured up in other chapters, such as "Aeolus," for instance, where it appears in the debate in the form of a comparative study of Greek, Roman, Semite, and British civilizations—the whole argument functioning as an allegory of the Celtic Revival. (Here again, the rhetorical character of this discussion is quite explicit: this is a discursive construction, that is, a matter of phrasing things.)

We also find the Greek and Roman element at the beginning of "Nestor," where Stephen checks whether his pupils have learned their history lesson by heart and questions them on a particular event deemed to be crucial to the foundation of the Roman Empire and the defeat of the Greek civilization, namely, the battle of Asculum, which, although it was won by the Greeks, was so costly that it led to their domination by the Romans. The student's ignorance of this official version leaves Stephen wondering about the inscription of such historical periods in our culture, the extent to which they determine the present and the alternative course history might have taken.

This passage is commonly interpreted as an expression of Stephen's desire "to break away from the traditional view of the past as a collection of dead, unalterable moments" (Rickard 5) and as a recognition of the facticity of such history. This is because it is an authoritative and univocal narrative that leaves no space for creative vision, that is, an inferior form of storytelling that does not acknowledge its fictive status.

Can one dispose of the past? That is certainly the question, but one cannot be sure that the text is a plea for liberation from the thralls of history. If history is a succession of different eras of civilization giving way one to another and oriented in one decisive direction, with no possibility of reversing the movement, this means that what has passed is past and gone forever, so there is no reason to fear enslavement, unless it returns. Conversely, if one rejects that construction, one is far less safe from such encroachments.

The historical approach delineated here undoubtedly suggests a deconstruction and reconstruction of the past, as opposed to the monumental version that has become solidified in textbooks and collective consciousness, but the episode offered as an illustration of this trend remains nonetheless extremely ambivalent. The paradox of Asculum, of a victory that spells defeat, is also evoked by Professor MacHugh under the headings "MEMORABLE BATTLES RECALLED" and "THE GRANDEUR THAT WAS ROME" in "Aeolus" (U 7.358 and 7.483). He does so in reference to a lyrical piece written in imitation of the classics, or judged with reference to the classics, and discarded as "a recently discovered fragment from Cicero" (the "title" of this episode or "fragment" being "HIS NATIVE DORIC" [U 7.326]).

But let us consider Mulligan first, since he is the one who opens the book with his praise of Hellenic culture as an antidote to Christianity. It is he again who enjoins Stephen to free himself from the paralyzing forces of negativity and evacuate memories by means of a liberating joy. Conversely, it is Stephen who resists these entreaties, turns down Mulligan's offer of a journey to Greece, and wishes to leave room in his existence for the work of the negative, retaining the "bitter mystery of love" and the "phantasmal mirth" associated with the mother.

The forces of reaction are apparent in this passage: Mulligan labors under the illusion that since Christianity has gained ground by obliterating the heritage of a healthier ancient paganism, all it takes to bring this paganism back is to reject Christianity. The whole cultural arrangement that has preceded it, against which it has been set up as a negative image, will thus be recovered by the systematic rejection of what has superseded it. Yet Mulligan's encomium on motherly waters is derisory, and his Homeric epithets "snotgreen . . . scrotumtightening" hardly a sign of reverence (U 1.78).

Conversely, Stephen remains enthralled by the paralyzing forces of Christianity because he sticks to the form of theological thinking and its set of intellectual representations. In his very execration of the Christian turn of mind, he remains a Jesuit. The Jesuitical "essence" keeps working at cross-purposes in him, and Mulligan diagnoses his illness as the general paralysis of the insane, denoting an incapacity to renew or reinvent himself.

At all events, there are many traces of the revival of a Greco-Roman spirit to be found in *Ulysses* coupled with a praise of sensual life. And one may wonder whether this results from the author's acknowledgment of nineteenth-century culture—a culture that, as it has frequently been remarked, has no form that it can call its own and which ostensibly recycles history (neo-medievalism, pre-Raphaelism, neo-Gothicism, neoclassicism, neo-Renaissance). In this case, what we would simply have here is an instance of artistic appropriation of the figures and *topoi* of the nineteenth century by Joyce as the raw material of his novel.

But alternately, one may argue that we are dealing with a much more personal endorsement, and it would testify to Joyce's conformity with what Jeffrey Perl has described as the implicit goal of the modernist project: carrying out the enterprise that had been aborted at the Renaissance (*Tradition* 20–24; *Skepticism* 4–5).

Among the many signs in the novel that can be related to the classics and the ancients in one way or another, the Joycean reader soon finds that a considerable amount of them lend themselves more easily to the first hypothesis than to the second.

For instance, it is the conflation of revised Nietzschean hubris and Arnoldian culture in Mulligan's speech (although these ingredients are hardly compatible) that convinces the young medical student that he has emancipated himself from Roman Catholic culture and is a fit spokesman for an older culture of heroism. "Ah, Dedalus, the Greeks!" he expostulates in "Telemachus," "I must teach you. You must read them in the original. *Thalatta! Thalatta!* She is our great sweet mother. Come and look" (*U* 1.79–81). Or a little bit further down: "God, Kinch, if you and I could only work together we might do something for the island. Hellenise it" (*U* 1.157).

Vincent Cheng contends in *Joyce, Race and Empire* that the Arnoldian reference that "textures" the whole chapter divides civilizing forces between the Hellenic and the Hebraic/Jewish (154). The Hellenic rationale is culture, while the Jewish turn of mind is based on unquestioned creed: Arnold dismisses it as archaic, rigid, and culturally inferior. This dichotomy, Cheng holds, is part of the ideological justification that ensures the dominant position of the British in Ireland.

This certainly tallies with the way Mulligan debases his own country in order to secure an alliance with the English as a provider of financial support. Thus, he ingratiates himself with Haines by providing him access to an Irish experience that fits into his prejudiced view of the Irish as a picturesque but archaic civilization and eventually confirms the whole ideology that keeps Ireland in a subordinate position.

Yet one is less sure that the Greek inheritance that Mulligan claims for himself is not precisely that of a brutal force which has been superseded by the Arnoldian culture of the more advanced nations. At this point, it seems that Nietzsche comes back at cross-purpose, and with a vengeance, so to speak.

It is our opinion that all this web of allusions refers us to a more complex and contradictory cultural mesh of nineteenth-century influences. It is made up of a quantity of incompatible elements that nonetheless lend themselves easily to amalgamation and derive a rhetorical force from that collusion, which may explain why they have fed the ideology of different counter-public spheres.

Rolf Lessenich notes, for instance, that "the Decadents pitted an idealized neopagan Renaissance against the reality of Victorian dogmatism and restriction, just as the Victorians had pitted idealized Middle Ages against the reality of egoism, capitalism, and materialism. By consequence, the revolutionary Decadents replaced the ideal of Victorian neo-medievalism by a provocative new idealization of Renaissance and Romantic cultures,—culture in the sense of ethical and aesthetic values" (1).

At this point, let us briefly interrupt this inquiry into the cultural sources of the passage to make sure that our position and intention are clear. The discursive trait we wish to emphasize in *Ulysses*—and it is actually a structural trait, at least this is what we will try to demonstrate—is not the denial that a Greek spirit can be brought back. This position is already articulated in "Hades" by Bloom, who is strongly hostile to the hypothesis of a return of the dead either in the spirit or in the flesh. His reticence eventually leads him to thin the possibility of afterlife down to its biological basis ("of course the cells or whatever they are go on living" [*U* 6.780–81]), as if he wished to convince himself of the finitude, or closure, of human life. "Broken heart, a pump after all . . . Old rusty pumps: damn the thing else. The resurrection and the life. Once you are dead you are dead" (*U* 6.673–77). But Bloom's argumentation hardly conceals his anxieties about being haunted by the figures of the past, and it eventually backfires at him in "Circe."

Neither is it the refutation of a Judaic heritage, nor a liberal conciliation or a *discordia concors* ("Greekjew is jewgreek."). Rather, it is the recognition of a dialectic rapport. The issue, then, would be the relationship established with past and dead generations, the modalities under which they can remain present, and the forms under which they can return (be it metempsychosis, theatricality, etc.).

More generally, "Telemachus" and "Aeolus" (and probably "Scylla and Charybdis" as well) problematize the concepts of origin and past, and the very possibility of returning to an original, or even an earlier state, when there remains no "live stock," no living "specimen," to represent them. Eventually it all comes down to this problem, which is the problem of intertextuality: How does one inherit the vitality of another age, be it "dark" or "golden"? How can a contemporary society start anew or enjoy a second lease of life? The question poses itself in terms that are political and cultural as well as linguistic and poetical, for the incantatory force of an invocation relies on the resources of rhetoric, and the past is only accessible through traces that are revived—as pastiche and parody. We are talking about a dialectic here, because the wholesale rejection of a prevailing order or establishment or discursive apparatus or "dispensation," as Yeats would call it, leaves its trace and these traces are still at work, under cover presumably, but vividly present nonetheless, manifesting themselves as insuppressible contradictions, aporia, paradoxes. This is the significance of the throwaway.

But before we can point at a few of these indicators of a paradoxical continuity or permanence, let us briefly return to the cultural dispensation of the late nineteenth century.

Among the voices that speak for the Renaissance in *Ulysses*, a few are particularly conspicuous, namely, the aesthetes, Havelock Ellis and Yeats. All of them trace discursive lines in the text, and they seemingly circumscribe a common project, incorporating recognizable elements such as spiritualism, science, mysticism, individualism, the ideal of the great man, paganism, Greek models, in such a way that, against all odds, it is possible to make these lines or boundaries coincide, to bring them into alignment, in spite of strong divergences. Pater writes in his essay on Leonardo da Vinci: "The movement of the fifteenth century was twofold; partly the Renaissance, partly also the coming of what is called the 'modern spirit,' with its realism, its appeal to experience. It comprehended a return to antiquity, and a return to nature. Raphael represents the return to antiquity, and Leonardo the return to nature. In this return to nature, he was seeking to satisfy a boundless curiosity by her perpetual surprises" (90). Here, it seems that in order to overcome the contradiction that lies in such a theoretical construction, Pater has to dissociate its elements, projecting them in the antithetical figures of Raphael and Leonardo, a Janus of sort, pointing toward both the past and the future.

Because, against all expectations, the "return to nature" is evidently future oriented: this is the modern spirit, the progressive impetus. The suggestion is that in ancient times things were on their way, but the Middle Ages cast man back into ignorance and obscurity, science became suspect, and innovation was discouraged.

In aestheticism, in its insistence that beauty should come first, prior to any moral estimation (rather than the other way round), and that piety and reverence and religious feeling should be detached from the exclusive figure of God in order to be redirected toward a variety of objects, it seems that the Nietzschean note can be heard: not one God but as many gods as necessary, one for each man. Perhaps such an account of aestheticism is amenable to the same criticism: this is precisely the sort of naturalization of aestheticism that has neutralized the subversiveness of Wilde and Pater, the reactionary or reactive assimilation of what was first an attack against Victorianism.

Whatever the case might be, these are the sort of analogies that produce the syncretic theory of "new paganism" to which Gibbons devotes a whole chapter in *Rooms in the Darwin Hotel* (39–67). In these pages he shows how a compilation of arguments drawn from Nietzsche, pragmatism, Bergson, Vico, and Spengler defined such a line of argumentation. (We may note parenthetically that it is the conflation of such cultural trends in the figure of Mulligan that endows this character with his colorful eccentricity.) To return to Gibbons, whose purpose is to trace the consequences of evolutionism in public debate, he remarks, for example, how "mystical and occult doctrines, in particular, gained a new lease of life as a result of the spread of evolutionistic thinking during the late nineteenth century" (7). This juxtaposition of hermeticism, magic, and science may indeed look like a contradiction, when envisaged from a contemporary vantage point where the *doxa* is a form of economical materialism or scientism. But with reference to the Renaissance the contradiction dissolves, as illustrated, for instance, by the figure of Giordano Bruno, whose natural philosophy and vitalism was just taken to be magic, indeed could not be anything but magic.

Yeats also figures prominently in the ranks of the advocates of a neo-Renaissance. *A Vision*, for instance, is an attempt at periodization that unavoidably produces dichotomies, dualisms. But Yeats's endeavor undoubtedly has a special status, first because it flaunts its artificial poetic nature at the reader, but more importantly, perhaps, because the two gyres, antithetical and primary, are interlocked and caught in the same cyclical movement. As one waxes, the other wanes. There may be a mathematical operation of quantification here, but there is also the admission that one principle cannot be separated from its opposite. And that is certainly more to Joyce's taste.

Now, as the reader will certainly have understood, what we wish to emphasize in this essay is the opposite pull, or perhaps the complementary principle that adjoins itself to all attempts at periodization positing and constructing a neo-renascent spirit, or any ancient spirit susceptible to return. It is this dialectic pull (the word *dialectic* can only be used tentatively in such a context) that forces us to recognize a continuity between what is authoritatively given as a series of separate and competing spirits, essences, or principles. This last principle seems to be in conformity with Joyce's general sense of correspondence, his belief in the recurrence of a limited set of archetypes.

Of course, the whole question is fraught with ambiguity. A cyclical conception of history, although opposed to a linear one, also requires that portions of time, episodes, and incidents be isolated before they can be repeated. This is why, insofar as the question of chronological ordering is concerned, the reader should pay attention to all that dramatizes it in *Ulysses:* divisions and subdivisions of the narrative into phases and sequences, for instance (in that respect the belated addition of titles in "Aeolus" is particularly significant), the interruptions of the flow of consciousness (the obstacles causing Bloom's coach to come to a halt in "Hades"), the oversize final sign of punctuation in "Ithaca" and conversely the almost total absence of punctuation in "Penelope" (this in relation to Molly's periods, of course).

As a conclusion, let us sketch briefly some of the ideas that directly follow from the observations made above. First of all, it is tempting to construe heresy as the renascent pause or stance, since it manifests itself by a staunch affirmation of the individual worldview and a refusal to comply with the *doxa*. This is why, in spite of their comical treatment in *Ulysses,* one may argue that Joyce is not taking a radical stand against theosophy, aestheticism, or neo-paganism. Undoubtedly, there is a heretical element in each of them that Joyce acknowledges. One may sense that this is the missing link with the miscarried project that had been revived in the fifteenth century but failed again, for ever since its inception it has only manifested itself in this failure. ("Loyal to a lost cause" [*U* 7.569] is Professor MacHugh's phrase for the spiritual endeavor of the Greeks.)

One may also suggest, albeit more tentatively, that the original intent of Greek philosophy (before it lapsed into metaphysics) had been an inquiry into the conditions of a just government, namely, a democracy. It is a project whose aesthetic counterpart may well be what Bakhtin describes as hetero-glossia, the juxtaposition and fitting together of conflicting fragments of discourse (a flexible method consciously pursued by Joyce). Of course, as every Joycean reader knows, democracy isn't exactly Mulligan's political priority (neither was it Arnold's, Yeats's, Eliot's, or Pound's). Consequently, if we align our definition of modernism with our definition of the Renaissance (that is, viewing the former as a product of the latter), then we must accept that it does not only consist of an emancipation from the fixed models offered by a theological tradition but that it also includes the painful recognition that the concurrent worldviews coexisting in society are irreconcilable without the authoritarian power of the prince or state that silences them. Bakhtin implies that much. He makes it clear that the Renaissance was heir to the spirit of free thinking and impiety that had dominated the carnival, to its leveling trend and its polyphonic contest of voices. But he also recognizes that if literature can become an open forum, most voices can only make themselves heard sporadically, just before their suppression.

Works Cited

Bakhtin, Mikhail. *The Dialogic Imagination: Four Essays.* Austin: U of Texas P, 1982.

Cheng, Vincent John. *Joyce, Race and Empire.* Cambridge: Cambridge UP, 1995.

Gibbons, Tom. *Rooms in the Darwin Hotel: Studies in English Literary Criticism and Ideas 1880–1920.* Perth: U of Western Australia P, 1973.

Lessenich, Rolf. "Ideals versus Realities: Nineteenth-Century Decadent Identity and the Renaissance." *Erfurt Electronic Studies in English* EESE 1/2004, http://webdoc.gwdg.de/edoc/ia/eese/cont24.html (accessed September 12, 2010).

Pater, Walter. *The Renaissance.* Cosimo: New York, 2005.

Perl, Jeffrey. *Skepticism and Modern Enmity: Before and after Eliot.* Baltimore: Johns Hopkins UP, 1989.

———. *The Tradition of Return: The Implicit History of Modern Literature.* Princeton, NJ: Princeton UP, 1984.

Rickard, John. "Stephen Dedalus among School Children: The Schoolroom and the Riddle of Authority in *Ulysses.*" *Studies in the Literary Imagination* 30.2 (1997): 17–38.

2

Textual Atomism in *Finnegans Wake*

JONATHAN POLLOCK

Giordano Bruno of Nola is mentioned over a hundred times in *Finnegans Wake*, under various denominations: "Nolan" (50.05), "Father San Browne" (50.18), "Padre Don Bruno" (50.19), "Fratomistor Nawlanmore and Brawne" (50.22), "O'Breen" (56.32), "Nolans Brumans" (93.01), "brulobrulo" (117.12), "O'Bruin" (128.24), "Bruno Nowlan" (152.11), "Nolan Browne" (159.22), "Davy Browne-Nolan" (177.20), "Brawn . . . Nayman of Noland" (187.24–28), "B. Rohan" (251.33–34), "N. Ohlan" (251.34), "Browne and Nolan" (268.08–9), "*nolens volens*" (271.20), "brune in brume" (271.21), "*Jordani*" (287.24), "Boehernapark Nolagh" (321.09), "The Nolan of the Calabashes" (336.33), "Saint Bruno" (336.35), "the widow Nolan" (380.31), "the Brownes girls" (380.32), "*Nolans*" (418.31), "*Bruneyes*" (418.31), "Bruno and Nola" (488.04), "Nola Bruno" (488.07), "egobruno" (488.08), "alionola" (488.09), "brunoipso" (488.09), "Bruno at being eternally opposed by Nola" (488.10–11), "Bruin" (488.14), "Nolans" (488.15), "Nolan" (490.07), "Mr Nolan" (490.08), "pronolan" (490.15), "Mr Nobru" (490.26), "Mr Anol" (490.27), "Browne" (503.34), "Nolan" (503.35), "brigadier-general Nolan" (567.22), "buccaneer-admiral Browne" (567.22–23), "Bruno Friars" (569.09), "Senior Nowno" (569.32), "Senior Brolano" (569.32), "Browne yet Noland" (599.23), and so forth. The name of Bruno's birthplace, Nola, becomes that of his alter ego, in keeping with the doctrine of the *coincidentia oppositorum* that Bruno and Joyce gleaned from another Renaissance philosopher, Nicholas of Cusa. As Umberto Eco points out, Joyce is given to quoting the following passage from Coleridge's essay on Bruno in *The Friend*: "Every power in nature or in spirit must evolve an opposite as the sole condition and means of its manifestation; and every opposition is, therefore, a tendency to reunion" (Eco 297). "The contraries are in the contraries," says Filoteo in *De l'infinito, universo e mondi* (Bruno 1958, 165), one of three metaphysical dialogues that Bruno published in London in 1584. We know that Joyce was familiar with Toland's eighteenth-century English translation, *An Account of Jordano Bruno's "Of the Infinite Universe and Innumerable Worlds."* And Eco has taught us how Joyce, in *Finnegans Wake*, transposes the doctrine of the coincidence of opposites to the linguistic material itself, by creating thousands of *Mischworte*, or portmanteau words, "the metamorphic nature of [which], of each and every etymology, [is] always on the point of becoming "other," of exploding in new semantic directions" (Eco 272). We all have our favorites, I imagine: "laughtears" (*FW* 15.09), "folsage" (119.05), "playguehouse" (435.02), "truefalluses" (506.18), and Anna Livia's "lothe" in the last pages of the novel (627.33), mixture of *love* and *loath*, for which Jacques Lacan's "hainamoration" (98), is the psychoanalytic equivalent. Such words, "by the coincidence of their contraries[,] reamalgamerge in that indentity of undiscernibles" (*FW* 49.35–50.01) that Bruno attributes to all natural and spiritual powers. However, it is another dimension of Bruno's influence that I wish to examine in this essay: his atomism. In this respect, Bruno is to be seen as participating in the revival, during the Italian Renaissance, of a scientific and ethical doctrine that the early Christians and the medieval church had done their utmost to vilify and suppress.

A manuscript of Lucretius's *De rerum natura* was discovered in an Alsatian monastery in 1417; copies circulated throughout Europe until a printed version appeared in Brescia around 1473. The edition to which Bruno refers is Lambin's, a collation of several manuscripts published in Paris in 1564. Bruno quotes extensively from *De rerum natura* at both the beginning and end of *De l'infinito*, and his trilogy of Latin poems, *De minimo, De monade,* and *De immenso* (1591, in Bruno, *Opera*), is impregnated with the manner and the matter of Lucretius. For the purposes of the present essay, I will limit my analysis of Bruno's doctrine to *De l'infinito*, as this text is quoted in *Finnegans Wake*. My underlying presupposition is that Epicurean atomism not only provided Renaissance thinkers with a means of challenging the medieval world picture, largely inspired by Aristotle's physics and metaphysics, but has also proved to be a major source of aesthetic and literary innovation from the sixteenth century to the present day. That *Finnegans Wake* is itself an experiment in atomist aesthetics becomes plausible when one considers the extent to which Bruno was indebted to the Epicurean tradition.

What are the essential aspects of atomism as they appear in *De l'infinito*, and where does Bruno part company with Lucretius? In his preliminary epistle to Michel de Castelnau, Bruno quotes *in extenso* the famous passage in which Lucretius explains that there is no boundary to the universe, because you can always throw a javelin from wherever you consider that boundary to be (*De rerum natura* [hereafter *DRN*] 1.968–79). Rather than being limited and organized in concentric spheres, the spatial void (*spatium profundum*) is a field or matrix of infinite extent. Bruno goes on to quote the lines (*DRN* 1.998–1007) in which Lucretius describes the universe as the "vast reservoir" (*ingens copia*). And then at the end of the fifth dialogue, he quotes the passage in which the Latin poet deduces the plurality of worlds from the initial premises of his doctrine, namely, that the void has no limits and that it contains an infinite number of microscopic atoms moving eternally in all directions. If this is indeed the case, then their interactions, stochastically speaking, must on rare occasions lead to the creation of worlds similar to our own.

Such hypotheses do not exclude cosmic and ontological unity: for both Lucretius and Bruno, all the worlds are in the same void, and they are all made out of the same matter. But this is also where the two authors differ: in Bruno's cosmology, the atomic *materia prima* is one of two eternal principles, the other being the *anima mundi,* from which derive the individual *animae* that determine the growth and movements of complex bodies. Epicurean atomism is a strict materialism that allows for emergent properties such as life and thought. Bruno's atomism is an animism. Like Pierre Gassendi in the following century, Bruno considers the material atoms to be the secondary cause of things: finite infinity, or Nature, proceeds from infinite infinity, or Providence. The *explicatio* of God in the universe is the counterpart of the *complicatio* of Nature in God.

Apart from this crucial difference, Bruno abides by most of the teachings of the ancient atomists. Like Lucretius, he believes that matter is in a constant state of flux. Although corpuscular in form, atoms move about in waves and currents. They are "endowed with infinite movement by infinitely changing their position from one moment to the next, leaving this body, penetrating that one, joining one composition, then another, passing through this or that formation, [as they cross] the immense space of the universe" (Bruno, *Dialoghi metafisici* 142). Such a supposition leads Bruno to adopt the Epicurean attitude to death. According to Lucretius, "death does not destroy anything to the point of annihilating the corpuscles of matter; it simply dissolves their union, and then joins them to others" (*DRN* 2.1002–3).

Likewise, Bruno claims that "neither ourselves nor any other substance suffer death; for nothing is substantially diminished in reality, but everything, wandering through infinite space, changes its aspect" (Bruno, *Dialoghi metafisici* 52). Joyce renders this idea in the following way: "Yet is no body present here which was not there before. Only is order othered. Nought is nulled. *Fuitfiat!*" (*FW* 613.13–14). As we shall see, these bodies or *corpora* behave in the same way as the letters of the alphabet.

According to Bruno, "Nothing comes to rest, but everything turns and eddies" (Bruno, *Dialoghi metafisici* 102). Renaissance animism and Copernican astronomy taught him that "everything that moves naturally either spins upon itself or turns in circles around another centre" (113). However, even here, and despite very real differences in their premises, his conclusions do not contradict those of the ancient atomists. According to Democritus and Epicurus, the infinite number of atoms that populate measureless space would remain in a state of statistical chaos were they not capable of forming immense whirls and vortices from which emerge worlds such as our own. In several passages of his poem, Lucretius describes how a *turba,* or state of pure atomic turbulence, may give way to regular processes of a cyclical nature, or *turbi,* explaining such transitions by the spontaneous declination of certain atoms. Given that the model of the vortex is not only cosmological but meteorological—Epicurus's *Letter to Pythocles* and the last book of *De rerum natura* are given over to meteorological observations—I can think of no better word than Joyce's "Ouraganisation" (*FW* 86.21) to describe the atheological process by which worlds come into being and enjoy a certain equilibrium despite the atomic fluctuations to which they are prone. *Ouragan* is the French word for hurricane, whirlwind, or tornado. Of course, the similarity in English of the words *whirl, whorl,* and *world* could not have escaped the eager ear of the Punman. However, as so often in *Finnegans Wake,* the fortuitous nature of the pun finds a hidden necessity at another level, in this case at the level of Joyce's use of atomist doctrine. Inasmuch as *Finnegans Wake* is a world in its own right, it corresponds to the non-creationist atomist model: "whorled without aimed" (*FW* 272.04–5), "whirled without end to end" (*FW* 582.20–21). Like the universe of Bruno and Lucretius, it embodies an order, or cosmos, never fully disengaged from an underlying disorder, or chaos: as Joyce himself writes, "every person, place and thing in the chaosmos of Alle . . . was moving and changing every part of the time" (*FW* 118.21–23).

Let it not be objected that Joyce's "chaosmos" is a purely self-contained literary one, whereas the atomists attempted to describe the real world as they imagined it to be. Not only do the formal properties of *Finnegans Wake* reflect the image of the world bequeathed us by relativity theory and quantum mechanics, but *De rerum natura* is by necessity a poem. Only "by writing thithaways end to end and turning, turning and end to end hithaways writing" (*FW* 114.16–17), according to the very definition of *versus*—here given by Joyce in the form of a chiasmus—could Lucretius hope to reproduce the spiraling motion of the cosmic *vertex*. This is why we need to explore the affinities not only between Joyce and Bruno but also between Joyce and Lucretius. When we say of Joyce's novel that it effectuates a kind of verbal sublimation of the physical world and of human history, we are suggesting that Joyce eliminates the difference between language, on the one hand, and physical and historical phenomena, on the other. This is equally true of *De rerum natura,* for the simple reason that the principal paradigm used by Lucretius to explain the ways atoms relate to one another is the Latin alphabet. The "lines of litters slittering up and louds of latters slettering down" (*FW* 14.17) that compose both his poem and Joyce's novel are no different from the atoms that compose Tim Finnegan's ladder. "Every letter is a hard" (*FW* 623.33), and as hard as atoms, and whirled together they form "livestories" or "whirlworlds," as the case may be: "Countlessness of livestories have netherfallen by this plage, flick as flowflakes, litters from aloft, like a waast wizard all of whirlworlds" (*FW* 17.26–29). The word *plage*, here, is not only a mixture of *page* and *plage*, the French word for "beach," but also includes the Latin word *plaga,* which Lucretius always uses to designate the shocks between atoms. Let us then forget Bruno for an instant and see to what extent Joyce may have been directly influenced by the ancient atomists.

I doubt whether the Jesuit education Joyce received at Conglowes Wood and at Belvedere College encouraged a close perusal of *De rerum natura.* Joyce mentions the name of Lucretius just once in *Finnegans Wake,* one of the many classical and biblical names that Shaun inscribes in the margins of his homework (*FW* 306.L3–12). It corresponds to the title "The Uses and Abuses of Insects," a veiled reference to the famous passage in book 4 of *De rerum natura* in which chance sexual encounters are advocated as a remedy to amorous passion. A dozen pages earlier, we find this marginal annotation: "*The Vortex. / Spring of Sprung / Verse. The Ver-tex*" (*FW* 293.L5–8). Apart from the obvious allusions to Wyndham Lewis's Vorticist movement and to Gerard Manley Hopkins's metrical innovations, there is also a play on the Latin words *ver,* "spring," and *vertex,* which is how Lucretius spells *vortex.* Not only does *De rerum natura* begin by a marvelous description of the coming of spring under the aegis of "alma Venus" (*DRN* 1.2)—with whom, be it said in passing, "Alma Luvia, Pollabella" (*FW* 619.15) has numerous traits in common—but, as we have seen, the figure of the vortex is at the very heart of Lucretius's cosmogony.

Epicurus is also mentioned only once. More precisely, the substantive derived from his name and meaning "pleasure-seeker" is associated with the name of his school, the Garden: "epicures waltzing with gardenfillers" (*FW* 475.11). The name of Democritus is conflated with the Greek adjective *kritikos*, meaning "critical" or "capable of judging," to form the word *democriticos* (*FW* 551.31). Here the reference is probably to the Democritus portrayed in the apocryphal Letters of Hippocrates, and whose incessant laughter is in fact a sign of moral reprobation. Joyce would have been familiar with the English transcription of these letters by Robert Burton, alias Democritus Junior, in the prologue to the *The Anatomy of Melancholy*.

References to the principal element of atomism, the atom, are also fairly scant. When Joyce writes, speaking of Anna Livia, that "her birthright pang . . . would split an atam" (*FW* 333.23–24), the allusion is to the biblical story of Adam and Eve and to nuclear physics. Epicurus's atom cannot be split, as the very word means "undividable." Or when he evokes, in the Butt and Taff chapter, "the bounds whereinbourne our solied bodies all attomed attaim arrest" (*FW* 367.28–29), the idea of lying down motionless "at home" is contrary to the property of incessant movement that characterizes the atom in all classical and Renaissance theories. And it would probably be stretching things a little to see a reference to Lucretius's theory of vision and to the emission of simulacra in the expression "the pitcher [may] go to aftoms on the wall" (*FW* 598.20–21). Having said this, neither Cicero nor Lucretius employs the Latinized Greek word *atomi*. Cicero prefers the literal equivalent, *individua*, whereas Lucretius makes use of a whole gamut of periphrastic expressions: *genitalia corpora, corpora prima, primordia caeca, corpuscula materiai, principia*, but above all, *elementa* and *semina rerum*, the semen or seeds of things. If we bear this in mind, it is possible to find references to ancient atomism in a great number of passages from *Finnegans Wake*. Joyce invites us to identify the "humble indivisibles in this grand continuum, overlorded by fate and interlarded with accidence" (*FW* 472.30–31) as being the letters, or *elementa*, that make up the text of the letter addressed by Anna Livia to Earwicker, and which is none other than the novel itself: "a miseffectual whyacinthinous riot of blots and blurs and bars and balls and hoops and wriggles and juxtaposed jottings linked by spurts of speed"

(*FW* 118.28–30). In the work of Joyce, the "spurts of seed," the *semina rerum,* are thus equated with "onanymous letters" (*FW* 435.31) and other such nefarious habits: "yunker doodler wanked to wall awriting off his phoney" (*FW* 464.21–22).

Joyce knew the passage in *Metaphysics* where Aristotle attempts to illustrate the properties of Democritus's atom by referring to the letters of the alphabet (Aristotle 1.4.985b). The capital letters A and N differ in terms of "rhythm" (*rhusmos*), or "figure"; the syllables AN and NA (AN NA is Aristotle's example, not mine!) differ in terms of arrangement (*diathigè*); and the capital letters Z and N exhibit the same form (they are both composed of three lines) but differ in terms of position (*tropè*). The translation of *rhusmos* by "figure" needs to be properly understood. In the fragments that have come down to us of Democritus's writings, *rhusmos* designates not only atomic form (which is immutable) but also the configurations that result from combinations between atoms. As we have seen, such configurations are eminently mobile. If I may be allowed to anglicize Democritus's Greek, the verb he uses to indicate a transformation is not "to metamorphose" but "to metarhythmose": changes of shape (*morphè*) are due essentially to changes of rhythm. It is precisely this aspect that Lucretius highlights when he compares atoms to letters: "in our verses, the order of the characters and their combinations are equally important. Those which designate sky, sea, land, rivers, sun also designate harvests, trees, animals. Most of them, if not all, are identical, but create different meanings according to their positions. The same is true of the corpuscles of matter: if their intervals, pathways, connexions, weight, shocks, meetings, movements, order, position and forms change, then the things they compose must change as well" (*DRN* 2.1013–22). This is precisely what Joyce does to the English language: he alters the "*interualla, uias, conexus, pondera, plagas, / concursus, motus, ordo, positura, figurae*" which commonly determine the letters of words and their distribution in sentences. Frank Budgen reports him as saying: "I always have the right word. What I have to slave over, on the other hand, is the order which best suits the words in the sentence. Each case has an appropriate order" (Eco 255; Budgen 20). On occasions he changes not only the order (*diathigè*) but also the position (*tropè*) of the letters: "Face to Face" is written with the first F turned to the ground and the second F lying on its back, as it were (*FW* 18.36); two capital Fs face each other "at gaze" in the twins' homework chapter (*FW* 266.21); and the capital E of Earwicker is turned onto its side in the form of a dolmen or cricket stumps to become "the meant to be baffling chrismon trilithon sign" (*FW* 119.17). However, what remain remarkably un-altered in *Finnegans Wake*, and which explain why the text is still more or less legible, are the many speech and song rhythms that underlie the words. Just as, in Epicurean physics, the microscopic movements and atomic com-binations are conditioned to a large extent by the macroscopic rhythms and statistical fluctuations they contributed to producing in the first place, the order of the elements that compose each sentence of *Finnegans Wake* is more often than not subject to the speech rhythms of the English language. This is most obvious in the use Joyce makes of popular songs and nursery rhymes, or "nonsery reams" (*FW* 619.18), such as "Humpty Dumpty," "Sing a Song of Sixpence," "This is the House that Jack Built," "Old King Cole," "Tea for Two," and so forth. I've already quoted Joyce's rendering of "Yanky Doodle." The following rendition of "Sing a Song of Sixpence" introduces the leitmotiv of Tristan and Isolde: "the king was in his cornerwall melk-ing mark so murry, the queen was steep in armbour feeling fain and furry, the mayds was midst the hawthorns shoeing up their hose, out pimps the black guards (pomp!) and pump gun they goes" (*FW* 134.36–135.04). Or, if you prefer: "Three for two will do for me and he for thee and she for you" (*FW* 584.10–11).

Of course, the "whirlworld" of the atomists is "ouraganised" as a result of purely chance factors, such as atomic deviation and emergent forms of auto-regulation. There is no providential author poring over his material in search of the best possible order. In this respect, Joyce's atomism is much closer to Bruno's than to Lucretius's. Nevertheless, from the reader's point of view, *Finnegans Wake* is a dream experience in perfect keeping with the way Lucretius himself explains the power of dreams. The atomists believed that every material thing continuously emits from its surface invisible mem-branes, or simulacra; and when a sufficient number of simulacra affect the eye, they provoke vision in the form of an *imago*. The air is full of such simu-lacra, and when we shut our eyes or when we sleep they are liable to tickle the atomic tissue of our very soul. Lucretius points out that people in the same room may think and dream of completely different things; our minds are constantly penetrated by all manner of simulacra, but we are only aware of those we pay attention to, either because we expect to see them or because they correspond to our interests and passions. Now, is not this precisely the experience of all readers of *Finnegans Wake*? The number of meanings and images are potentially infinite. We only perceive those we want to see, or are capable of seeing.

Works Cited

Aristotle. *Aristotle's Metaphysics.* Ed. W. D. Ross. 2 vols. Oxford: Clarendon, 1924.

Bailey, Cyril. *Titi Lucreti Cari De rerum natura libri sex.* Oxford: Clarendon, 1947.

Bruno, Giordano. *Dialoghi italiani.* Vol. 1, *Dialoghi metafisici.* Ed. Giovanni Gentile. Florence: Sansoni, 1958.

———. *Opera latine conscripta.* Ed. F. Fiorentino, F. Tocco, H. Vitelli, V. Imbriani, C. M. Tallarigo. 3 vols. Naples-Florence: Morano, 1879–91.

Budgen, Frank. *James Joyce and the Making of "Ulysses."* Bloomington: Indiana UP, 1960.

Burton, Robert. *The Anatomy of Melancholy.* Ed. H. Jackson. 3 vols. London: Dent, "Everyman Library," 1932.

Eco, Umberto. *L'œuvre ouverte.* Trans. C. Roux de Bézieux. Paris: Seuil, 1965.

Epicurus. Letters. *Diogenis Laertii Vitae philosophorum.* Ed. H. S. Long. Oxford Classical Texts, vol. 2 (book 10). Oxford: Clarendon, 1964.

Hippocrates. *Opera omnia.* Ed. E. Littré. 10 vols. Amsterdam: Hakkert, 1962.

Lacan, Jacques. *Encore: Le séminaire, livre 20.* Paris: Seuil, 1999.

3

James Joyce and Giordano Bruno

An "Immarginable" and Interdisciplinary Dialogue

FEDERICO SABATINI

Joyce's interdisciplinary and "intermedial" method famously relies on a mixture of literary genres and kinds of narratives, as well as on a concoction of techniques derived from various artistic disciplines, such as painting, sculpture, music, and cinema. As in *Ulysses,* where a different art or discourse was used to shape each chapter, in Joyce the structural laws of visual arts are always employed to shape the writing itself and the structure of the texts. It is my intention here to connect this stylistic peculiarity to Giordano Bruno, who also advocated a tangled combination of arts and sciences and whose work was overtly praised by Joyce, starting from his essay "The Philosophy of Bruno" (1903) and later becoming a philosophical source for the structure and language of *Finnegans Wake.* Besides the elevated number of references to Bruno in the *Wake,* Joyce especially created the mot-valise "immarginable" (*FW* 4.19), a term that summarizes the whole philosophy and subversive cosmology of Bruno, containing ideas of margin and "lack of margin" together, absolutism and relativity, ideas of innumerability, of thinkable and unthinkable, imaginable and unimaginable, illimitable imagination for an unbounded universal space. According to Bruno, in fact, there were infinite worlds that spread throughout space, a structure of the universe made of suns and clusters of suns circling in grand orbits without any fixed center. The theory, which profoundly influenced the structure of *Finnegans Wake,* strikingly fascinated Joyce, who was also sympathetic to Bruno's heroism (in relation to the Inquisition) and intellectually attracted to "his constant and inextinguishable appetite for every form of experience"

(Pater 234–44) and to his atomistic coincidence of the infinitesimally large and the infinitesimally small, as in the words on Bruno by Walter Pater:

> Considered from the point of view of a minute observation of nature, the Infinite might figure as "the infinitely little"; no blade of grass being like another, as there was no limit to the complexities of an atom of earth, cell, sphere, within sphere. But the earth itself, hitherto seemingly the privileged centre of a very limited universe, was, after all, itself but an atom in an infinite world of starry space, then lately displayed to the ingenuous intelligence, which the telescope was one day to verify to bodily eyes. (239–40)

Bruno's atomistic theory and assertion of an ubiquitous center in a constantly enlarging circumference of the universe inform both the themes of his works and, especially, his style, so as to strikingly resemble Joyce's literary method, in which the style itself was a semantic vehicle for the content. Starting from his critical essays, it is well known that Joyce had a keen interest in the Renaissance, considering it a breakthrough period and a phase of amazing innovations. In "The Universal Literary Influence of the Renaissance" (1912), the writer praises the "struggle against scholastic absolutism" and against that "system of philosophy that has its fundamental origins in Aristotelian thought." He considers the Renaissance as a "hurricane amidst all (this) stagnation" and praises the "tumult of voices" that arose throughout Europe, and he particularly refers to Bruno's theory of contraries: "Giordano Bruno himself says that all power, whether in nature or the spirit must create an opposing power without which man cannot fulfil himself, and he adds that in every such separation there is a tendency towards a reunion. The dualism of the great Nolan faithfully reflects the phenomenon of the Renaissance" (OCPW 188). The theory is then further enacted by Joyce in the end of the essay, where he makes the *Maximum* and the *Minimum* coincide in a manner very akin to Bruno's: "All modern conquest, of the air, of land, the sea, disease, ignorance, melts, so to speak, in the crucible of the mind and is transformed into a little drop of water, into a tear" (OCPW 190).

Joyce simultaneously presents the antithesis between a vast space and a large portion of matter (the air, the sea) and the infinitesimal part of them, symbolized by a drop of water, which nevertheless contains the whole and can be taken as the whole. The passage, besides re-creating Bruno's ideals and style, also evokes notions of pantheism and, to an extent, mirrors Bruno's theory of the human point of view with respect to the philosophical debate between absolutism and relativism, the same one that is crucially enacted in *Ulysses* and *Finnegans Wake*. According to the philosopher, the static and central world conceived by Aristotle had no more reason to exist, since the plurality of worlds in the infinite universe caused it to be that every world constituted one of the possible and countless centers. At the same time, the human being couldn't possibly be at the "center of the universe," because of the plurality of such centers. According to Bruno, man was still the absolute center because of his personal and irreplaceable vision, because of his being the only source of representation of the world and of the universe. For this uniqueness, therefore, the point of view must be considered *absolute*. And yet, at the same time, all other points of view are also to be considered absolute centers, so as to become at the same time relative ones. Such a relativity, which is not at odds with its absoluteness, means that although a viewpoint identifies with no other one, it is simultaneously in a constant relation with all other potential viewpoints. According to Bruno, the infinity of the universe and of the points of view had forcibly to mirror the infinity of our mental being, of our infinite potential knowledge and of a thought that appears as unlimitedly self-nourishing. In the same way, the universe continuously changes, due to a conception of matter that never disappears but becomes something else within the perennial movement, recombination, and fusion of the atoms. Consequently, an absolute vision of space goes together with a relative one: the all-encompassing space of the universe is retraceable not only in the smaller places in which our thought is enacted but even in the smaller particles of them. That Joyce was interested in such a vision of the great space merging with the smallest places is now well known as a major influence both for his re-creation of phenomenological space and, most notably, for the non-closing nature of *Finnegans Wake*, with its liquid and continuous structure in which all particles of language, like atoms for Bruno, continually move and co-create new semantic beings for an inexhaustible period of time.

The philosophy of the coincidence of contraries, which informs all of Bruno's thought and aesthetics, becomes in *Finnegans Wake* a hyperbolized poetics of the "cocoincidences" (*FW* 597.01), namely, a poetics that involves the paradoxical, and yet realized, aim of making coincidences themselves converge, in a sort of continuous chiasmus relationship that unifies, by means of repetition and reversal, series of binary oppositions. These, therefore, are all reunited in order to re-create the infinite complexity of the real world and of the human thought, the "varietas," the infinite and never graspable variety of human experience. Most importantly, such a cosmological philosophy finds its linguistic counterpart in a style that, in both authors, appears to be surprisingly similar. Both Bruno and Joyce operated a real breakthrough with respect to their previous literary traditions, and both employed inventive weapons that, despite their different backgrounds, show a strong intellectual affinity. Bruno's *coincidentia oppositorum* and his *varietas* of experience could be considered as two forces that guide Joyce's writing as well, as they are both embodied in a language that is the equivalent *signifier* of such a complex and revolutionary vision of life and art. More precisely, there are three main aspects of Bruno's language and literary style that I would like to underline and to compare to Joyce: first, *Bruno's poetics of the enlarging style*, which, by mirroring his cosmologic expansion, presupposes the literary self-enlarging form of the *dialogue*, as well as the invention of new words, the use of amplified figures of speech, particular lexical choices, and a vortex-like use of syntax; second, the *mixture of literary genres*, conceived by Bruno as an instrument to aesthetically achieve the "varietas" of human existence; and third, the above-mentioned *overlapping of word and image*, which presupposes a mixture of literary techniques and visual techniques deriving from spatial arts.

The infinity of the universe and the infinity of a "universal knowledge" (Bruno, *Expulsion* 135) are for Bruno two parallel concepts; in fact, his investigation in cosmology was never separated from a more general gnoseologic investigation. That is why he was searching for the perfect idiom to re-create this kind of world, a language meant to be plastic and "visible" so as to express the infinite world of our existence, the inexhaustible potential and enlargement of knowledge, and, especially, the ever-growing variety of reality:

> . . . he who sees unity, understands unity, the one and the number, the finite and the infinite, the end and goal of intelligence, and the *abundance* of all things; and he's able to perform all things, not only in the universal but also in the particular. So since there is no particular that is not contained in the universal, there is no number in which unity is more truly contained than number itself. Thus then, Jove, without difficulty or annoyance, provides for all things, in all places and times, just as being and unity are necessarily found in all numbers, in all places, in all times and atoms of time, places, and numbers; and the only principle of being is in infinite individuals who were, are, and will be. (Bruno, *Expulsion* 136)

To express such a "varietas," such an "abundance of all things," Bruno chose the form of the dialogue, the only one being infinitely expandable and potentially infinite, namely, open to the "not yet said," "not-yet-discussed," "not-yet-known," "not-yet-gnosible." That gnoseology was characterized by infinity (like cosmology) is made evident by the fact that all knowledge stems, in the first place, from language, which Bruno conceived in its infinite permutations and combinations. For this main reason, Bruno (like Joyce) could not accept the restrictions imposed by rhetorics and classical poetics. He felt that language had infinite possibilities, that it developed in time and space, and that it was not to be seen as an instrument to communicate but it could represent itself communication. Experience to be communicated *in* language and not *through* language: a revolutionary assumption that will find its natural echo in Beckett's famous description of *Finnegans Wake* as being "not *about* something; *it is that something itself*" (Beckett 14). For this reason, besides the mixture of genres and of media, Bruno even declared the possibility, and the urge, to invent new meanings and new voices when a new form of thought needed them: "We will be of use when we will extract from the abyss of darkness the dogmas of the sages, with their ancient words, for the sake of the novelty of things, and with these words taken from the source, we will be authors of new voices" (Ordine, *La cabala dell'asino* 149). That the "new voices" are not only a metaphorical expression for new ideas in opposition to the scholastic and rhetorical ones is then explained by the extreme innovative use of language enacted in all his vernacular works, in which words, as expressed many times in *The Expulsion of the Triumphant Beast* and in *The Heroic Enthusiasts*, are new voices, new instruments to be molded for our specific purposes.

These considerations are notably mirrored in *Finnegans Wake*, both from a thematic point of view and from a stylistic and linguistic one, reproducing and condensing Bruno's ideas concerning the creation of new voices by means of new ideas and, simultaneously, new ideas by means of new words:

> The mixer, accordingly, was bluntly broached, and in the best basel to boot, as to whether he was one of those lucky cocks for whom the *audible-visible-gnosible-edible* world existed. That he was too cognitively conatively *cogitabundantly* sure of it because, living, loving, breathing and sleeping morphomelosophopancreates, as he most significantly did, whenever he thought he heard he saw he felt he made a bell clipperclipperclipperclipper. (*FW* 88.04–11; italics mine)

This sought-after world appears here to the "lucky cock" in its elements of visibility and audibility, two categories that, it is well known, inform the writing of Joyce from its beginning to the climax of *Finnegans Wake*. Such a world is also defined as "gnosible," referring to the possibility of knowing and comprehending it, namely, the possibility of making it exist through thought and reflection. At the end of the compound adjective we find the word *edible*, which, on one hand, refers to a metaphorical physical relationship between man and the world, but on the other hand, it may also represent an explicit reference to Bruno, who identifies the variety of desires and of intelligences with the variety of tastes (especially in *Ash-Wednesday Dinner*). The connection to Bruno is further reinforced in the continuation of the passage in which the lucky man is first described as "cogitabundantly sure" and then as a person who "morphomelosophopancreates." "Cogitabundantly" could be seen as the philosophical Joycean counterpart of Brunonian "immarginable": the latter describing the infinitely imaginable universe and knowledge, and the former the infinite dimensions of our thought. As an adverb, "cogitabundantly" explicitly unifies the Latin *cogito*, the noun *abundance*, and the adverb *abundantly*, so as to refer both to an overabundance of thought (which mirrors the overabundance of the "varietas" of reality) and to an "abundantly thoughtful" awareness that comes from the many-sided human experience, expressed by that list of vital activities of "living, loving, breathing and sleeping." All of these activities are meant to lead to that complex kind of creation which Joyce expresses in the long mot-valise "morphomelosophopancreates." Besides the ironic reference to the "pancreas" which reinforces the edible character of knowledge, the verb contains the Greek root word *morpho* ("shape"); *melo*, which means "music" but potentially contains references to the minor genre of "melodrama"; "philosophy"; "Sophocles," that is, a reference to drama (both canonical tragedy and minor genres as "satire," of which Sophocles was also an author with *The Tracking Satyrs*). All of these elements of knowledge, deriving from different disciplines (philosophy, drama, literature, and music), are able to shape a "creation" which in Joyce become a "pancreation." Interestingly enough, there are countless references to the myth of Pan in Bruno and, as I'll argue, in Joyce too. As noted by Maria Pia Ellero, Bruno drew on the Neoplatonic tradition of the Renaissance that interpreted the myth of Pan as a symbol of the multifarious aspect of nature, often in opposition to Jove. As in Agrippa, the two myths were taken together to achieve a whole portrait of the universe: the sitting Jove to signify the immutability of God, and the standing Pan, being also in motion, to signify the course of nature and the evolution of the world. Such an idea provided a fervent enthrallment to Bruno, who advocated a "stability within mutation" together with a "mutation within stability" (Bruno, *Expulsion* 181; later reenacted in *Finnegans Wake* as "stabimobilism" [*FW* 308.39]), another dichotomy to be reunited by means of *coincidentia oppositorum*. This is mostly evident in *The Expulsion of the Triumphant Beast*, and especially in its third dialogue, when Saulino and Sofia discuss the immanent presence of the divinity in the physical world ("natura est deus in rebus," i.e., "by nature God is in things"), revealing Bruno's pantheistic approach to God and nature: "Whence all of God is in all things (although not totally, but in some more abundantly and in other less). . . . Because just as Divinity descends in a certain manner, to the extent that one communicates with nature, so one ascends to divinity through nature, just as by means of a life resplendent in natural things one rises to the life that presides over them" (236–37). The simultaneous movement from God to things and from things to God, typical of pantheism, is strikingly reinforced, sometimes with a distancing irony, by Joyce. In *Portrait*, for example, we are shown Stephen while experiencing such an ecstatic moment of contemplation and participation to a transcendental reality: "And he remembered an evening when he had dismounted from a borrowed creaking bicycle to pray to God in a wood near Malahide. He had lifted up his arms and *spoken in ecstasy* to the sombre nave of the trees, knowing that he stood on holy ground and in a holy hour. And when two constabulary men had come into sight round a bend in the gloomy road he had *broken off his prayer* to whistle loudly *an air from the last pantomime*" (P 252; italics mine).

Stephen is immersed in nature and able to pantheistically feel the presence of God in all things ("holy hour"; "holy round"), a concept that is reinforced by the symbolic transformation of the forest into a church, whose naves are delimited by trees. The effect is, however, ironical, since the experience ends in the anticlimax of the sudden interruption: the mystical dialogue with God is violently substituted by the music of a pantomime and, more precisely, by the music of "the last pantomime," that is, the one that could more easily and mechanically get impressed in his memory. The combination, and simultaneous presentation, of pantheism and pantomime will be a constant motif in *Finnegans Wake*. As Cheryl Herr has argued, although Joyce criticized the excessive simplicity of the minor theatrical genres, he had nonetheless a passion for them, especially due to their intertextual character:

Like Joyce's works, which forever quote themselves to the consterna-
tion of many readers, the theatre of Joyce's day was *highly and self-con-
sciously intertextual*. Melodrama begat burlesque, pantomime begat
extravaganza, pantomime quoted burlesque, and music hall interpen-
etrated the lot. . . . Joyce exploits this *intertextuality of form* in composing characters, showing the presence in their thought and behavior
of material that emanates from the *self-quoting stage*. (120–21; italics
mine)

As I've stated before, in *Finnegans Wake* a vast number of terms are con-
structed with the prefix "pan" and, apart from the very relevant meaning of
panning as in photography or cinema, they all refer to a general idea of all-
pervasiveness, a spatiotemporal amplification that turns a single unilateral
concept into a hyperbolized concept of infinity and "immarginable vast-
ness": "pancosmos" (*FW* 613.12), "pancosmic urge" (394.32), "panthoposo-
pher" (365.05), "panssion" (230.19), "panful" (140.31), "panesthetic" (173.18),
and the very famous and very Brunonian "panaroma of all flores of speech"
(143.03). The more evident combination of pantheism and pantomime,
however, occurs in two instances referring to the Gaiety Theatre, which
was famous for its annual Christmas pantomime and which becomes very
meaningful if set in this dialogue with Bruno: "noblewomen flinging every
coronetcrimsoned stitch they had off at his *probscenium,* one after the others, inamagoaded into *ajustilloosing* themselves, in their *gaiety pantheomime*"
(*FW* 180.01; italics mine).

"Pantheomime," combining the cult of Pantheon ("the totality of gods")
with "pantomime," underlines the all-pervasive nature of the popular theatrical genre characterized by an intersection of other genres and disciplines
and of sociopolitical motives, which so deeply fascinated Joyce. On one
hand, God manifested himself in all the phenomena of the universe, and
on the other hand, the pantomime covered all aspects of life and the arts,
"adjusting" all their static and "still" elements with their constant "loose-
ness." In another Brunonian passage, Joyce speaks of a "pantaloonade" (pantomime and harlequinade) and especially of a "*Pantharhea* at the Gaiety,"
which explicitly refers to "panta rei," the riverrun-like conception of becoming in Heraclitus (another source for Bruno's philosophy), and ironically
hints at "diarrhea," focusing again on the physical and visceral aspect of
biological life which was not at all avoided by Bruno himself in his countless
metaphorical images of eating and digestion. The dialogue with Bruno here

is dual: on one hand, "pantheomime" converses with his representation of the cult of the Pantheon; on the other, it communicates with Bruno's urge to achieve the same concoction of genres and of "all flores of speech" to re-create reality. Explicit references to the Pantheon are also made in *The Expulsion of the Triumphant Beast*, where the Pantheon is a signifier for a kind of divinity that assumes all the characteristics of the single gods, so as to reverse and, at the same time, to parallel the pantheistic assumption of a divinity that communicates itself by descending upon the manifold elements of nature.

Like Joyce's "intertextual pantomime," Bruno's writing is characterized by a constant intersection of literary forms (*"the same tragedy or comedy is being directed and acted in the same theatre"* [Bruno, *Expulsion* 159]), which purposely included a treatment of the so-called minor genres. In order to find new stylistic means that could express his new vision of man and of the world, Bruno also showed a keen interest in burlesque or erotic litera-ture, which was obviously deemed inferior to poetry. In *The Expulsion*, So-fia explains that the Gods also read Aretino and burlesque poetry, and she advocated the necessity of a "communal library" containing the manifold representation of all things:

> There is no lesson, no book, that is not examined by the gods and that, if it is not altogether without salt, is not used by the gods and that, if it is not altogether senseless, will not be approved and chained to the shelves of a public library ("biblioteca commune"). For they take delight in the multiform representations of all things and in the mul-tiform fruit of all minds, because they are pleased with all things that exist and with all representations that are made; they are no less con-cerned that these should exist, and give orders and permission that they be made. (Bruno, *Expulsion* 160)

Comic literature, blended with the serious one, was for Bruno a source for the above-mentioned "varietas," and this interest also mirrored his rebel-lion against the static dogmas of classicism and Petrarchism in literature. As Giorgio Bàrberi Squarotti has argued, Bruno's main influences were writ-ers considered "minor," such as Berni, Aretino, Doni, and Folengo, authors of comic, burlesque, or erotic literature that offered him an assortment of styles and devices that he reenacted and reinterpreted in his own writing. Among these, it is worth remembering the use of vernacular proverbs, ob-scene metaphors, and parodic caricatures which fueled a revolutionary use of lexicon, and especially an extremely innovative use of syntax, where the long sentences were disarticulated in numerous subordinate clauses that lost their connection. The result was an extreme use of hypotaxis, and especially of the figures of *accumulatio* and of *enumeratio,* that is, series of long listings of concepts, often disharmonious or even antithetical, which tended to dissolve the sentence into an open linguistic construct made of reciprocal influences of all its single units. This led to an amplifying stylistic accumulation of speeches, techniques, and registers which, in their totality, were not only a stylistic means but reflected, more poignantly, the manifold and potentially infinite activity of the human thought, as vast and limitless as the innumerable worlds in the infinite universe.

Related to this urge to combine different stylistic approaches to literature and to philosophy, Bruno's language combines images, letters, symbols, and numbers, which were all masterfully fused in his new stylistic constructs. Hence, Bruno's proclamation of a "filosofia-pittura" (philosophy-painting; see Ordine, Introduction 151, and Ciliberto 120) which had to teach people "to see thought" and to combine objects and ideas in order to set a system of direct correspondence between the daily material world and the immaterial world of thought. This brings us back to the source of this analysis, which has started with a reflection on Joyce's concoction of literature and visual arts, namely on his visual "poetographies" (*FW* 242.19) and "*verbivocovisual*" (*FW* 341.19) writing, which derived scenes from painting, relief from sculpture, and movement, as it is well known, from cinema. Joyce's employment of all these devices implies a disintegration and a simultaneous recombination of literary genres and of artistic techniques, which had in fact to be deconstructed and further recombined in new "concreations" (*FW* 581.29) in order to achieve the same "varietas" sought after by Bruno. This is also expressed in the following famous passage inspired by Vico, which, nonetheless, seems also to contain a forceful Brunonian echo: "smeltingworks exprogressive process, (for the farmer, his son and their homely codes, known as eggburst, eggblend, eggburial and hatch-as-hatch can) receives through a portal vein the dialytically separated elements of precedent decomposition for the verypetpurpose of subsequent recombination" (*FW* 614.31).

The amplifying "meltingworks of exprogressive progress" deals with elements that come directly from a "portal vein," another reference to bodily functions and biological life in the association with "dialysis" (in Greek "dissolution"), that is, a physical procedure that separates one or more substances melted in a liquid and, from 1854, also the medical procedure to cleanse the blood in presence of the kidneys' failure. Most significantly, however, these elements are said to be *dialytically* separated, in order to be recomposed in further reconfigurations. The innovative adverb unifies a series of other adverbs: "dialectically" and "dualistically" (referring to Bruno's *coincidentia oppositorum*), "deistically" (in opposition to *fideism* and closely related to *pandeism*, for which God is the universe), and "dialogically," namely, following the open and unlimited procedure of the dialogue. This could be referred to the same principle that pushed Bruno to choose the dialogue as his privileged writing form, but also to the same purpose that Bruno and Joyce had in creating a "dialogue" between all forms of languages, of experiences, and of arts. Like Joyce, Bruno employs several artistic and literary methods to signify, refer to one another, and to indicate an integrated vision of the universe and of all the elements within it. In order to pursue his desire to "teach people to see thought," Bruno advocated a philosophy-painting, a discipline that had to make the invisible become visible and the unspoken become spoken, or even "dialogical." His works contain a vast number of references to the relationship between painter and philosopher, because, for him, they both had to use images in order to re-create reality and to uncover the shadow or the veil that makes us see only partially through it. In *The Ash-Wednesday Dinner*, for instance, Bruno metanarratively speaks of the work as a "tela," a word that stems from the Latin *textum* and refers to the plot and to the textual web but also to the art of painting, since *tela* in Italian also means "canvas," or, by extension, "painting." *The Ash-Wednesday Dinner*, in fact, is often described as a particular form of portrait (Ordine, Introduction 147), while in *The Expulsion* Bruno proclaims the impossibility to go beyond "some mysterious and undetermined features and shadows, as for the painters" (167). The function of the image is to mediate between the visible and the invisible, to suggest a possibility to gain free access to the world of ideas and to a kind of knowledge that comes only from direct observation of and participation with the natural phenomena of the unlimited universe. Bruno underlines the fragmentary nature of pictorial reproductions, the nuances of colors, and the partiality of the reproduced features. In *The Cabbala* he praises the value of details, once more by setting them in direct relation with dialogue. He affirms that this work ("operetta") contains "a description and *a painting*," and that for such painting to be effective, it is sufficient to re-create a "single" detail, such as, for instance, "one head without the rest of the body." Bruno considers an excellent "artifice" to "paint" a single hand, a foot, an eye, a "swift ear." The importance of detail and of a prose that transcends the classical distinction between static descriptions and dynamic narration are also and famously typical in Joyce. Opposite to long and seemingly exhaustive descriptions, this kind of writing turns the readers into spectators, increases their fantasy, and allows them to take an active part in the aesthetic and philosophical process. In the incompleteness of the text, of the description and of the images, the readers can pick up a profound meaning, always different and always partial. The hermeneutic procedure and the construction of meaning become infinitely susceptible to multiple interpretations and unlimited visualizations, as it clearly happens in *Finnegans Wake*. In *The Heroic Enthusiasts,* Cicada and Tansillo discuss the impossibility of a single unilateral interpretation and suggest that the meaning will be disentangled, if it might ever be, only through time and space, a procedure that fiercely resembles our still-vibrant and "immarginably" open readings of *Finnegans Wake:*

TANSILLO: *This seems more like an enigma than anything else, and I do not feel sure that I can explain it at all;* yet I do believe that it means that the same fate vexes, and the same torments both the one and the other—that is, *immeasurably,* without mercy and unto death, *by means of various instruments or contrary principles,* showing itself the same whether cold or hot. But this, it seems to me, requires longer and special consideration.

CICADA: Let us go, and *by the way we will seek to untie this knot—if* possible.

Works Cited

Barberi Squarotti, Giorgio. *Parodia e pensiero: Giordano Bruno.* Milano: Greco e Greco, 1997.

Beckett, Samuel. "Dante . . . Bruno. Vico . . Joyce." Samuel Beckett et al., *Our Exagmination Round His Factification for Incamination of Work in Progress.* 1929. London: Faber, 1972.

Bruno, Giordano. *The Expulsion of the Triumphant Beast.* Trans. Arthur D. Imerti. Lincoln: U of Nebraska P, 1964.

———. *The Heroic Enthusiasts, An Ethical Poem.* Part the First. Trans. L. Williams. Project Gutenberg. http://www.gutenberg.org/files/19817/19817-8.txt (accessed 20 Oct. 2008).

Ciliberto, Michele. *Introduzione a Bruno.* Bari: Laterza, 1996.

Ellero, Maria Pia. "Comment on" Giordano Bruno, *Spaccio della bestia trionfante,* in *Opere italiane.* Torino: UTET, 2002.

Herr, Cheryl. *Joyce's Anatomy of Culture.* Urbana: U of Illinois P, 1986.

Ingegno, Alfonso. *Filosofia e cosmologia nel pensiero di Giordano Bruno.* Firenze: La Nuova Italia, 1978.

Ordine, Nuccio. *La cabala dell'asino: Asinità e conoscenza in Giordano Bruno.* Napoli: Ligouri, 1987.

————. Introduction to Giordano Bruno, *Opere italiane.* Torino: UTET, 2002.

Pater, Walter. "Giordano Bruno." *Fortnightly Review* 46, no. 272 (1889): 234–44. Project Gutenberg. http://www.gutenberg.org/etext/4228 (accessed 25 Oct. 2008).

4

The Dream and the Wake

An Alchemy of Words and Scenes
in the *Hypnerotomachia Poliphili* and *Finnegans Wake*

James Joyce's interest in François Rabelais is well documented. But in his 1959 study of Joyce's sources, *The Books at the Wake,* James Atherton makes no mention of one of Rabelais' own principal sources of inspiration, the 1499 erotic dream novel, the *Hypnerotomachia Poliphili.*[1] This incunabulum, published anonymously at the humanist press of Aldus Manutius in Venice, is noteworthy for its beautiful illustrations yet historically little read because it is written in an invented language. In research to date I have not discovered any confirmation that Joyce—Italophile as he was—did read the *Hypnerotomachia,* but certain lines and themes in *Finnegans Wake* strongly suggest that he had it in mind.[2] Superficial similarities of language and dream form stirred me to examine the parallels between the two books. While no short essay could do justice to two books of rival complexity and literary significance, I will outline some general similarities that can cast new light on both works. Assuming a readership more familiar with *Finnegans Wake,* I will focus the comparison through the *Hypnerotomachia* (HP).

This unique title is compounded of three Greek roots: *hypnos,* a dream; *eros,* love; and *machia,* strife or battle. The story is narrated in the first person by its own "ideal reader suffering from an ideal insomnia" (*FW* 120.14)—Poliphilo—whose name means both "he who loves all (or many)" and "lover of Polia."

"Hic cubat edilis"

Poliphilo's *insomnium* (nightmare) occurs at dawn, as he finds himself lost in an unknown wilderness, searching for Polia, who does not requite his love. In a series of misadventures, in a dream within the dream, he wanders through a mysterious realm that interweaves archetypal city with rural landscape, examining the ruins of classical antiquity—Egyptian, Greek, Roman—describing in phenomenal detail the ornate and beautiful

arboſcelli,& di floride Geniſte, & di multiplice herbe uerdiſſime, quiui uidi il Cythiſo, La Carice, la commune Cerinthe. La muſcariata Panachia el fiorito ranunculo,&ceruicello,o uero Elaphio, & la ſeratula,& di uarie aſſai nobile,&de molti altri proficui ſimplici,& ignote herbe & fio ri per gli prati diſpenſate. Tutta queſta læta regione de uiridura copioſamente adornata ſe offeriua. Poſcia poco piu ultra del mediano ſuo, io ritrouai uno ſabuleto, o uero glareoſa plagia, ma in alcuno loco diſperſamente, cum alcuni ceſpugli de herbatura. Quiui al gliochii mei uno iocundiſſimo Palmeto ſe appræſento, cum le foglie di cultrato mucrone ad tanta utilitate ad gli ægyptii, del ſuo dolciſſimo fructo fœcúde & abun dante. Tra lequale racemoſe palme,& picole alcune, & molte mediocre, & laltre drite erano & excelſe, Electo Signo de uictoria per el reſiſtere ſuo ad lurgente pondo. Ancora & in queſto loco non trouai incola, ne altro animale alcuno. Ma peregrinando ſolitario tra le non denſate, ma interuallate palme ſpectatiſſime, cogitando delle Rachelaide, Phaſelide, & Li byade, non eſſere forſa a queſte comparabile. Ecco che uno affermato & carniuoro lupo alla parte dextra, cum la bucca piena mi apparue.

4.1. Poliphilo dreaming among the many architectural remains and statuary fragments of classical antiquity. *Hypnerotomachia Poliphili* (Venice: Aldus Manutius, 1499). Photo: Bibliotheca Hertziana–Max-Planck-Institut für Kunstgeschichte, Rome.

buildings, gardens, statuary, and rituals he encounters, as well as ruins and a necropolis, reading inscriptions in the languages of the *prisca theologia* and the ancient poetic wisdom: hieroglyphic, Attic Greek, Latin, Hebrew, Arabic, and Etruscan, always translating for the reader—though not necessarily into vernacular Italian.

Eventually he finds Polia, and after a sequence of initiatory ceremonies she tells her own story, nested within his, often logically contradicting what we (the readers) already "know." Polia's story fills most of Book II and includes detailed descriptions of her own dreams and nightmares. Finally, as Poliphilo is on the point of consummating his burning love with his muse, the Sun—whose image initiates the book—rises (out of jealousy) and awakens him from his marvelous dream.

Poliphilo and Polia are archetypal characters in the literary ancestry of HCE and ALP. Poliphilo is, like HCE, a somewhat foolish, lustful everyman. His narration and vocabulary amply hint to the reader that in the "real" world he, like "Bygmester Finnegan . . . freemen's maurer" (*FW* 4.18–19), the hodcarrier or master builder, and like HCE, is involved in the architectural art.

Poliphilo is also, within his dream, a species of landscape deity, a lesser god or demiurge, dreaming the world in his own image. Early on, wandering the ruins of an ancient city, he encounters a bronze colossus sprawled on the ground as if asleep—just like him, moaning in torment (*HP* 39–40). The pneumatic statue is so huge that he is able to climb inside through its mouth, and while exploring its inner spaces he finds modeled organs museologically labeled in three antique languages, with their names, diseases, and cures. This is a visual, not verbal, Rosetta stone, a clue that every materialized and externalized setting is a mirror of his inner self, metaphorical for the contents of his imagination framed in architectonic form.[3]

"riverrun past Eve and Adams"

Polia, her name suggesting both the Athenian *polis* (whose tutelary deity was Athena Polias) and material plurality, is a Plurabelle figure. In contrast to the stable geometries, the solid objects, in which Poliphilo is reflected, she is named a *nymph*, having a liquid, volatile reality—a watery spirit like ALP, whose "riverrun" (*FW* 3.1) generates the story's flow. In Book II of the *Hypnerotomachia,* a tearful Polia describes her genealogy, descended from a Rhoa or Rhea—meaning *flow* (*HP* 387)—and explains how the goddess

no fci

4.2. The fountain in the Palace forecourt, showing the devolving watery *spiritus* of the nymphs fecundating the sculpted heads. *Hypnerotomachia Poliphili* (Venice: Aldus Manutius, 1499). Photo: Bibliotheca Hertziana–Max-Planck-Institut für Kunstgeschichte, Rome.

Venus punished her ancestral family's hubris by transforming its members into the geographical water features of the Veneto landscape: a system of several rivers and tributaries, along with rainwaters, *fata morgana,* and various aquatic creatures.

Polia's characterization as a nymph refers to the power of fluids in nature to purvey form from within—like blood, or sap. Renaissance gardens used this metaphor, directing the movements of water to convey the Neoplatonic philosophy that *light* gives form to the material world from the inside. Though Polia is not a letter writer like ALP, Poliphilo describes her as the source of eloquence—and her fluency and liquidity in the context of the story indicate that she is consubstantial with the rarefied substance *spiritus,* present in the brain's ventricles, in which the virtual images forged by the imagination, with which to think, are imprinted and mutate.

In consequence of liquids representing significant form, Rabelais, following the *Hypnerotomachia,* used thirst to symbolize the desire for knowledge, the recovery of memory. Poliphilo frequently finds garden statuary with magical fluids spurting from eroticized orifices, and in an early episode he slakes his thirst by drinking from the breast of a marble nymph sculpted in a fountain (*HP* 77). This causes his head to become infused with *spiritus,* for immediately his visual perceptions of the garden and descriptive vocabulary blossom expansively.

As Poliphilo explores buildings and colossal sculpture, he repeatedly enters literally or metaphorically into a *head,* "the humptyhillhead of himself" (*FW* 3.19), thematizing heads, "The cranic head on him, caster of his reasons" (*FW* 7.29), brains, and the inner and outer senses; feting the image-making faculty of inner spaces. What lies within the brain, the reader must decode, is a species of ever-burning lamp—and the monumental stone Elephant containing one such perpetual illumination is inscribed "*The brain is in the head*" (*HP* 41).

"babble towers"

With a view to the texture of *Finnegans Wake,* I now turn to the relationship between the architectural theme and the language in the *Hypnerotomachia.* Italian scholars term it *macaronic;* it combines ancient Greek with Latin (both classical and medieval), Tuscan, and Paduan dialects, while transgressing the boundaries of textuality by incorporating text within the

numiſmati in circo. Vno ſacello cum patefacta porta,cum una ara i me-
dio. Nouiſſimamente erano dui perpendiculi. Lequale figure i latino cu
ſi le interpretai.

DIVO IVLIO CAESARI SEMP. AVG. TOTIVS ORB.
GVBERNAT. OB ANIMI CLEMENT. ET LIBERALI
TATEMAEGYPTII COMMVNIA ERE.S. EREXERE.

Similmente in qualūque fron
te del recenſito ſuppoſito qua-
drato, quale la prima circulata
figura, tale unaltra ſe p̄ſtaua a li
nea & ordie della prima a la de
xtra planitie dūque mirai ancora tali eleganti hieroglyphi,
primo uno uiperato caduceo.
Alla ima parte dilla uirga dil-
quale, & de qui, & deli, uidi u-
na formica che ſe creſceua i ele
phanto. Verſo la ſupernate æ-
qualmente dui elephāti decreſ
ceuano in formice. Tra queſti
nel mediaſtimo era uno uaſo PACE, AC CONCORDIA PAR-
cum foco, & dalaltro lato una VAERESCRESCVNT, DISCOR
conchula cum aqua. cuſi io li DIAMAXIMAEDECRESCVNT.
interpretai. Pace, ac concordia
paruæ res creſcūt, diſcordia ma
ximæ decreſcunt.

4.3. Two species of the language of objects in the hieroglyphic inscriptions, with
Poliphilo's translations for the reader. *Hypnerotomachia Poliphili* (Venice: Aldus Ma-
nutius, 1499). Photo: Bibliotheca Hertziana–Max-Planck-Institut für Kunstgeschichte,
Rome.

illustrations, where the woodcuts picture funerary monuments whose en-graved first-person narratives form stories told by the dead nested within Poliphilo's story, and fictive Egyptian hieroglyphs—illustrating proverbs and mottoes.

The astute reader can recombine the hieroglyphs Poliphilo translates to generate a basic pictographic lexicon for "reading" the same archetypal im-agery in the physical settings of the dream—an early psychoanalytic struc-ture. C. G. Jung, who originated the theory of archetypes in dreams, indi-cates that this book provided his first clue.[4]

Joyce offers such codes himself; for example, using a "middenhide hoard of objects!" to spell out the Hebrew alphabet: "Olives, beets, kimmells, dol-lies . . ." (FW 19.9–10).[5] In the Hypnerotomachia, leaping beyond the medi-eval metaphor of Creation as the Book of Nature, these convert the physical world into a legible book, marvelously conflating the spaces of the world and the printed page. Through Poliphilo's depictions of classical antiquity, the reader can seek to "solve and salve life's robulous rebus" (FW 12.34).

"pollyfool fiansees"

Not only is Poliphilo's language hybrid, a verbal grotesque, forging neol-ogisms from Greek and Latin roots, but the author deliberately amplified these and various Italian vernaculars, most notably Tuscan and Venetian, by consulting lists and lexica of specialized terms, arcane words, notably reusing *hapax legomena* as signposts to their original contexts. As a remark-able strategy in composing language, it seems inevitable to compare this to Joyce's language in the *Wake*, again with or without the mediation of *Gar-gantua and Pantagruel*.

In mythology, the superfetation of language is linked to the myth of the Tower of Babel. This theme of the human race attempting to climb to the heavens by means of architecture runs through both works as a repeated and varied motif. Poliphilo finds it sculpted in its classical form as a gigan-tomachy (HP 32), in which the earthborn Giants storm Jupiter's citadel on Mount Olympus, only to be struck down with a thunderclap—a thunderclap that first resounds prominently (FW 3.16) as the unpunctuated primordial language accompanying Finnegan's fall. Joyce touches on the pagan story[6] but foregrounds the biblical version, with repeated mentions of Babylon and its tower, in which God multiplies the human languages to prevent such unity of meaning again.[7] It is thus significant that among "The babbelers"

Sopra qualũque delle quale, di charactere Ionico.Romano. Hebræo.
& Arabo, uidi el titulo che la Diua Regina Eleuterilyda haueami prædi-
cto & pronosticato, che io ritrouerei. La porta dextra haua sculpta que-
sta parola. THEODOXIA. Sopra della sinistra q̃sto dicto . COSMO-
DOXIA. Et la tertia haua notato cusi. EROTOTROPHOS.

Da poscia che nui quiui applicassimo imediate, le Damigelle comite
incominciorono ad interpretare disertamente, & elucidare gli notandi
tituli, Et pulsando alle resonante ualue dextere occluse, di metallo, di uer-
daceo rubigine infecte, sencia dimorare furon aperte.

4.4. Queen Telosia's grotto of the Three Portals, inscribed in the languages of ancient
wisdom. *Hypnerotomachia Poliphili* (Venice: Aldus Manutius, 1499). Photo: Bibliotheca Hertziana–Max-Planck-Institut für Kunstgeschichte, Rome.

(*FW* 15.12) he places a certain pair of "pollyfool fiansees" (*FW* 15.14–15). This looks to be Joyce's nod to Polia and Poliphilo, younger and wilder, yet recognizable precursors to ALP and HCE.

In the story of the Tower of Babel, the architectural rise is part of a cycle completed by the linguistic fall: we need only look to the builder, Tim Finnegan, whose fall from his ladder (*FW*-3.17–18) enacts the myth in miniature, triggering the dream-Wake.[8] Among HCE's triadic names are "Hic cubat edilis" (*FW* 7.22–23), *here the builder dreams,* and "Humpheres Cheops Exarchas" (*FW* 62.21), suggestive of the *Hypnerotomachia*'s soaring white pyramid, whose vast statuary base portrays those fallen Giants who stormed the heavens, a myth Poliphilo reenacts by climbing to its vertiginous top (*HP* 31).

"Hung Chung Egglyfella now speak he tell numptywumpty"

That the dreamer is "archetypt" (*FW* 263.30) or "masterbilker" (*FW* 111.21) suggests the demiurgic power to re-create or forge cosmic order, for Joyce a "chaosmos" (*FW* 118.21), and two mythic variations on the creation myth form leitmotifs in both books—the cosmogonic dream and the cosmic egg.

In Orphic theology, the cosmic egg, a primordial unity, symbolically equivalent for Renaissance philosophy to the Neoplatonic One, is shattered by the serpent of Time to give birth—just as Finnegan's skull cracks open in what we might call a "Haroun Childeric *Eggeberth*" (*FW* 4.32)—to *Phanes,* the luminous power of Eros, an inner sun latent in the shell.

At Finnegan's wake, the opening of his cranium produces as "ontophanes" (*FW* 13.16) the dream as his experience of the otherworld through the language of the world reveals the soul's faculty of *phantasia,* creative imagination, as a modality of Phanes, the source of the oneiric phantasmagoria.

While in the *Hypnerotomachia* images of the cosmic egg are sublated as the astrological solar symbol, an umbilicated circle, in the *Wake* they are conveyed often and openly as Humpty-Dumpty—the Orphic egg continuously cracking open in everyday life.[9]

Philosophically, the inward Sun, correlate of the Neoplatonic One—in that "creation myth"—emanates through the orders of existence taking on material specificity, finitude, the illusion of time, as it becomes increasingly separate and multiple—defined, as the Many. This progenitor imprints its primal form on all natural objects that devolve from it, so each

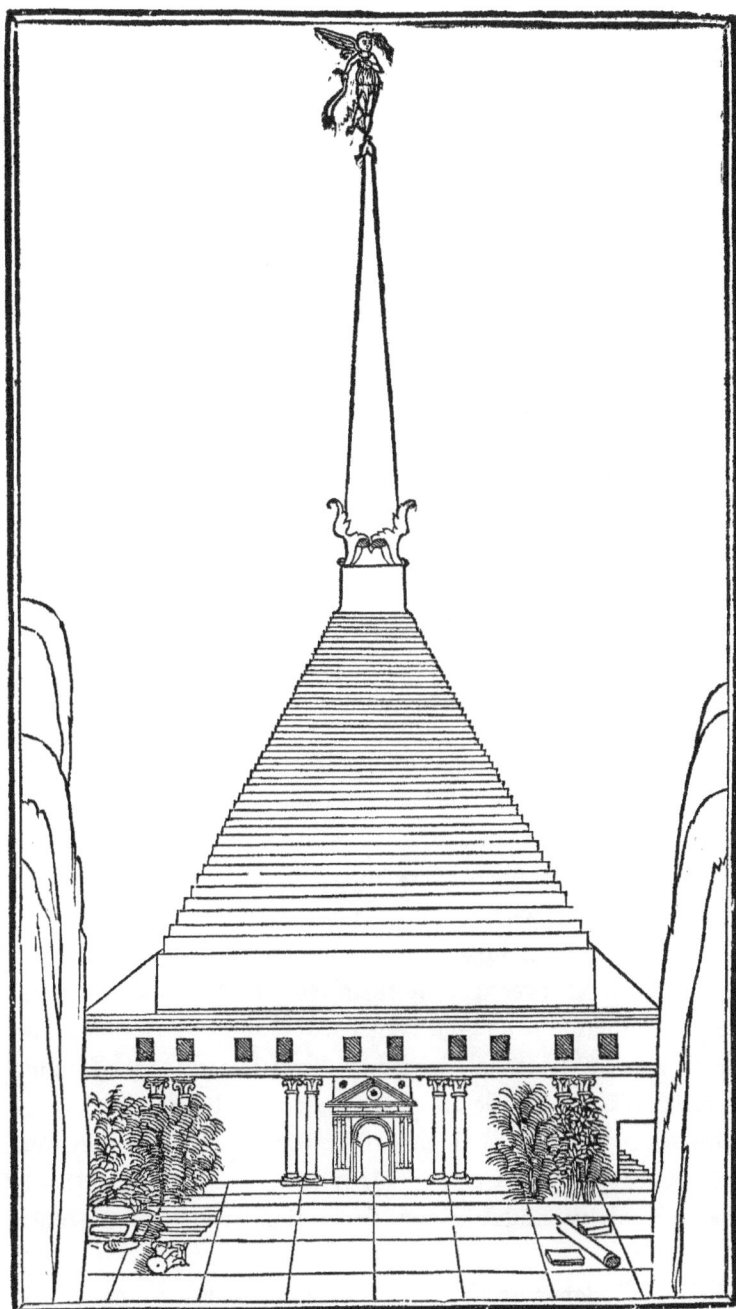

Ritorniamo

4.5. The Great Pyramid of the Sun, which Poliphilo climbs, surmounted by its fiery obelisk. *Hypnerotomachia Poliphili* (Venice: Aldus Manutius, 1499). Photo: Bibliotheca Hertziana–Max-Planck-Institut für Kunstgeschichte, Rome.

thing, bearing the trace, can be seen as one rung on a ladder leading back to original unity, from which, as from Eden, out of which a "riverrun" (*FW* 3.1), our souls have fallen in this cosmic game of snakes and ladders. In the multiplication and refraction of separate objects, man's game is *naming*, and (following Adam, and the Babylonians) words are invented to reflect the cosmic process.

The dream-vision of Poliphilo's soul—descending toward the material world in words that one stumbles over like concrete objects, and rising through image-building—moves through a sequence of settings or environs in which the form of the One—as the Sun—is impressed. This solar *symbolon*[10] is identical with the alchemical symbol for gold: the ultimate goal of the transmutation of base matter.

"the Bringer of Plurabilities"

In the *Hypnerotomachia*, this ovular figure appears in the woodcuts and is implied in the ekphrases, concealed in images of cosmic fecundity, wherein the transcendent One seeds the physical sphere from within. A gleaming altar paneled with carvings of the four Seasons is dedicated to Priapus, the god of gardens (*HP* 199), and around this marked center circle four ornate chariots, parading Jupiter's children by mortal women, in ascending ontological order representing the cosmic elements of Earth, Water, Air and Fire. This fourth "**H**aveth **C**hilders **E**verywhere with Mudder" (*FW* 535.34–35) is represented by Bacchus-Dionysus—a function of the One imprinting on its offspring, while Joyce's Bacchanalian cry of celebration including HCE paints a parallel: "all over again in their new world through the germination of its gemination from Ond's outset till Odd's end. And encircle **h**im **c**iruly. **E**vovae!" (*FW* 505.13). Earlier, HCE participates in the fecundation of the world as "**h**eavengendered, **c**haosfoedted, **e**arthborn" (*FW* 137.14) and offers the suggestion that vital formative powers are hidden in matter, "**t**umulous under **h**is **c**hthonic **e**xterior" (*FW* 261.18), reminding us that HCE, like Poliphilo, always finds his inner abstractions reflected in the outward, and the visible.

Poliphilo's reader must trace this theme to its ultimate center-within-a-center, where in the center of a circular island (whose concentric rivers, not unlike ALP, flow in circles), in the center of a circular amphitheater, in the geometrical center, of a circular fountain, suspended from a cupola

4.6. The altar of Priapus, symbol of cosmic fertility and patron deity of gardeners. *Hypnerotomachia Poliphili* (Venice: Aldus Manutius, 1499). Photo: Bibliotheca Hertziana–Max-Planck-Institut für Kunstgeschichte, Rome.

of sparkling crystal hangs a gigantic "golden egg, like a carbuncle flashing lightning in every direction, the size and shape of an ostrich egg" (*HP* 364). This shimmering egg is the ultimate representation of Poliphilo's own essence to himself: a creative light flashing from within his dreaming skull, and an affirmation of his status as demiurge, not forgetting the feminine *spiritus,* enabling the masculine hero's mind to become a proxy womb in which artifacts gestate.

"with larrons o'toolers clittering up and tombles a'buckets clottering down"

Yet the forward impulse of Poliphilo's phantasmagoria is directed by the soul's progress, the moral represented by the spatial, indicated by the transformations of architectural settings into increasingly abstracted geometrical order, using cosmological symbolism to reintegrate those forms disintegrated and distorted by the fall into matter. The *Hypnerotomachia* and *Gargantua and Pantagruel* both use a textual device that Joyce favored: the list, which provokes the reader to seek a Universal from Many; like his recollection of all the colors of the spectrum from refraction (devolving into parts) of white sunlight: "like a rudd yellan gruebleen orangeman in his violet indigonation" (*FW* 23.1–2).

The soul's ascent, thus using language, verbal or hieroglyphic, to harmonize and unify multiplicity on the path back to the One, culminating in a direct experience of union with the divine, a union beyond thought, is theurgy, or god-working. The fifth-century philosopher Proclus[11] saw the poetic word as a magical hinge by which the invisible world is coupled with the visible, tactile realm. The impossibility of fixing meaning, poetic ambiguity, meant regarding a word as a vehicle to move in either direction, toward the abstraction of Mind or the tangible, sensible world of objects, depending on active interpretation. In *Hypnerotomachia* and *Finnegans Wake* the titles alone amply demonstrate the tensions implicit in the verbal *coincidentia oppositorum.* Joyce's invented language resonates with Poliphilo's parlance, using verbal paradox as a reconciliation of opposites in what Jung describes as the process of individuation (Jung 265).

Proclus invited the reader to participate in theurgical interpretation using his own soul as the symbolic token involved in the rite—in a foreshadowing of modern psychoanalysis, making the soul itself subject to the hermeneutic process—enfolding its plurality and viewing the Platonic forms within itself (Rappe 176). Theurgic writings, an important resource for the

CLAVSVRA · DE MYRTO

VNO · TERTIO · P. CCC XXXIII

CLAVSVRA · DE NEMORI

LITTORE

CLAVSVRA · DE · NARANCETO

FLVME

PERISTYLIO

BOSCO · P. XX. SILICATO · P. XIIII. THEATRO · P. XXV.

SEMITERTIO · P. CLXVIJ

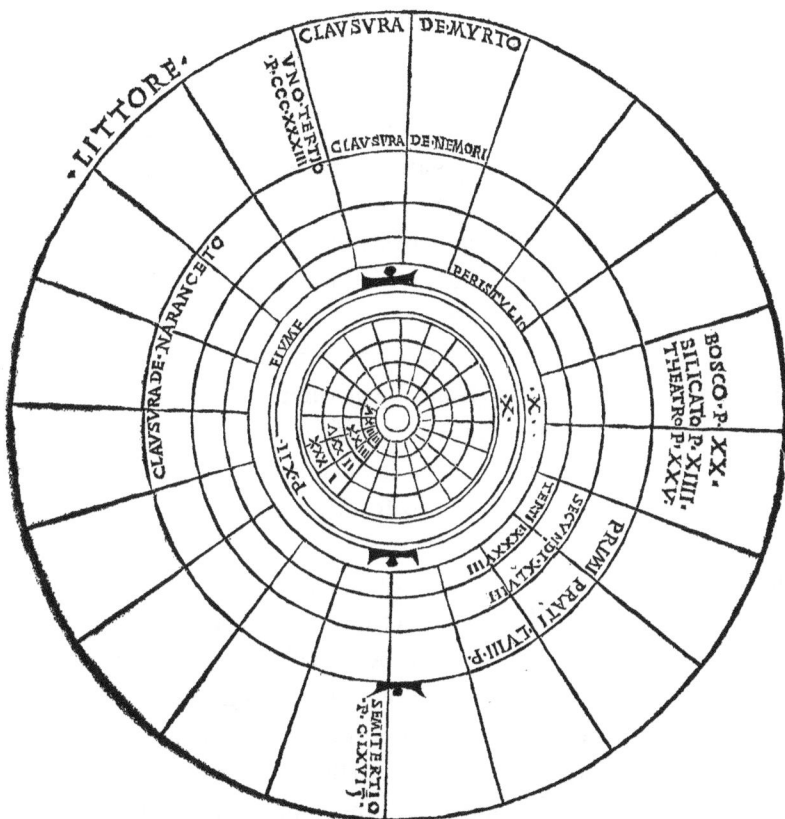

Per piu euidente dimonſtratione, Il circuito di queſta delitioſa & amœ-
niſſima inſula di circūmenſuratione conſtaua di tre milliarii. La figura
dillaquale di uno milliario il ſuo diametro præſtaua. Ilquale in diuiſione
tripartito, uno tertio. 333. paſſi continiua uno pede, & dui palmi, & alquā
to piu dalextremolabro dille litorale ripe fina al clauſtro naranceo. La
menſura di uno ſemitertio, paſſi. 166. & palmi. 10. occupaua. Daqueſto ter
mine ícominciauano gli prati uerſo il centro tendenti, altro tanto ſemitertio. Diſtributo dūque acconciamente uno integro tertio, rimane uno
ſemitertio a diſpenſare fina al meditulo, paſſi. 166. & palmi. 10. Dal periſty
lio antediſto, era conceduto alquanto di ſpatio rimaſto per la contraſtio
ne degli prati ſopradiſti, ad euitare láguſtia dille quadrature. Gliquali
non haueuano il ſuo termine fina al cōpimto dil tertio, et queſto ſolertem
teaduene p proportionarealquáto il q̃drato ultimo p le linee al púſto di
duſte. Ilqualeſpatio tra il flume & il periſtylio intercalato, tuto gratioſa-

4.7. The umbilicated plan of the Island of Cythera, a solar *symbolon*, showing its circular
rivers. *Hypnerotomachia Poliphili* (Venice: Aldus Manutius, 1499). Photo: Bibliotheca
Hertziana–Max-Planck-Institut für Kunstgeschichte, Rome.

Hypnerotomachia, engaged a full spectrum of genera in language and textual forms, filtering down into the literature of the Renaissance, especially marked in Rabelais, and ultimately to modernity. In the *Hypnerotomachia,* as in the *Wake,* the cognitive functions must find order through recollection, in the confusion of languages and memories of events, indicating "This the way to the museyroom" (*FW* 8.9) through which the psyche pursues its goal anagogically, by interpretation of symbols, such that through the forest of the visible which eclipses the invisible world, abstract forms and ideas emerge—and the soul is elevated.

Order, particularly narrative and mnemonic order, is found in both microcosm and macrocosm, detail and big picture; likewise the *Hypnerotomachia* hides an acrostic sentence in the initials of the chapters.[12]

While Poliphilo's Neoplatonic hermeneutics propel the *Hypnerotomachia*'s world more or less consistently toward higher order, as if in the morass of history's documents and artifacts, verbal and architectural, a bridge could be found by which the Renaissance could reinvent the Golden Age, Vico's cycle shifts the *Wake* ever closer to chaos and degeneration. However, within *this* philosophical construct, time is an illusion fostered by the separateness of the Many, and the emanation from the One into physical objects takes place simultaneously with the upward climb through the orders of existence powered by the desire to return to the One. The *symbola* or forming powers in objects are *both* approaching the stable, recognizable archetypes *and* melting into the grotesque hybrids whose most evident modality is the language itself. An interesting further research might compare Shaun and Shem (Hebrew for *name*) to these opposite streams coursing between their father and mother.

Inevitably, the process of interpretation—often treated in the text as translation or mnemonic association—may err. In both the *Wake* and the *Hypnerotomachia* this process is repeatedly symbolized as incomprehension or misprision (especially by tropes like homophone, the common pun)—so that the reader of the *Hypnerotomachia* is prompted to treat the naive narrator skeptically by revising his train of thought.

In his story, most of the hieroglyphs Poliphilo interprets are found engraved on obelisks. An element in common between page and landscape, the term represents both architectonic *axis mundi* and printer's mark. The obelisk was first used in Homeric manuscripts to mark lines of dubious authorship, and became a printer's device (†) marking typographical errors on a page—principally omissions.[13]

At critical points in the *Hypnerotomachia,* the presence of Egyptian obelisks—which symbolize rays of sunlight and the transference of the solar
luminosity into the brain—indicate the reader's need for philosophical
interpretation—usually reassessment—of the concretized "hieroglyphic"
objects composing the physical environment.

The first of Poliphilo's obelisks, which he compares to one at Heliopo-
lis (present as "Healiopolis" on *FW* 24.18), made of red fire-granite, soars
upward from the summit of the white marble pyramid. In the *Wake* Joyce
provides a reading of its second meaning: "as were it sentenced to be nuzzled
over a full trillion times for ever and a night till his noddle sink or swim
by that ideal reader suffering from an ideal insomnia: all those red raddled
obeli cayennepeppercast over the text, calling unnecessary attention to errors, omissions, repetitions and misalignments" (120.11–15)

Poliphilo's obelisks play off asterisks (*), which appear as decorative elements throughout the printed text. Asterisks stand for the souls transmi-
grating home to the stars by using hermeneutics to range up ladders of words
and things. Thus a text lying between the space of a printed page and the
narrated landscape carries the points of entry onto and exit from the world-
stage, using printer's marks to dramatize the recirculation of erotic energy.
In the *Wake* the simultaneity of the Neoplatonic universe is perceptible in
the unconscious, in which, Freud speculated, time does not exist; this experience of atemporality Virgil attributed to the Delphic oracle under Apollo's
influence.

In this kind of dream, by grace of the solar Musagetes who governs the
nine goddesses of poetry, the true cosmic laws become visible, and in the
Wake arguably audible. Besides representing the form of the city as Athena
Polias, eloquent Polia's verbal self is Polyhymnia, muse of sacred poetry,
another modality that ALP shares. Through the flotsam and jetsam of history,[14] the letter the hen (Greek "one," for the primordial One) scratches
up is equated with or translated to the egg she lays, the living world that
contains all things.[15] Poliphilo and Finnegan, whose thematized brains both
represent the world's potentialities, attest to the humanist confidence in the
infinite creative capacities of the human mind. Their words, in both cases
the text of the book, show as well as tell the story, verbal objects in a "museyroom" that is ultimately the printed book.

Ultimately, both books are cosmogonic dreams, journeys through an underworld tracing the restoration of order in the absence of the sun, and culminating in the sunrise. In both, the murky, ambiguous nightmare landscape

supports the hero's metaphorical descent or fall into the underworld, where he taps into the source of erotic energy, and awakens the *logoi spermatikoi* buried in the fluid feminine matrix. Thus in the *Hypnerotomachia* and in *Finnegans Wake*, the sunrise that interrupts the respective dreamers is itself doubly charged, playing off symbolism of resurrection, individuation, and illumination with a plunge back into the phenomenal world, though now adumbrated by the dream—both an awakening and an effective wake of the imagination.

Notes

1. The pages are unnumbered; my references are to the digital facsimile in the Herzog August Library, Wolfenbüttel, Germany.

2. First published in 1499, it gained its large readership in France through the first vernacular translation made in 1546 as *Le songe de Poliphile*, later followed by other French editions, including two new translations in the nineteenth century. (Thus the timely impact for Rabelais, as well as the double entendre of "pollyfool fiansees" [*FW* 15.14–15] as "parlez-vous français.") As well, a substantially abridged English translation was published in 1592 titled *The Strife of Love in a Dreame*. During Joyce's lifetime, however, no Italian translations were made, nor was an English translation completed.

3. A similar project is at work in *FW* 13.4–5, with "So This Is Dyoublong? Hush! Caution ! Echoland !" reading Dublin as "do you belong" and especially "doubling," because Echoland is where Narcissus falls in love with his reflection without realizing it is himself. The *Hypnerotomachia* elsewhere uses the same trope of Echo to cue the reader.

4. Carl Gustav Jung, in his foreword to *Der Liebestraum des Poliphilo* by Linda Fierz-David, referring to a French version, *Le tableau des riches inventions,* edited by François Béroalde de Verville, published by M. Guillemot in Paris in 1600.

5. Nearer the end of the book, and thus further "devolved" and recombined, we find the beginning of the Greek alphabet: "alphabeater cameltemper" (*FW* 553.2–3).

6. *FW* 167.22 reveals "The thundering legion has stormed Olymp," and at *FW* 613.28 we find "The folgor of the frightfools is olympically optimominous."

7. As some examples, "the turrace of Babbel" (*FW* 199.31); "babble towers" (*FW* 354.27); "having successfully concluded our tour of bibel" (*FW* 523.31–32).

8. *FW* 4.26–5.4 outlines the tale: "during mighty odd years this man of hod, cement and edifices in Toper's Thorp piled buildung supra buildung pon the banks for the livers by the Soangso. . . . Oftwhile balbulous, mithre ahead, with goodly trowel in grasp and ivoroiled overalls which he habitacularly fondseed, like Haroun Childeric Eggeberth he would caligulate by multiplicables the alltitude and malltitude

until he seesaw by neatlight of the liquor wheretwin 'twas born, his roundhead staple of other days to rise in undress maisonry upstanded (joygrantit!), a waalworth of a skyerscape of most eyeful hoyth entowerly, erigenating from next to nothing and celescalating the himals and all, hierarchitectitiptitoploftical, with a burning bush abob off its baubletop and with larrons o'toolers clittering up and tombles a'buckets clottering down."

9. Joyce doesn't ignore the Chinese creation myth; "Hung Chung Egglyfella now speak he tell numptywumpty" (*FW* 374.34) refers to Hun-Tun, the primordial chaos described as "like a chicken's egg" in which Heaven and Earth are inextricably commingled (Bodde 384).

10. For the Neoplatonic term, see Shaw 162.

11. In his commentary on Plato's *Republic,* Proclus expressly compares poetic expression to theurgic activity: poetry works in the same way as the hieratic art, since each taxis of being contains attributes pervading the entire hierarchy in all its classes, from sensible particulars up to the gods. These attributes, Proclus elaborates, "instantiate and refer to events by means of which the poets clothe their secret vision of the first principles" (qtd. in Rappe 176).

12. The presence of this acrostic accounts for the attribution of the book to a Francesco Colonna. This attribution, however, remains problematic and circumstantial.

13. The signs as used in manuscripts by Origen "consisted of the obelus which was prefixed to words or lines which were wanting in the Hebrew and found in the Greek, and the asterisk, which noted words or lines wanting in the Greek but present in the Hebrew" (Fritsch 171).

14. Beginning I:5, "Her untitled mamafesta memorialising the Mosthighest has gone by many names at disjointed times" (*FW* 104.4–5) is followed by a list, a rhetorical device straight from the heterogeneous pages of Rabelais, conveying the plenitude and even the multiplication of the Book. ALP begins the alphabet from whose plurality flows all possible books.

15. ALP is "the Everliving, the Bringer of Plurabilities" (*FW* 104.2).

Works Cited

Atherton, James. *The Books at the Wake: A Study of Literary Allusions in James Joyce's "Finnegans Wake."* New York: Viking, 1959.

Bodde, Derk. "Myths of Ancient China." *Mythologies of the Ancient World.* Ed. Samuel N. Kramer. New York: Doubleday, 1961. 367–408.

Fritsch, Charles T. "The Treatment of the Hexaplaric Signs in the Syro-Hexaplar of Proverbs." *Journal of Biblical Literature* 72.3 (1953): 169–81.

Hypnerotomachia Poliphili. Venice: Aldus Manutius, 1499.

Jung, C. G. *Dreams.* London: Routledge, 2002.

————. Foreword to Linda Fierz-David, *Der Liebestraum des Poliphilo*. Zurich: Rhein-Verlag, 1947.

Rappe, Sara. *Reading Neoplatonism: Non-Discursive Thinking in the Texts of Plotinus, Proclus and Damascius*. Cambridge: Cambridge UP, 2000.

Shaw, Gregory. *Theurgy and the Soul: The Neoplatonism of Iamblichus*. University Park: Pennsylvania State UP, 1995.

5

"As Great Shapesphere puns it"

The Name Game in Shakespeare and Joyce

FRANÇOIS LAROQUE

"Names! What's in a name?"

Ulysses 9.901

Thanks to Vincent Cheng's *Shakespeare and Joyce: A Study of "Finnegans Wake"* (1984) as well as to Adeline Glasheen's remark that "Shakespeare (man, works) is the matrix of *FW*" and that "*FW* is about Shakespeare" (260), the reader's vague feeling that Shakespeare and his oeuvre lie at the core of the proliferating text of Joyce's most fascinating and controversial work has now become an established fact.

This essay aims at showing that Joyce is systematically quoting, as well as making parodies and (dis)integrations of, the Shakespearean text in the *Wake*, which amounts not only to what Harold Bloom called the "anxiety of influence" and to some ingrained desire on the part of Joyce/Shem to topple down the main father figure of English drama and literature in general, but also to what probably remains as a most perceptive reading and understanding of the bard's own vision and revision of language presented as a "name game," as a "proteiform graph" and "polyhedron of scripture" (*FW* 107.8). This associates orality, acoustics, songs, and music with the written word and the letter. When the page is thus twinned with the stage ("our world-stage's practical jokepiece" [*FW* 33.3]), word and letter become slippery and make for a proliferation of meanings and for multiple, protean games of echo and association. Shakespeare calls this "equivoquation" in *Macbeth*, thus "moralizing two meanings in one word" (*Richard III* 3.1.81) when his characters are "to double business bound" (*Hamlet* 3.3.41).

So, among many other things, the *Wake* is a very perceptive, even revolutionary reading of Shakespeare, the great "worldwright" (*FW* 14.19), the playwright of the world, of the Globe, and the master wordsmith ("he was himself a lord of language" [*U* 9.454]). I will argue that James Joyce is as much the heir of the Renaissance as he is the son of the Jesuits. If Joyce is indeed more than aware that the Church of Rome was founded on a pun on the name Petrus, meaning both Peter and stone, Shakespeare was also indebted to the numerous learned Greek and Latin quibbles of the humanist writers, such as Thomas More's coinage of the word "U-topia" to mean both a "good place" (*eu*-topos) and a "place of nowhere, a never never land" (*u*-topos), or Erasmus's making his famous *Encomium moriae* a *Praise of Folly* as well as a "praise of More." Indeed, in the first decade of the sixteenth century, amphibology, paronomasia, and equivocation were often resorted to in those texts and thus contributed to the creation of a space for what was later to become Shakespeare's technique. Far from being accidental or neurotic, his way of weaving meaning in a subtle web of associations or arrangements was reinforced by poetic and prosodic resonances. Moreover, his revival of the character of the Fool and of the Clown onstage allowed him to give the various quid pro quos or sexual double entendres a particular dramatic dimension and power. Because his text was first and foremost a "playtext," a piece of scripture meant to be orally performed onstage and heard by mixed audiences, this specific as well as idiosyncratic manner of multiplying meaning(s) became what might be called Shakespeare's own specific "trademark" in the theatre.

"Shaping the Sphere"

Reading Shakespeare in the *Wake* first consists in the recording of the various literary echoes and verbal transmogrifications that his name is subject to: "Shikespower" (*FW* 47.19), "Shapekeeper" (123.24), "shake-again . . . shakealose" (143.22–23), "Chikspeer" (145.26), "Shakespespill and eggs" (161.31), "Shakhisbeard" (177.32), "Shopkeeper's wives" (183.26), "for the laugh of Scheekspair" (191.2), "Sheepcopers" ("shopkeepers" turned inside out) (229.8–9), "As Shakefork might pitch it" (274.4), "As Great Shapesphere puns it" (295.4), and "Will Breakfast" (575.29). What sounds like some series of almost childish jingles or like an equivalent of the *serio ludere* verbal transvestism associated with the carnivalesque jokes of early modern England does in fact correspond to the fact that names and name spellings were far from fixed in those days, so that, alongside Shakespear(e), one finds such variants as "Shakeshaft," "Shaxper," "Shaxberd," "Shaksper," and so forth. If, on the other hand, we consider that the poet indulges in an incredible series of puns on his own first name, "Will," in the sonnets, we may then become convinced that the playwright's identity was deliberately meant to be kept uncertain, ambiguous or even obscure. As Richard Wilson puts it,

> Shakespeare's apparent invisibility is not a simple fact, it is an act ... The most obvious material pre-condition of this author's disappearing trick was, after all, his use of the recusant tactic of dual residence, allowing him to slip between parish pump and state intelligence as habitually as his own characters go "To liberty, and not to banishment" (*As You Like It*, I.3.132). And it may be that this alternation of different locations, and the constant recourse in his plays to some estranged "world elsewhere" (*Coriolanus*, III.3.139), are indeed clues to the negative capability which Greenblatt honours as Shakespeare's unique genius for inhabiting the identities of others through the extinction of his own. (22)

This also explains why generations of so-called critics or pseudo-biographers have engaged in "Will-hunting," desperately hoping to find the keys to the Shakespeare mystery and revealing to the world the true face of the "real" Shakespeare. In this perspective, he then becomes a champion of multiple identity, "Rutlandbaconsouthamptonshakespeare," according to Stephen's formula in *Ulysses* (9.866), before Haines later jeers that "Shakespeare is the happy huntingground of all minds that have lost their balance" (*U* 9.1061). Shakespeare's name is indeed one that, like Joyce's, lends itself to many quibbles, thus contributing to make it the penman's doppelgänger or alter ego in the world of the *Wake*, where history and literature are marked by the successive cycles of a fall, of a digging in a middenheap followed by a retrieval or *ricorso*. Thus Shem/James Joyce becomes Will Shakespeare *redivivus*. In a "renascent Joyce" perspective, the Renaissance phoenix of English drama and literature becomes a "second-best bet" as it were, living a sort of second life in a text where the manifold latent meanings and submerged puns are allowed to come out into the open by being "actualized" by Joyce's irreverent and subversive reading/writing. In such a view, the word machine of the *Wake* literally recycles an almost infinite number of name games in Shakespeare, in a method marked by iteration, echo, deformation, and defamation ("Shem was a sham and a low sham"

[*FW* 170.25]) as well as parody and rewriting ("the last word in stolentell-ing" [*FW* 424.35]). The systematic compression of meaning in a number of key words, jingles, set and recurrent phrases, and echoic tags and alliterative verbal patterns are evocative of song and musical leitmotifs just as they are reminiscent of the techniques of commercial ads. The phrase "Putting Allspace in a Notshall" thus echoes and compresses Hamlet's "O God, I could be bounded in a nutshell, and count myself king of infinite space" (1.2.251–52), while simultaneously alluding to the style of the Ten Com-mandments' "Thou shalt not . . ."

Shakespeare's "Dreariodrama" (*FW* 79.27–28)

Another common point between the Shakespearean canon and the world of *Finnegans Wake* is the fact that Joyce places language at the center of his "worldstage," just as Shakespeare did at the Theatre, the Globe, or the Blackfriars. "All the world's a stage," *totus mundus agit histrionem*, are two mottoes that Joyce also made his by constantly calling attention to orality, pronunciation, stammering, singsong tunes, nursery rhymes, airs, and old Irish ballads ("Finnegan's Wake" being precisely one of them), folksongs, and opera. There is no need to repeat how important the world of music and bel canto was to Joyce, who is said to have hesitated between becoming a writer or being trained as an opera singer. Song and music are also part and parcel of Shakespeare's plays—in the comedies, of course (*As You Like It, A Midsummer Night's Dream, The Merchant of Venice, Twelfth Night*), but also in the tragedies (Ophelia's songs in *Hamlet*, the Fool's snatches of old tunes in *King Lear*) and in the romances (most prominently in *The Tempest* with Ariel's sweet songs and airs). As Seamus Deane writes in the introduction to the Penguin edition of *Finnegans Wake*, "Joyce often renders philosophical and linguistic problems in the spirit of a great slapstick comedian" (x). So his "drema" (*FW* 69.14) of "The Mime of Mick, Nick and the Maggies," to be played at the Phoenix, seems emblematic of this. Incidentally, the Phoe-nix was also the name of one of the Jacobean playhouses in London, which corresponded to the old roofed Cockpit in Drury Lane when Christopher Beeston converted it into a private theater. After it was reopened at the Restoration in 1660, the first play to be performed there was Shakespeare's *Pericles*. "The Mime of Mick, Nick and the Maggies" is indeed playing "Every evening at lighting up o'clock sharp and until further notice in Feenichts Playhouse" (*FW* 219.1–2). The play, like the Cockpit, a playhouse sacked and partially burned down by the London apprentices on Shrove Tuesday 1617, indeed seems to be constantly reborn out of their own ashes like Egypt's mythical bird.

In a similar way, *Finnegans Wake* is presented as the play of world history, as a "Christmas pantomime," a pandemonium and a mumming play ("rainborne pamtomomiom" [*FW* 285.15–16]), as a mine of puns ("punnermine" [*FW* 519.3]), a *puntomime* ("our theoatre Regal's drolleries puntomime" [*FW* 587.8]). If "Shapesphere" remains the playwright of the Globe ("she is spherical, like a globe," says Dromio of Syracuse of Nell, the kitchen wench, in *The Comedy of Errors* [3.2.112]), Joyce is also the "worldwright" with such exclamations as "How frilled one shall be as at the taleotold of Formio and Cigalette" (the Ondt and the Gracehoper masquerading here in as French versions of Romeo and Juliet [*FW* 563.27–28]). The theater brings excitement and light to the world: "What a dumpty daum earth looks our miseryme heretoday as compared beside the Hereweareagain. Gaities of the Afterpiece when the Royal Revolver of these real globoes lets regally fire of his *mio colpo* for the chrisman's pandemon to give over the Harlequinade to begin properly SPQueaRking Mark Time's Finist Joke" (*FW* 455.24–29). The earth is but an empty dome, a vacant space (*Raum*), compared with the glories of the Globe. "The eeriedreme . . . From Topphole to Bottom" (*FW* 342.30–32), which refers to Bottom's dream in *A Midsummer Night's Dream* where *Pyramus and Thisbe*, the play performed by the Athens mechanicals, constantly creates hilarity at the expense of the amateur players among the aristocratic onstage audience. This is the occasion of a fireworks display of obscene innuendoes (the wall's hole and stones), malapropisms, and preposterous non sequiturs. Joyce's "funferal . . . puddenpadded very like a whale's egg . . . sentenced to be muzzled over a full trillion times for ever and a night till his noddle sink or swim by that ideal reader suffering from an ideal insomnia" (*FW* 120.10–14), in spite of the word "Wake" in its title, is essentially a book of dreams. So, this may be why there are so many references to Bottom's dream in *A Midsummer Night's Dream*, the most quoted play after *Hamlet, Macbeth,* and *Julius Caesar:* "Methought as I was dropping asleep somepart in noland of where's please . . . I heard at zero hour as 'twere the peal of vixen's laughter among midnight chimes" (*FW* 403.17–21). This passage blends allusions to Bottom's dream and to Falstaff's "chimes at Midnight" when, in the company of Justice Shallow, he celebrates the good old days of yesteryear in *2 King Henry IV* (3.2.209). Joyce further alludes to the "many wiles of Winsure" (*FW* 227.1–2), that is, to Falstaff being disguised as Herne the Hunter at the end of *The Merry Wives of Windsor*, when he is wearing deer's antlers on his head and then deceived, exposed, and punished by the two merry wives, Mrs Ford and Mrs Page: "One bed night he had delysiums that they were all queens mobbing him. Fell stiff" (*FW* 379.17–19). This rolls into one many successive hints at Falstaff's ("Fell stiff") nightly delusions when he is undeceived and pinched by a troop of boys disguised as fairies, as well as to the "Illyria/Elysium" paronomasia at the beginning of *Twelfth Night* (1.2.4–5), at Mercutio's Queen Mab in *Romeo and Juliet*, and finally at the "mobled queen" in the First Player's tirade in *Hamlet* (2.2.493). The long sequence of Clarence's dream in *Richard III* (1.4.9–63) before he is murdered in the Tower (drowned in a butt of malmsey wine), and Iago's fictitious dream in *Othello* ("Oldfellow" [*U* 15.3828] and "oldfellow" [*FW* 410.4]) are other occurrences linking Shakespeare and Joyce (as well as Chaucer and the whole medieval dream tradition).

Shakespeare as "Pelagiarist" (*FW* 182.3)

If Shem the penman, alias James the punman, is presented as a fake and as a notorious forger in the *Wake* ("Shem was a sham and a low sham" [*FW* 170.25]), he is also an "alshemist" (*FW* 185.35) and, like Friar Laurence in *Romeo and Juliet*, a "holy friar" who turns into a fairly dubious monk figure when he ventures into forbidden ground to become a sorcerer's apprentice who will "hoist with his own petard" (*Hamlet*, 3.4.196) in the end. The "peliagiarist pen" of the palimpsest writer becomes the site where contraries and contradictions meet in the most funny cacophony. The penman is indeed described as "an Irish emigrant the wrong way out . . . an unfrillfrocked quackfriar . . . (will you for the laugh of Scheekspair help mine with the epithet?) semi-semitic serendipist . . . Europasianised Afferyank! (*FW* 190.36–191.1–4). The "Europasianised Afferyank" turns the emigrant writer into the figure of the wandering Jew, into "an extravagant and wheeling stranger, / Of here and everywhere" (*Othello* 1.1.134–35), like the Moor Othello who has traveled from Mauritania to the Serenissima and who has become a general at the service of the Venetian Republic.

Now, at the beginning of his dramatic career Shakespeare was accused of plagiarism by the University Wit and polygraph writer, Robert Greene, in a deathbed pamphlet entitled *Greenes Groatsworth of Wit bought with a Million of Repentance:* "Yes trust them not: for there is an upstart Crow, *beautified* with our feathers, that with his Tygers heart wrapt in a player's hyde, supposes he is as able to bombast out a blanke verse as the best of you: and beeing an absolute *Iohannes fac totum* is in his own conceit the onely Shake-scene in a countrey" (Greene 84–85). Shakespeare, the jack-of-all-trades, is here blamed as a notorious impostor who, through the Aesopean allusion, appears as a plagiarist who is quite happy to steal from his better contemporary fellow playwrights and who prides himself on having become the very best "Shake-scene" in his country. Greene's name-dropping and name game in this passage was a transparent allusion to the young playwright whom he so violently denounces as dramatic upstart. Shakespeare was probably shocked, as he later felt the need to retaliate in the passage in *Hamlet* when Ophelia comments on Hamlet's letter: "'To the celestial, and my soul's idol, the most *beautified* Ophelia'—That's an ill phrase, a vile phrase, 'beautified' is a vile phrase" (*Hamlet* 2.2.109–11). This ironic reminder of the word "beautified" is clearly meant as a counterblast against Greene's earlier attack. It is also possible to read Iago's famous description of jealousy as "the green-eyed monster" (*Othello* 3.3.169), rendered as "the greeneyed mister" in the *Wake* (*FW* 88.15), as a bitter, belated quip against Greene, who is thus indirectly described as "green with envy" at Shakespeare's meteoric rise on the London stage of the early 1590s. Joyce was obviously quite familiar with the quarrel and, in his typical manner as parodist and plagiarist, he turns into another *ben trovato* quibble, where Greene's *Iohannes fac totum* is rewritten as "faketotem" (*FW* 516.24). As always with Joyce, one word is enough to compress a whole debate and to serve as an ironic, deflected commentary about it. The name game seems to work here like a ping-pong match between Shem the penman and Shake-scene-Shapesphere, while Greene is put in the position as referee and envious onlooker.

The Name Game as Letter Game

Several critics have remarked that Shakespeare uses the "O" exclamation some 152 times in *Romeo and Juliet,* a frequency that can be explained by the mourning ejaculations in the lamentation scene in 4.2, when Juliet is found dead in her bed on the morning of her intended marriage to Count Paris. But it is also used as a reference to the "nothing" of female genitalia, to "the O of woman" (*FW* 270.25–26) as well as to the outer circle of the "wooden O" (*Henry V,* Prologue, l. 13), that is, to the theater and to the stage world as a whole. Furthermore, the name Romeo, with its double "O" like the name Othello, rhymes with *echo* and *woe*, while Mercutio is keen to parody his friend's infatuation with Rosaline with a series of magic and mock-erotic associations already present in his name:

> 'Twould anger him
> To raise a spirit in his mistress' circle
> Of some strange nature, letting it stand
> Till she had laid it and conjured it down:
> ... My invocation
> Is fair and honest, in his mistress' name:
> I conjure only but to raise up him
>
> . . . .
>
> If love be blind, love cannot hit the mark.
> Now will he sit under a medlar tree
> And wish his mistress were that kind of fruit
> As maids call medlars when they laugh alone.
> O Romeo, that she were, O that she were
> An open-arse, or thou a popp'rin pear (2.1.24–39)

Here, Mercutio may well have had in mind some kind of Renaissance erotic alphabet like Peter Flötner's, which was then apparently quite well known and widely circulated. Moreover, the expression "open-arse," often deleted by editors (replaced by "etc" or suspension marks), can also be read as "open R's" as in Jonathan Goldberg's *"Romeo and Juliet's* Open R's" (Goldberg 271–85). We find an echo of this in the Nurse's question to Romeo:

> Nurse
> Doth not "rosemary" and "Romeo" begin
> Both with a letter?
>
> Romeo
> Ay, Nurse, what of that? Both with an "R."
>
> Nurse
> Ah, mocker, that's the dog's name. "R" is for the _____, no, I know
>   it begins with some other letter (2.3.195–99)

More generally, the play modulates the sounds "I" and "O" present in the names of Juliet and Romeo, while simultaneously inverting gender roles, since the phallic "I" is doubly present in the girl's name ("J" and "i"), while the boy's is somehow contained between two Oes. The bawdy associations of the two letters is clearly unveiled in Mercutio's obscene retort to the Nurse:

Nurse
Is it good e'en?

Mercutio
'Tis no less, I tell ye, for the bawdy hand of the dial is now upon the
    prick of noon (2.3.105–7)

The play further combines the sounds [U-*you*] and [I-*Ay*], so that "Jule" (which is what the Nurse keeps calling young Juliet) and "Ay" combine in *July*, the month when Juliet was born and whose name also evokes the "creator" of the calendar (still used in the Elizabethan era after Gregory's reformation was refused by the English Church authorities), Julius Caesar:

Nurse
Thou wilt fall backward when thou hast more wit, wilt thou not Jule?
    And by my holidam, the pretty wretch left crying and said "Ay"
    (1.3.44–46)

But the words *Jule* and *jewel* also coalesce when Romeo discovers Juliet among the dancers at Capulet's ball, so that name, birth date, and poetic blazon coincide at this magic moment of mutual recognition (Romeo becoming the "pilgrim"—which is the translation of the Italian etymology of the name) in the sonnet the lovers exchange before their kiss starts and seals the career of their "star-crossed" love. This name game may be echoed in *Finnegans Wake* in the word "Yuletide" (*FW* 97.3), which combines *Julius*, *Juliet*, and *July* as well as *Yuletide*, the Celtic word for Christmas (indeed, in Brooke's poem, *Romeus and Juliet*, Shakespeare's main source for his love tragedy, the story is situated at Christmas rather than in mid-July). The name game thus makes for an intriguing association or even a fusion of space and time.

Such a concern with letters is to be found almost on each page of the *Wake*, this "abcedminded . . . claybook" (*FW* 18.17–18):

For if the lingo gasped between kicksheets, however basically English, were to be preached from the months of wicker churchwardens and metaphysicians in the row and advokaatoes, allvoyous, demivoyelles, languoaths, lesbiels, dentelles, gutterhowls and furtz, where would their practice be. . . . If juness she saved! Ah ho! And if yulone he pouved! The olold stolioleum! From quiqui quinet to michemiche chelet and a jambebatiste to a brulobrulo! It is told in sounds in utter that, in signs so adds to, in universal, in polygluttural, in each auxiliary neutral idiom, sordomutics, florilingua, sheltafocal, flayflutter, a con's cubane, a pro's tutute, strassarab, ereperse and anythongue athall. (*FW* 116.25–30, 117.10–16)

"Yulone," which comes after "juness" (June and "jeunesse"), associates July, Jule, and Yule, while the allusion to Giordano Bruno, who was burned at the stake in 1600 in Rome ("brulobrulo"), may here be reminiscent of the canicular atmosphere of Shakespeare's love tragedy, where torches burn bright in Verona and where "heretical" desire leads the lovers to their doom. As Romeo exclaims,

> When the devout religion of mine eye
> Maintains such falsehood, then turn tears to fire;
> And these who, often drowned, could never die,
> Transparent heretics be burnt for liars (1.2.91–94)

In *Twelfth Night,* where the figure of Echo lies at the heart of the play's imagery and soundscape, there are also many letter games to be found, including the famous conundrum ("MOAI doth sway my life . . . what should this alphabetical position portend?" [2.5.106–17]) that baffles and mystifies Olivia's Puritan steward, Malvolio. But the letter game also provides Shakespeare with an opportunity for obscene and scatological double entendres ("thus makes she her great P's" [2.5.87]), which alludes to Olivia urinating, and "These be her very c's, her u's and her t's" [2.5.86]), the word *CUT,* which suggests both cunt and castration. This is exactly the sort of letter game that the *Wake* presents us with and which must have rejoiced its author enormously, as when Shem is being accused of "shemming amid everyone's repressed laughter to conceal [his] scatchophily" (*FW* 190.33–34).

Mercutio the "grave man," Bottom the ass-man, Suffolk who suffocates in water and drowns after being called Walter de la Poole by the Lieutenant and Whitmore in 2 *Henry VI* (4.1 70–72), Joan of Arc who is successively identified as Puzzel/Puzzle and Pucelle, the rebel Jack Cade, whose own name makes for several successive jokes ("cade of herrings") and who ends up killed by Lord Iden in his Eden-like garden of Kent, the Plantagenet king who is "planted" by York, or Shakespeare's own wife, Ann Hathaway, whose name is inscribed in sonnet 145 in the famous line "'I hate' from 'hate away' away she threw"—examples such as these are innumerable in Shakespeare's plays, so much so that Samuel Johnson wrote of what he considered as a serious defect in his famous critique of the bard that "A quibble, poor and barren as it is, gave him such delight, that he was content to purchase it by the sacrifice of reason, propriety and truth. A quibble was to him the fatal Cleopatra for which he lost the world and was content to lose it" (Johnson 309). If Shakespeare indeed calls upon all sorts of puns and quibbles in his dramatic and poetic name game, he does so in order to multiply meaning in an overall poetic strategy founded on the principle of echoic language. Similarly, history, for Joyce, appears as what Seamus Deane calls a "whispering gallery," a Babel of voices, while writing provides him with a means of reestablishing the body as the locus of language, so that letters, in their various slippings and strange arrangements, are intimately associated with desire (the equivalent of Shakespeare's "fatal Cleopatra"): "If you spun your yarns to him or the swishbarque waves I was spelling my yearns to her over cottage cake" (*FW* 620.34–36). Contrary to Romeo's love for Rosaline, which, according to Friar Laurence, "did read by rote, that could not spell" (*Romeo and Juliet* 2.2.88), Shem's "cantraps of fermented words, abracadabra calubra culorum" (*FW* 184.26) sound like the new literacy and like some modern liturgy of desire.

Works Cited

Cheng, Vincent John. *Shakespeare and Joyce: A Study of "Finnegans Wake."* Gerrards Cross: Colin Smythe, 1984.

Deane, Seamus. Introduction to James Joyce, *Finnegans Wake*. London: Penguin Classics, 2000.

Glasheen, Adaline. *Third Census of "Finnegans Wake."* Berkeley: U of California P, 1977.

Goldberg, Jonathan. *Shakespeare's Hand*. Minneapolis: U of Minnesota P, 2003.

Greene, Robert. *Greenes Groatsworth of Wit bought with a Million of Repentance*. Ed. D. Allen Carroll. 1592. Binghampton, NY: Medieval & Renaissance texts & studies, 1994.

Johnson, Samuel. *Selected Poetry and Prose*. Ed. Frank Brady, William Wimsatt, and William Kurtz Wimsatt. Berkeley: U of California P, 1977.

Shakespeare, William. *Hamlet*. Ed. G. R. Hibbard. Oxford: Oxford UP, 1987.

———. *King Richard III.* Ed. Antony Hammond. London: Methuen, 1981.

———. *Othello.* Ed. E. A. J. Honigmann. Walton on Thames: Thomas Nelson & Sons, 1997.

———. *Romeo and Juliet.* Ed. Jill L. Levenson. Oxford: Oxford UP, 2000.

———. *Twelfth Night.* Ed. Keir Elam. London: Cengage Learning, 2008.

———. *2 King Henry IV.* Ed. A. R. Humphreys. London: Methuen, 1987.

Wilson, Richard. *Secret Shakespeare: Studies in Theatre, Religion and Resistance.* Manchester: Manchester UP, 2004.

6

"Marked you that?"

Stephen Dedalus, Pierrot

MARIA-DANIELLA DICK

C iting the now phantom *Hamlet* lectures, Joyce incorporated his ex-
pounding of Shakespeare to docile Trieste into the fragments of *Giacomo Joyce*: "Hamlet, quoth I, who is most courteous to gentle and simple
is rude only to Polonius. Perhaps, an embittered idealist, he can see in the
parents of his beloved only grotesque attempts on the part of nature to produce her image. . . . Marked you that?" (*GJ* 10). In the fragment directly following this allusion to the lecture series appears the female object, Amalia
Popper or Annie Marie Schleimer, not only as Ophelia but also recalling
the Beatrice of Dante as well as of Shelley; "So did she walk by Dante in
simple pride" (*GJ* 11). If Joyce thought that "Italian literature begins with
Dante and finishes with Dante" and that "In Dante dwells the whole spirit
of the Renaissance" (R. Ellmann 218), the convergence of these two writers, Shakespeare and Dante, is again figured through the theme of Hamlet
in the "Scylla and Charybdis" episode of *Ulysses*.[1] During the discussion of
the play, Stephen Dedalus will deny that the middle-aged Shakespeare, "a
greying man with two marriageable daughters, with thirtyfive years of life,
nel mezzo del cammin di nostra vita" (*U* 9.830–31), could appear in the play as
Hamlet, the "bearded undergraduate from Wittenberg" (*U* 9.832). Both instances, ostensibly treating of *Hamlet*, allude to the Dantean *vita nuova*, the
desire for the blank, a spacing and demarcation of the self that superscribes
canonical allusions onto a subject imagined in literary terms.

The *Hamlet* lectures place "Scylla and Charybdis" in a prosthetic relation
to Joyce. They do so because they are absent—the manuscripts lost—and

there is known of them only a partial reception, from reviews in the *Piccolo della Sera* (see R. Ellmann 776), and part of their composition, traced by William Quillian through a surviving set of sixty-two loose sheets and a *Quaderno Shakespeare* in the James Joyce Collection of the Cornell University Library, containing excerpts from the biographies of Sidney Lee, George Brandes, and Frank Harris, and from John Dover Wilson's 1911 anthology on the Elizabethan drama and life, *Life in Shakespeare's England: A Book of Elizabethan Prose.*[2] Delivered at the behest of Roberto Prezioso for the Minerva Society, the lectures were originally intended to be ten in number but were increased to twelve, possibly eleven if following Erik Schneider's reasoning that one would not have been given on the dates of December 23 or January 6, the feast of the Epiphany (Schneider 10). As the lectures are lost, they constitute a blank within the Joycean oeuvre, a spacing like the typographic spacing in Mallarmé's poems where the white of the page also comes to be part of the text, and they make of "Scylla and Charybdis" a site of infinite referral as the black of the text refers back to the blank of the lectures. It is easy to be tempted into a constative reading of that episode and seek to base a Joycean theory of aesthetics, of patriarchy, and of art around the chapter, which is then impoverished in what it is made to say, its excess contained and made to constitute a fixed statement. The absence of the lectures, albeit on the evidence most probably a largely historical summation for an Italian audience, shades the work in proffering the prospect of a lost genetic imprint of "Scylla and Charybdis." The desire for the blank contained in the *Vita Nuova* is a wish to begin anew through the radical break, symbolized by the appearance of Beatrice, which inscribes that beginning as a *tabula rasa* and then remarks itself in text as metaphoric of an elision of the past and a reinscription, as it did when Joyce gave Lucia a copy of the Dante after an episode of illness. The inscription of the blank space of the lectures into "Scylla and Charybdis," as a site of reference which is in fact non-reference and can be known only in the abstract, is a remarking of that desire, adding, as will be shown, an illusory reference that ultimately can gesture only to the act of reference itself.

In *Giacomo Joyce,* Joyce portrayed his infatuation in terms of the new life by comparing its object to Beatrice, the comparison evidently intending something of the impulse for a willed reinscription of his self prior to the episode. By July 1917, after having written of "Scylla and Charybdis" in April to Ezra Pound (*SL* 224–25),[3] he had told Georges Borach that the father and husband Ulysses, the most human subject in world literature, was appropriate to him, in *"mezzo del cammin"* (R. Ellmann 416), as Hamlet is said by Dedalus to be inappropriate to Shakespeare. The *Hamlet* lectures, *Ulysses,* and *Giacomo Joyce* fold in upon each other, but this folding should not, however, tempt us to an unfolding which would seek to uncover a Joyce at the center, as Stephen unfolds Hamlet only to expose Dante. *Giacomo Joyce* begins with the same question as *Hamlet:* "Who?" and in the terms of this article Francisco's challenge to "unfold your self" (*Hamlet* 1.1.1–2) reveals yet another figure—two, in fact—whose dialectic has already marked this argument. Through "The Double Session" Jacques Derrida reads Stéphane Mallarmé's chain of signifiers, concentrating, among others, on the mark, the fold, the blank. The title of this article is a citation across all of these figures: in *Giacomo Joyce,* in *Hamlet,* and in Derrida, reading Mallarmé. It makes the link between the deconstruction of mimesis effected by Derrida in *Dissemination* and that effected by Joyce in "Scylla and Charybdis," through Stephen Dedalus, who figures as the actor—the mime who is also linked to Mallarmé's Hamlet—and whose Shakespeare thesis mimes reference to the blank of the lectures. As such, Stephen can be compared to the Pierrot of Mallarmé's *Mimique* and its deconstruction by Derrida, who shows that the mime does not refer, but *mimes reference,* alluding always to that which does not exist either outside or prior to the mime itself.

•

New life begins for Dante with the first sighting of Beatrice in the *Vita Nuova,* when, at the beginning of that first "book of himself" Dante proclaims the stability of self through memory that Stephen Dedalus arrives at in episode 9 of *Ulysses,* and also a rebirth, writing, "In that part of the book of my memory before which there would be little to be read is found a chapter heading which says: 'Here begins a new life' (*Incipit vita nova*)" (3). The blank of the self before the advent of Beatrice could be compared to the "blancovide" (*FW* 43.24) of Mallarmé's page, for certainly Dante is faced with the anxiety of the *vita nuova* or *tabula rasa,* such that after her death he finds himself in a dark wood, the right path having been lost, the new life having been sullied. The desire for the blank, the illusion of rebirth of an originary self, is repeated from the dark night of the soul that is the *Inferno,* after his having marked—re-marked—the new beginning which serves in the former text as a rebirth of the self *ab origine.* Lost in the middle of the dark woods, the right path obscured, Dante again achieves a spiritual purgation through Beatrice that effaces his previous self. Compare Best, in "Scylla and Charybdis," iterating this trope of the subject as text: "—Mallarmé, don't you know, he said, has written those wonderful prose poems Stephen MacKenna used to read to me in Paris. The one about *Hamlet*. He says: *il se promène, lisant au livre de lui-même,* don't you know, *reading the book of himself.* He describes *Hamlet* given in a French town, don't you know, a provincial town" (*U* 9.112–16). The Mallarméan Hamlet, "haut et vivant Signe" ("Hamlet" 1564), takes part in a play staged in a provincial town as was Paul Margueritte's mime, *Pierrot assassin de sa femme,* about which Mallarmé would write in *Mimique* and on which Derrida would comment. This Hamlet has an affinity with the mime of Margueritte, as will later be shown, but it suffices now to note that the suggestion, the link of the mime to the Hamlet figure in French literature from Baudelaire to Laforgue to Mallarmé, appears here in *Ulysses.*

Kevin Nolan compares the Beatrice figure in *Giacomo Joyce* to Ophelia in act 2, scene 2 of *Hamlet* and to "La Béatrice" of Baudelaire, perceiving the connection also between Hamlet and the mime. He cites that poem's demons urging the speaker:

> Contemplons à loisir cette caricature
> Et cette ombre d'Hamlet imitant sa posture,
> Le regard indécis et les cheveux au vent.
> N'est-ce pas grand pitié de voir ce bon vivant,
> Ce gueux, cet histrion en vacances, ce drôle. . . .

and states that "from here the way is clear for the later Laforguean disfigurement of Hamlet as contemplative Pierrot." The concept of Hamlet as "caricature," an imitator and Pierrot, is a suggestive one, initially as introduced in Baudelaire's poem, already linked by Nolan with the Beatrice of Dante and Joyce's muse and thus touching once again upon the strange relation between Shakespeare's "absentminded beggar" and the will to self-effacement described in the *Vita Nuova,* but also because it is the figure used by Mallarmé to describe Hamlet, "a mime and a thinker" (Mallarmé, *Hamlet, Divagations* 128), the mime the scene to which "The Double Session" too gestures.

Placing Plato's *Philebus* alongside Mallarmé's short prose piece *Mimique* (Mimesis), Derrida questions the understanding of mimesis as, in Barbara Johnson's words, "fundamentally ontological . . . either the self-presentation of a being-present or a relation of adequation between an imitator and an imitated" (Derrida xxviii). The mime treated by Mallarmé in *Mimique, Pierrot assassin de sa femme,* was written as a booklet by its actor, Paul Margueritte, *after* its performance, and the mime presented as the remembrance of a murder,[4] itself fictive, rather than a present representation of the event. Margueritte himself was a sui generis Pierrot, in that he had never seen a mime before embarking on his own. He writes in the booklet that, "ignorant of all traditions," he "came up with a personal Pierrot, in conformity with my innermost aesthetic self. As I sensed him and translated him, it seems, he was a modern being, neurotic, tragic, and ghostly" (Derrida 290–91). This "modern being" has its affinity both with Mallarmé's absent-minded beggar and with Stephen Dedalus; as for Derrida the interest in the mime is that he follows no reality, whether external actual event, fictive event present in the mime, or a phenomenal text, so too these mimic figures mime reference, Stephen to a lecture and Hamlet to a murder. Derrida describes how in the mime no reality offers itself up as a present, to be perceived; the gestures themselves are not present, as they always "refer, perpetually allude, or represent" (Derrida 220), and *Mimique* is shown in "The Double Session" to posit an imitation of imitation, of mimesis itself. Mallarmé writes of a mime, the Pierrot inscribing and miming his wife's murder, and, as Johnson neatly explains that inscription, proceeding then to quote Mallarmé, "Writ(h)ing upon the conjugal sheets, the Mime plays both man and woman, pleasure and death, 'in a hymen (out of which flows Dream), tainted with vice yet sacred, between desire and fulfillment, perpetration and remembrance: here anticipating, there recalling, in the future, in the past, *under the false appearance of a present*'" (Derrida xxviii).

The mime has no referent beyond itself; reading the book of himself, the artist invites comparison with Stephen Dedalus, "the loveliest mummer of them all," Buck Mulligan's own Pierrot: "—But a lovely mummer! he murmured to himself. Kinch, the loveliest mummer of them all!" (*U* 1.97–98). And if Stephen is the mime, the imitator dressed in black as Mallarmé characterizes the actor who plays Hamlet—"a mime and a thinker" (Mallarmé, *Hamlet, Divagations* 128), a modern, neurotic being—narratologically he is his own father. His theory of *Hamlet*, expounded in 1904, is generally perceived—without referent—to be that of Joyce as author, perhaps that of the lost lectures, and it might be read as imitating those lectures, *avant la lettre*: before the text because, within the economy of the text, eight years prior to the lectures of 1912, yet imitative because, in its genetic context, written five years after their delivery. Joyce portrays Stephen as imitating reference, to the lecture that is now without referent, the I still to come (recalling Stephen's continuity and discontinuity of the form), for Stephen and for Joyce, in the fiction of the text. This is the illusion of a temporary present, "through which all future plunges to the past" (*U* 9.89). Conventionally read as the imitation of the Joycean model, Stephen's theory, and "Scylla and Charybdis," are made to mark, to fold, the blank of the lecture: the lecture that is without text, the theory that he does not believe.

As there is no reality or event to be made present in Margueritte's mime, and as the Mallarméan text refers to a textual representation that postdates its performance, similarly Stephen's theory is never present within the text. It gestures outside of itself as a reference to a wider Joycean system of perverted genealogy and therefore as a Joycean imitation, a representation of the *auctor* imitated. Yet this is valid only to a degree, as the author himself is never fully present in this representation either, for as "imitation" implies a representation that can be formally distinguished from an original,[5] the theory is a "perpetual allusion" to continually shifting textual instances, none of which are present or foundational—to the *Hamlet* lectures, to *Hamlet* itself, to Joyce the author and his life, "the book of himself," to Dante, to Shakespeare, to a negative theology.

It is not known if the lectures of Joyce shared a theoretical content with Stephen's discussion in "Scylla and Charybdis." As in *Mimique*, that discussion, like the mime, is a "perpetual allusion without piercing the veil or canvas"[6] causing the blank to fold upon itself, because the allusion is to a referent that possibly can never be or has never been present, which does not come before or after the mimodrama of the chapter and is not committed within it, whether real lecture or view held by Joyce as part of a sustained theory; while seeming to allude to the Trieste lectures, the discussion may converge with them—and with a Joycean view of *Hamlet*—only in its focus on the same play. The understanding of "Scylla and Charybdis" as a metatextual chapter that is always read as *referring*, as a *representation beyond itself* of a complete Joycean theory of patriarchy that illuminates the role of the artist, would be called into question if it were read as biographically anti-mimetic. In another of his *Scribbles at the Theater*, the previously quoted *Hamlet*, Mallarmé condemns the actor playing Laertes for forcing himself, his talent, into the drama, asking, "What do the most beautiful of qualities . . . matter in a story that extinguishes everything but an imaginary hero, half mingled with abstraction? To refer to the real is to break through the ambience using reality as a battering ram to punch through a vaporous canvas, around the emblematic Hamlet" (*Divagations* 126). This canvas is related to the figure of the hymen, that which is both inside and outside and, for Mallarmé "a pure medium of fiction" (*Mimique, Divagations* 141) located "between present acts that are never present" (Derrida 212). Thus does "Scylla and Charybdis" resemble the hymen, as both inside and outside of *Ulysses*, located between present acts that are never present. Derrida writes of the opening of *Crise de vers* that "Like *Mimique*, like *Or*, that essay begins with the simulacrum of a description, a scene without a referent" (309). It would be easy to fall (a word with all intended implications surrounding originary religious and family scenes for Stephen) into a Dedalean temptation to read the chapter psycho-biographically and to imagine ourselves listening to Joyce in Via Carducci, where the lectures were given; or rather, to imagine that Joyce was never in Via Carducci in any real sense: that what he undertook there was but the imitation of Stephen Dedalus. There is no presence, no actual action, as the two refer to each other, each marked by the spacing of the other, without real extant referent but not existing platonically. Each, rather, created out of the materiality of the other, the actual fact of the lecture, the actual text of Stephen's theory.

Interrogating Plato's concept of the *antre*, Derrida puns homophonically on the *entre*, the between, the syntax or spacing—the blanks—of Mallarmé's text, which allow the text to fold back upon itself and deny a search for a single meaning. "What takes place is only the *entre*, the spacing, which is nothing, the ideality (as nothingness) of the idea . . . only the memory of a crime which has never been committed . . . because on the stage we have never seen it in the present (the Mime is recalling it)" (224). In "Scylla and Charybdis" one sees the idea of the lecture past and to come. There is no present action that could be identified by a referent because whereas the Trieste lectures, delivered before the chapter was written, have been shown to be an unstable source for the text, within the economy of the text itself Stephen is not performing a lecture but is marking one to come for him. The lecture marks *différance*, as both a spatial and a temporal deferral from any present, and the chapter is thus released from the tyranny of totalising conclusion because that spacing resists an identification of it with the lost lectures. Stephen himself picks up on the performative demarcation of this *entre*, when, interrupted by Mulligan, he perceives himself to be *"Entr'acte,"* in the interval of performance (*U* 9.484).

Through the mark and gesture of his writing, Joyce mimes a lecture—Stephen's nascent presentation, conflated by readers with his own theory—which never took place in a reality. In doing so, he displaces it as a textual present, by inserting the fold of his own lecture into the hymen of the text. There is no way of knowing if "Scylla and Charybdis" was a faithful reproduction of a referent thesis (even one held by Joyce beyond the historical contextualization that the notes and newspaper review suggest constituted a large part of the lecture series), for there is no mimesis from model at work here and the text folds continuously. In this sense, and as Derrida writes, the "mime mimes reference. He is not an imitator; he mimes imitation" (229) as the hymen interposes itself. The hymen—between desire and fulfillment, perpetration (which is piercing) and remembrance—is not pierced. But Stephen is also recalling to us a lecture that now does not exist (Joyce's lecture), which takes its place in the text nonetheless, yet not as an *avant-texte* available to be studied. Rather, Stephen's imitation becomes the model for Joyce's text, especially through the searches within the arid bibliographic-anthropological *quaderno* that renders its fragments resistant to a coherent reconstitution. Mallarmé shows that this is how the mime operates, whose act is confined to "a perpetual allusion without breaking the ice or the mirror: he thus sets up a medium, a pure medium, of fiction" (*Mimique, Divagations* 141) the medium of the hymen.

This discussion is apophatic and not binary, for, like Stephen defining what the father *is* by what he *is not,* it seeks, in saying that "there is not," to ascertain an aesthetics of the "subject as writing" rather than a distinction between presence and absence that would be a simple subversion. The discussion in episode 9 is the prelude to an event as Stephen would understand it, for he is always gesturing toward something to come, his defining feature a *potentiality* for creation that is never realized in the present.[7] When urged by Best to publish, to make present his ideas which are here only being tested, he ironically concedes that "you can publish this interview" (*U* 9.1085), in a pseudo-Dialogue. Stephen operates within a textual system, constantly himself referring to another allusion, and his self is constituted by a *mise en abyme* of non-presence through reference to other, textual, marks.

Joyce calls attention to the perverse Platonism of Hamlet, railing at Polonius's reversed mimesis, in *Giacomo Joyce;* "an embittered idealist, he can see in the parents of his beloved only grotesque attempts on the part of nature to produce her image. . . . Marked you that?"[8] The parents are not the model but the distorted image of the child, who herself is an image of the parents, being the copy of their copies of her "image." Joyce thus destabilizes mimesis's supposed relation to truth or meaning through a referential reality, through the figure of Stephen. Like the mime that was not published until after the event, which refers to no actual present representation or external text, he is imitating only within the text of himself—he is imitating imitations with no referent reality. Invoking Dante, *nel mezzo del cammin,* in the dark wood of the *Inferno* which is a metaphor for middle-life spiritual crisis, Stephen does not read and compare it on its allegorical level but aesthetically, as a linguistic figure. It is thus that the concerns of reality are subordinated to a formalism that creates its own aesthetic theory by collapsing text into text in an anarchy (*an-arche*) of authority that erases the author to appropriate language *as language.* Even on the level of *Ulysses,* Dante is not referred to as an authority by the use of that phrase; rather, the aesthetic of the language is foregrounded, along with an excess that bespeaks "literature." The aesthetic stands alone, but the phrase is synecdochal for a formalism, a pure "writing." It is the "binding of the subject to writing"[9] through this phrase that enacts the idea of text as aesthetic commentary, and of the politics of a writing that through its formal capacity rather than through its content transfers the site of authority onto language and engages with the problematics of a subjectivity constituted by writing. Or, as Stephen attempts to show in his theory of intentionalism, the subject subsumes external realities to create the "book of himself"; there, as in *Hamlet,* Shakespeare is shown to be playing out his life in text, creating from himself as model in the same way that the narrator of *À la recherche du temps perdu* affirms the importance of life existing only insofar as it serves to be transformed into art.

Stephen, however, is imitating texts; he is himself not a model for a book, but the "book of himself" is written by the text of others. Like the mime of Margueritte, "white as a yet unwritten page" (Mallarmé, *Mimique, Divagations* 140), and like Mallarmé's Hamlet, himself in the mimic tradition, Stephen is a living sign, but a sign made up wholly of text. His name is but the signifier of text, his referent is not his body but his textually constituted psyche, perpetual allusion in overdrive. He understands himself, and models himself, on the imitations of others, and in this can be compared to the Sophist, miming the poetic that is itself mimetic, producing production's double. Not just his artistic image, but his psyche, is woven and unwoven through *text,* and while Stephen is represented, he is also a series *of* representations, which can never be fixed and are never fully present, are present only as fragments and citations. As has been argued, the character of Stephen functions to mime reference by imitating that which has not taken place, in textual referents and by "performing" a lecture that has never been. Like the lecture, he marks himself only to fold, again, over. The trace is the mark of difference, and thus these allusions that constitute Stephen are not one and the same but spatially and temporally different, unable to be reconstituted into a stable model for subjectivity, yet containing traces of each other, as the different representations of Hamlet carry within them the memory of the others. His memory of his self, the continuous "I," is the memory of a self defined by its imitations, which are themselves, from childhood, textual representations as the blank of Stephen is overwritten and folds upon its representations. His psyche is fundamentally figured through textual conversion, as he imagines his mother, in one instance, bidding him "list, list" (U 9.144).

Joyce's lost Trieste *Hamlet* lectures constitute a "silence" within the Joycean archive, thwarting a fetishization of origins and questioning patriarchy in the transmission of texts and the ideas that are inseparable from it: the text that is not, to paraphrase Beckett on Joyce, about something, but *is* that something itself, albeit that that "is" must remain provisional, untraceable to an origin, and always succumbing to the fold, its "is" the very status of inhabitation by other texts because the text is never fully present to itself. The text is its own progenitor, through text, giving birth to itself in the sense that, as also in *Finnegans Wake*, text is the signifier, but what is signified back is text itself. Stephen's speech apostrophizes himself, as he sends out a call to a self not present to him because his subjectivity is one that is created by and in writing.

Buck Mulligan, like Athena, has an unborn child, the play, bursting forth from his head (U 9.875–77). The idea of the Platonic become actual, the birth of the imitation of the ideal, is reversed in the folds of "Scylla and Charybdis," which continually places and displaces text in order that there be no ideal to be imitated, even the ideal of an imagined lecture. As Stephen cannot ultimately affirm knowledge because he does not place primary importance on belief, the desire for knowledge of the Trieste lectures is itself displaced as fragments of the lectures fold into and mark the texts of *Giacomo Joyce* and *Ulysses* and are disseminated, shifting the historical actual to an imagined ideal, conflating the known fragments with Dedalean theory to posit an ideal displaced from textual evidence but called forth by its prompting.

Arguing intentionalism in Shakespeare, Stephen's character shows that such an opposition cannot be maintained. He is a composite of textual fragments, Hamlet and Stephen in black, operating upon the white of the page, re-marking it and gesturing beyond it, as the allusions evoked by Joyce through Stephen cannot be contained in him but replicate from him. The image of Stephen the mummer, the Pierrot, in black, is mocked by Mulligan:

"Mournful mummer, Buck Mulligan moaned. Synge has left off wearing black to be like nature. Only crows, priests and English coal are black" (*U* 9.1155–56), and like Shakespeare, the upstart crow, Stephen is beautified with the feathers, the pens, of others. He is the imitator without model, like the mime of Margueritte, who wrote of his mime, published in 1882, the year of Joyce's birth:

> If anything is left of my mimic efforts, it is the literary conception of a modern, suggestive Pierrot, donning at will the flowing classical costume or the tight black suit, and moving about in uneasiness and fear. This idea, set down in a little pantomime, was one I later developed in a novel, and I intend to use it again. . . . *Henceforth I should be allowed to emphasise the dates of my works*. . . . It would be unjust if my forthcoming books should seem to be inspired by someone else, and if I should be accused of imitation or plagiarism. Ideas belong to everyone. . . . I am just affirming my priority and reserving it for the future.[10]

Notes

1. Although Joyce situates Dante (1265–1321) as a Renaissance rather than medieval figure, it should be noted that such a characterization would generally be considered atypical, though it seems clear that Joyce is referring to the manner in which Dante anticipates early modern linguistic and semiotic advances.

2. See Quillian, *Hamlet*, and Quillian, "Shakespeare."

3. Letter of April 9, 1917. Joyce writes: "As regards excerpts from *Ulysses*, the only thing I could send would be the Hamlet chapter, or part of it—which, however, would suffer by excision" (*LI* 101).

4. As Maud Ellmann notes in "The Ghosts of *Ulysses*," the same is true of King Hamlet's death: "this death, which never literally *takes place*, is *represented* time and again, by the dumb show and the mousetrap, by the testimony of the ghost, and by the carnage which completes the tragedy. . . . Thus it is telling that Hamlet exults in the success of the play-within-the-play as if he had already murdered Claudius by staging the destruction of a king: for he can only conquer theatre with more theatre, compelled to reenact the uncorroborable death which institutes the order of paternity" (105).

5. This conception of mimesis, which understands the stability of an original and its availability to representation, is as illusory as the logocentrism of Stephen, who in wishing to be his own father does not subvert a credence in origin but in fact desires its concretization.

6. See Mallarmé, *Mimique, Divagations* 140.

7. Compare Mallarmé's depiction of Hamlet in the eponymous prose piece within *Divagations*: "*the latent lord who cannot become, the juvenile shadow of us all*" (125).

8. See also *U* 9.434–35.

9. I am indebted to Julian Wolfreys for commenting on an earlier version of this article, and for the suggestion of this phrase.

10. Paul Margueritte, "Notice" to *Pierrot assassin de sa femme*, 2nd ed. (1st ed. 1882), in Jacques Derrida, notes to "The Double Session": I, *Dissemination*, trans. Barbara Johnson (London: Continuum, 2004), 291.

Works Cited

Alighieri, Dante. *Vita Nuova*. Trans. Mark Musa. Oxford: Oxford World's Classics, 1992.

Derrida, Jacques. *Dissemination*. Trans. Barbara Johnson. Chicago: U of Chicago P, 2004.

Ellmann, Maud. "The Ghosts of *Ulysses*." *The Languages of Joyce: Selected Papers from the 11th International James Joyce Symposium*. Ed. R. M. Bollettieri Bosinelli, C. Marengo Vallio, and Christine Van Boheemen. Amsterdam: John Benjamins, 1992. 105–19.

Ellmann, Richard. *James Joyce*. New and rev. ed. New York: Oxford UP, 1982.

Mallarmé, Stéphane. *Divagations*. Trans. Barbara Johnson. Cambridge: Harvard UP, 2007.

———. "Hamlet et Fortinbras." *Œuvres Complètes*. Ed. Henri Mondor and G. Jean-Aubry. Paris: Gallimard, 1945. 1564.

Nolan, Kevin. "Feydeau's Republic." *Hypermedia Joyce Studies* 3.1 (2002), online. Reprinted in *Giacomo Joyce: Envoys of the Other*, ed. Louis Armand and Claire Wallace. Prague: Litteraria Pragensia, 2006. 136.

Quillian, William. *Hamlet and the New Poetic*. Ann Arbor: U of Michigan P, 1983.

———. "Shakespeare in Trieste: Joyce's 1912 *Hamlet* Lectures." *James Joyce Quarterly* 12.1–2 (1974): 7–63.

Schneider, Erik. "Towards *Ulysses*: Some Unpublished Joyce Documents from Trieste." *Journal of Modern Literature* 27.4 (2004): 1–16.

Shakespeare, William. *Hamlet. The Norton Shakespeare*. Ed. Stephen Greenblatt et al. New York: Norton, 1997.

7

The Ass Dreams of Shaun's Bottomless Heart

Shakespeare and the Dream-Work in *Finnegans Wake* 403–407

JIM LEBLANC

As Book III of *Finnegans Wake* begins, it is midnight and the atmosphere of Joyce's narrative is especially somnolent: "Hark! . . . Pedwar pemp foify tray (it must be) twelve. And low stole o'er the stillness the heartbeats of sleep" (*FW* 403.1–5). We soon hear the voice of a dreamer, one who seems to be a protagonist in the dream of another, who narrates events surrounding and including a dream he had: "Methought as I was dropping asleep somepart in nonland of where's please (and it was when you and they were we)" (403.18–19). He thought he saw Shaun: "Shaun! Shaun! Post the post!" (404.07) as he, the speaker, was "jogging along in a dream as dozing I was dawdling, arrah, methought" (404.3–4). Later, as this dreamer's vision becomes clearer: "Yet methought Shaun . . . Shaun in proper person . . . stood before me" (405.07–11). By this point we know that the narrator of Book III's overture is the donkey that accompanies the four old men throughout the text of the *Wake*: "but I, poor ass, am but their four-part tinkler's dunkey" (405.6–7).

Vincent Cheng, in his monograph on Shakespearean elements in *Finnegans Wake*, has outlined parallels between the narrative of the opening pages of Book III and Nick Bottom's dream vision in *A Midsummer Night's Dream*. There is the occurrence of the phrase "dhove's suckling" in Joyce's text (*FW* 403.16–17), echoing Bottom's "sucking dove" in Shakespeare's play (*MND* 1.2.82–83; cited in Cheng 36). Then there are the repeated variations of the Elizabethan phrase "methinks" and the fact that both events occur around midnight (Cheng 36). The ass's dream, Cheng notes, is "perhaps incomprehensible, resisting rational analysis or decoding," like Bottom's, and since *Finnegans Wake,* like *A Midsummer Night's Dream,* "is both dream and drama, the Ass's dream vision thus finds a parallel in Bottom's dream" (37–38).

Those familiar with Shakespeare's work will recall that the mischievous sprite, Puck, on orders from Oberon, the fairy king, gives Bottom a donkey's head as part of a ruse to embarrass Oberon's fairy wife, Titania. After having her eyelids anointed by Puck with the juice of a magic flower while she sleeps, Titania awakens to dote on the first creature she sees, which Puck ensures will be the buffoonish and cranially transformed Bottom. Titania lavishes her affections on the perplexed but pleased mortal for a brief period before the two fall asleep, with Titania entwining Bottom in her arms. Puck then breaks the spell. When Nick Bottom returns to consciousness, he remembers the strange events as a dream. Here is his reaction to the dream's contents:

> I have had a most rare vision. I have had a dream, past the wit of man to say what dream it was: man is but an ass, if he go about to expound this dream. Methought I was—there is no man can tell what. Methought I was,—and methought I had,—but man is but a patched fool, if he will offer to say what methought I had. The eye of man hath not heard, the ear of man hath not seen, man's hand is not able to taste, his tongue not able to conceive, nor his heart to report, what my dream was. I will get Peter Quince to write a ballad of this dream: it shall be called Bottom's Dream, because it hath no bottom. (*MND* 4.1.204–16)

Nick Bottom wants his dream to be named after him, and after precisely what his fuzzy recollection of his dream is not: a text with a "bottom." And if anyone is foolish enough to try to explicate this dream, then he or she is an ass—precisely what Bottom was in his enchanted state. This paradoxical commentary on one of the several oneiric moments in Shakespeare's play by one of the dream's participants could well serve as a general observation regarding the reading of *Finnegans Wake:* it is difficult to ascertain exactly what the dream is about, except that one feels like an ass when trying to interpret it. It seems indeed to have no bottom, this text of Joyce. In the following pages I aim to explore the implications of this notion of bottomlessness in Book III's overture, and in *Finnegans Wake* as a whole, and what it means for the unique kind of reading and interpretation that Joyce's book demands.

Just how bottomless is the dream within the dream, the ass's dream about

Shaun? We see Shaun, through the eyes of the dreaming donkey, as very large: "He was immense, topping swell for he was having a great time of it, a twentyfour hours every moment matters maltsight" (*FW* 405.21–23 [Ger. *Mahlzeit*, "meal"]). This observation recurs later in III.2 when we find "Jaun" dining on "gracious helpings, at this rate of growing our cotted child of yestereve will soon fill space and burst in systems" (429.11–12). As Shaun himself remarks, "I never open momouth but I pack mefood in it" (437.19–20). Shaun eats like a hungry bandit, "three-partite pranzipal meals *plus* a collation" (405.31–32), which the dreamer describes with Rabelaisian fervor. We also discover, in a detail indicative of the dream-work's penchant for absurdity, that the food is "all free of charge, aman . . . And the best of wine *avec*" (406.21–22). The statement that follows seems patently incongruous: "For his heart was a big as himself, so it was, ay, and bigger!" (407.23–24). Shaun's heart seems to defy the logic of space, and furthermore, what's so big-hearted about this fellow, anyway? His gargantuan eating habits and the fact that his meals are provided "all free of charge, aman" (406.21–22) would hardly lead us to conclude that Shaun is of a generous disposition, ay, even more generous than generosity itself. Clearly, there are other facets of Shaun's persona that glimmer just below the surface of the ass's narration at this point. We might surmise, for example, that it is actually Shaun's belly that is "as big as himself," and that the signifier "heart," having been separated from its suffix through a kind of pruning mechanism in the psychic formation of the ass's dream, really serves to describe Shaun's appetite, which is certainly heart-y. This potential linguistic transformation from hearty to heart suggests another one of Shaun's appetites: the heart to which we ascribe so-called "affairs of the heart." In the previous chapter (*FW* II.4) we find the following words in a description of Issy: "nothing under her hat but red hair and solid ivory (now you know it's true in your *hardup hearts*) and a firstclass pair of bedroom eyes, of most unhomy blue" (*FW* 396.9–12; emphasis added). This juxtaposition of the would-be lover's heart and the loved one's eyes is reflected in the ass's narration when he remarks *à propos* of Shaun that "in the sighed of lovely eyes while his knive of hearts made havoc he had recruited his strength by meals of spadefuls of mounded food" (*FW* 405.28–30). It is immediately following this passage that the donkey's description of Shaun's gastronomic orgies begins. Shaun eats to keep his strength up, to keep his "knives of hearts" honed, to keep his "hardup heart" up hard, this knave of hearts who will need all the energy he can muster when he encounters the twenty-nine leap year girls of St. Bride's later in Book III and becomes the more and more prolific HCE he has come to replace. Already, he is "so jarvey jaunty with a romp of a schoolgirl's completion sitting pretty over his Oyster Monday print face" (*FW* 407.6–8) and "on the . . . mash" (407.8–9 [sl. *on the mash*, "making amorous or flirtatious advances"]). Finally, the "lovely bedroom eyes" appear once again, homophonically at least, in the "ay" (i.e., "eye"), the affirmation in the ass's declaration that Shaun's "heart was as big as himself, so it was, *ay*, and bigger." Thus, at this moment in the donkey's narration are condensed the ravenousness of Shaun's appetite in the dovetailing of both its alimentary and sexual aspects, Shaun's seemingly bottomless capacity for satisfaction, desire itself, the infinite, the unfathomable—all economically loaded into the apparently misplaced, or at least mischosen, signifier, "heart."

It is easy to construe Shaun's heart, as it appears in the manifest content of the ass's dream, as an emblematic figure for the entire text of *Finnegans Wake*. Joyce's book indeed overflows itself. Its content is immense (and "topping swell"), and both the writer, we presume, and the enthralled reader are, as the donkey puts it, "after having a great time of it, a twentyfour hours every moment matters maltsight." Paradoxically, time and space seem to be almost infinitely expanded as they are condensed and compacted in the *Wake* where "the park is gracer than the hole" (*FW* 512.28). The text seems as bottomless as Shaun's drives and, in fact, we can discover figures of the text as a (w)hole almost anywhere in its 628 pages, so deep are the semantic, visual, and auditory overtones of each passage, word, and syllable.

In this way, reading the *Wake* is like the interpretation of a dream. In his major treatise on dreams, Freud examines the way in which chiefly latent dream-thoughts, previous day's events, and external stimuli are woven (*gewebt*) into the dream's condensed and distorted manifest content. There are two phenomena in what Freud calls the "dream-work" (the mechanism with which the mind transforms the latent dream-thoughts into the manifest dream-contents) that are of particular interest with regard to the notion of "bottomlessness" in the *Wake*: nodal points (*Knotenpunkte*, literally "knot points") and navels (*Nabel*). Both are elements in the dream's content at which the dream-thoughts intersect in a dense, tortuous, thematic entanglement that is condensed into a single word or phrase. In his analysis of his own "Dream of the Botanical Monograph," Freud states that the verbal element "botanical" constitutes "a regular nodal point [*Knotenpunkt*] in the dream" and that "numerous trains of thought converged upon it" (4: 283). In interpreting dreams, Freud seems to focus on these moments of dream-thought entanglement, of "overdetermination," as he calls it (283), not only as points packed with valuable information about the dream's latent content and structure but as signifiers whose interpretation is absolutely crucial to a reading of the dream.

A dream's navel is similar, but crucially different. In his analysis of his dream of "Irma's Injection," Freud notes that "There is at least one spot in every dream at which it is unplumbable [*unergründlich*, literally, "without a discernible bottom"]—a navel [*Nabel*], as it were, that is its point of contact with the unknown" (4: 111). Later in his text, Freud revisits the idea of dream navels:

> There is often a passage in even the most thoroughly interpreted dream which has to be left obscure; this is because we become aware during the work of interpretation that at that point there is a tangle [*Knäuel*, also denoting "a ball of thread or yarn, a skein, or a knot"] of dream-thoughts which cannot be unraveled and which moreover adds nothing to our knowledge of the dream. This is the dream's navel [*Nabel*], the spot where it reaches down into the unknown. The dream-thoughts to which we are led ... cannot ... have any definite endings; they are bound to branch out in every direction into the intricate network of our world of thought. (5: 525)

In other words, though the terms "nodal point" and "navel" both denote moments in the manifest content of a dream at which various thematic threads from the dream-thoughts converge and entangle themselves in a knot of linguistic associations, Freud appears to embrace the nodal point as a nexus of linguistic overdetermination and as a useful source of interpretive information, while shying away from the navel's concentration of dream-thoughts that "branch out in every direction" without "definite endings." It may be that Freud's own mental censorship is at work here; there is certainly something unspoken and sexual in his lengthy analysis of his dream of "Irma's Injection," in which Freud admonishes his female patient in the dream for not opening "her mouth properly" (4: 143). However, for the purposes of the current argument I'd like to take his distinction between the two different kinds of dream nodes at its face value: some points of overdetermination in the dream-work lead us to relevant interpretive threads (nodal points), while other points of associative convergence in the dream-work "branch out in every direction" and reach down into what seems to be a bottomless abyss" of "our world of thought" (navels).

Joyce famously purported to be uninterested in Freud and his theories of psychoanalysis, claiming that the Austrian thinker had been anticipated by Vico.[1] We know, however, that Joyce apparently did learn a lot about psychoanalysis through his Italian friends and that he held pamphlets by Freud, Ernest Jones, and Carl Jung in his Triestine library (Ellmann 340). It is difficult to believe that Freud's ideas did not play a part in Joyce's creation of his "book of the night." John Bishop argues this point convincingly in *Joyce's Book of the Dark,* stating that "It seems . . . impossible for any reader seriously interested in coming to terms with *Finnegans Wake* to ignore *The Interpretation of Dreams*" (16)—or the "intrepidation of our dreams," as Taff evokes it in II.3 (*FW* 338.29–30). It is no surprise, then, that Freud's notions of nodal points and navels, and especially the language he uses to describe these dream phenomena, might be particularly useful in dealing with the night language of the *Wake.*

Readers of Shakespeare's play may recall that Nick Bottom is a weaver. This character's surname, Bottom, suggests "a bottom of thread, or the clew or core on which the weaver's yarn is wound" (Shakespeare, 2003 ed., 65 n.). Thus the asinine dreamer in *A Midsummer Night's Dream,* evoked by Joyce in chapter III.1 of *Finnegans Wake* in the guise of the dreaming donkey, represents not only the bottomlessness of a particular dream that he wishes to name, paradoxically, "Bottom's Dream, because it hath no bottom," but also those points in the dream at which there is a certain density of latent threads of thought—both those that can be profitably unwound (like the weaver's bottom or a dream's nodal point) and those "cannot be unraveled" (like Bottom's dream and Freud's dream navel). And in the ass's narration (with its Shakespearean overtones) of Shaun as a figure of bottomless appetites, with a heart that is bigger than himself, Joyce's text reads like an overdetermined moment in the manifest content of a dream at which the dream-work's entwining of various mental threads threatens to engulf the book's readers in the intricate, bottomless network of "our world of thought." But does this thematic convergence in the *Wake* represent an interpretive navel or a nodal point?

I would argue, both. Scholarly reading, and interpretation in general, are often concerned with the unraveling of nodal points in discourse, elements in a text at which "numerous trains of thought converge": double meanings, irony, layers of symbolism, unreliable narration—all discursive or rhetorical mechanisms that manifest themselves in overdetermined signification. Navels, as Freud describes them, are to be recognized, but avoided for the

purpose of serious exegesis, for they lead the reader down interpretive pathways with no "definite endings." They are traps in which the reader is especially prone to read "too much" into the text, as the clichéd caveat goes. The
distinction between these two types of discursive clustering is not always
clear, however, and in a text like *Finnegans Wake* it is positively "allmurk"
(*FW* 404.10). Crossing the line between universally accepted interpretive
conclusions into more impressionistic, "risky reading of risky writing" (as
Margot Norris terms it) is not necessarily a bad thing, though; it can sometimes even serve as a useful strategy for more adventurous and rewarding
reading. Gayatri Spivak makes an important observation in this regard when
she invokes Freudian dream navels in her especially lucid summary of the
art of deconstruction, which appears in the introduction to her English
translation of Derrida's *De la grammatologie*: "this tangle cannot be unraveled in terms of, and adds nothing to the contents of the dream-text within
the limits set up by itself. If, however, we have nothing vested in the puta-
tive identity of the text or dream, that passage is where we can provisionally
locate the text's moment of transgressing the laws it apparently sets up for
itself, and thus unravel—deconstruct—the very text" (Derrida lxvi). Thus,
deconstruction (or whatever one might wish to term the technique with
which readers turn texts-to-be-interpreted back on themselves) strikes at
the lawless, "unhomy" moment of discourse and treats it as a *nodal point,* not
as a navel—for the serious reader, one intent on presenting universally compelling conclusions about a particular discourse, would choose to ignore a
navel, if the textual element in question were perceived as such, as being
unreadable and, what's more, as being unimportant for an understanding of
the text as a whole.

In *Finnegans Wake,* Joyce created a novel of discursive entanglement, of
linguistic anarchy, and it is perhaps in a kindred spirit, or at least with a
light and somewhat foolhardy reader's heart, that we tend to confront this
bottomless, lawless text. Hélène Cixous, for whom such a stance is not only
noteworthy, but of prime importance with regard to *all* of Joyce's fiction, acknowledges the necessity, ramifications, and dangers of such an approach in
her essay, "Joyce: The (R)use of Writing." She describes Joyce's literary discourse as "(r)used writing, writing governed by ruse . . . you have to modify
the traditional mode of narrative which claims to offer a coherent whole,
utilizable down to its smallest detail, the author being tacitly bound to produce an account of his expenditure. This is writing which is prodigal and
therefore disconcerting because of its economy, which refuses to regulate

itself, to give itself laws" (Cixous 19). The paradox of both the dream text and *Finnegans Wake* is that although time, space, and sense are economically condensed into tight, concise packages of linguistic weave, the unwrapping of these little bundles, these signifying jacks-in-boxes, through the activity of reading unleashes a decidedly uneconomic blast of ever-expanding signification that has no "definite ending," that is "unplumbable." This bottomless latent discourse, "which refuses to regulate itself," is "hard to bear, just as it is difficult to accept that frustration is normal, especially in the intellectual sphere . . . yet it is at this point that you must stop demanding meaning. It is also at this point that academic discourse is brought to its limit, or its . . . discouragement, *loss of heart,* of moral fibre, of potency, in the face of danger or difficulty" (Cixous 21, emphasis added).

But we need not lose heart in the face of Joyce's most complex and demanding text, for the author's style in *Finnegans Wake* necessarily invites readers to transcend the limits of conventional interpretive discourse, academic or otherwise, ay, compels it. *Finnegans Wake* is like a Rorschach test: our glosses of words, phrases, and passages often reveal more about ourselves than about the latent narrative content of Joyce's text.[2] Faced with the constantly overdetermined language of the sleeping "narrator," we are pushed by a kind of interpretive imperative to apply an analysis that treats the *Wake*'s relentless multilingual puns, references, and syntactic ambiguities as nodal points, while necessarily becoming entangled, like Nick Bottom in Titania's sleepy embrace, in a relentless occurrence of textual navels that plunge us into the hermeneutic unknown. The boundary between these two linguistic dynamics is just too indistinct to be enforceable, and the latent thoughts we glimpse (or think we glimpse) behind the *Wake*'s elusive figures appear like Shaun in the ass's dream: "somewho might amove allmurk" (*FW* 404.10) and "who so swayed a will of the wisp" (405.15)—there, but not there. For this reason, we might reach consensus on some glosses, while more idiosyncratic readings may seem compelling to some readers, while implausible to others.

"Words, since they are the nodal points of numerous ideas, may be regarded as predestined to ambiguity," says Freud (5: 340), and never more so than in *Finnegans Wake*. Readers of the *Wake* therefore have to overcome their prudish concern over making asses of themselves in the face of Joyce's seemingly "unreadable" text, its "eyes of unhomy blue" seducing and teasing their expert readers' pride. They must take heart, a slightly arrogant heart perhaps—one that may be bigger than themselves, perhaps too big for their britches—and like Nick Bottom, the weaver, erstwhile ass, explore adventurously the delightfully allmurky depths of Joyce's nocturnal tale about everything and everybody, his dreamy carnival of language that yields to the lawlessness of a bottomless, prodigal discursive economy. There *is* something to be untangled and rewoven here, playfully, through a process of analysis similar to the "intrepidation of our dreams." To limit the satisfaction of this analytical appetite, no matter how gargantuan, would be to make a most "freudful mistake" (*FW* 411.35–36).

Notes

1. From an interview with Paolo Cuzzi, cited in Ellmann 340.
2. I owe this observation to Ana Rojas.

Works Cited

Bishop, John. *Joyce's Book of the Dark: "Finnegans Wake."* Madison: U of Wisconsin P, 1986.

Cheng, Vincent. *Shakespeare and Joyce: A Study of "Finnegans Wake."* University Park: Pennsylvania State UP, 1984.

Cixous, Hélène. "Joyce: The (R)use of Writing." Trans. Judith Still. *Post-Structuralist Joyce: Essays from the French.* Ed. Derek Attridge and Daniel Ferrer. Cambridge: Cambridge UP, 1984. 15–30.

Derrida, Jacques. *Of Grammatology.* Trans. Gayatri Spivak. Baltimore: Johns Hopkins UP, 1976.

Ellmann, Richard. *James Joyce.* New and rev. ed. Oxford: Oxford UP, 1982.

Freud, Sigmund. *The Interpretation of Dreams.* Vols. 4–5 of *The Standard Edition of the Complete Psychological Works of Sigmund Freud.* Trans. James Strachey. London: Hogarth, 1958.

Norris, Margot. "Risky Reading of Risky Writing." *Joyce in Trieste: An Album of Risky Readings.* Ed. Sebastian D. G. Knowles, Geert Lernout, and John McCourt. Gainesville: UP of Florida, 2007. 36–53.

Shakespeare, William. *A Midsummer Night's Dream. The Riverside Shakespeare.* 2nd ed. Boston: Houghton Mifflin, 1997.

———. *A Midsummer Night's Dream.* Ed. R. A. Foakes. Cambridge: Cambridge University Press, 2003.

8

"The Imprevidibility of the Future"

On Joycean Prophecy

PAUL K. SAINT-AMOUR

Beauty is not there. Nor in the stagnant bay of Marsh's library
where you read the fading prophecies of Joachim Abbas.

Ulysses 3.107–8

Behold, I make all things new.

Revelation 21:5

More than fifty years ago, Richard Ellmann characterized Joyce's relationship to his readers and scholars as one of enduring untimeliness:
"We are still learning to be James Joyce's contemporaries, to understand our
interpreter" (*JJ* 1). Ellmann's was a Joyce so advanced as to have outrun not
only his own contemporaries but also those generations of readers who still
lay in the future. Even the future, in other words, was belated with respect
to Joyce, as if it already belonged to a stable, interpretable past.[1] Ellmann's
formulation may be better understood as addressing the decryption time
demanded by Joyce's work—the centuries' worth of enigmas and puzzles
Joyce claimed would ensure his immortality—than its powers of prevision
(*JJ* 521). Nonetheless, Ellmann mantles that strategy of deferred reception in
the rhetoric of earliness and prophecy, a move that has been repeated many
times since by Joyce's critics. Intimations of foreknowledge or untimely perception confer a powerful frisson. But in this essay I wish to look elsewhere
for the shiver of alterity in Joyce's work, resisting the notion that its author
had some special prognostic access to a future that included several generations of his readers. Prophecy, I argue, was not Joyce's gift or mode but one of

his great subjects—one of a variety of discrepant temporalities that *Ulysses,* in particular, wants to probe, anatomize, and exhibit in a critical light.

One might have expected prophecy to be absent from Joyce's book, its absence serving as one of the indices by which the novel's 1904 setting measures its distance from the oracle-haunted world of Homer, the prophets of the Hebrew bible, the vaticinations of early Christian mystics, and certain early modern seers. But instead *Ulysses* positively teems with allusions to prophets and prophetic texts, with diegetic instances of prognostication, and with skeptical anatomies of prophecy's social function. It is almost as if Joyce's book were an encyclopedia of prophecy, a kind of latter-day answer to that chapter of Isidore of Seville's seventh-century *Etymologies* titled "Man and Portents." In the course of cataloguing varieties of prophecy, I suggest, *Ulysses* partly undertakes to demystify prophecy by assimilating it to its historical moment, making it one of many discourses competing for attention. Yet this deprivileging of prophecy is not the end of the story, for *Ulysses* also engages in acts of premonitory, if conditional, *hope* that may be the true locus of untimeliness in the text, as against prophecy's false untimeliness. "Behold, I make all things new," intones the Book of Revelation. Even as *Ulysses* historicizes apocalyptic prophecy, the original news that stays news, it undertakes a renovation or renaissance of future-directed utterance in opener, less authoritative, less historical registers.[2] I will conclude by distinguishing prophecy from hopefulness and by imagining Joyce's book as a reservoir of unfulfilled futures that may still irrigate our political hopes today.

In addition to engaging Ernst Bloch's work on political hope, my discussion of *Ulysses,* prophecy, and the future is informed by two recent books. One is by a historian and the other by an anthropologist; both participate in a broad surge of interest across the humanities and the more qualitative social sciences in what we might call *critical futurities:* an application of literary and critical theory to past and present conscriptions of "the future," to the rhetoric and poetics of such conscriptions, and to their ethical, political, and historiographic import.[3] My first reference point in what I am calling critical futurities is Michael André Bernstein's *Foregone Conclusions: Against Apocalyptic History,* which mounts an ethical critique of "heavily forestructured" histories of mass trauma. Bernstein develops an immensely useful term, "backshadowing," which he defines as "a kind of retroactive foreshadowing in which the shared knowledge of the outcome of a series of events by narrator and listener is used to judge the participants in those events *as though they too should have known what was to come"* (1, 16). Treating futures-past as inevitable, Bernstein argues, is often the first step in chiding those who failed to heed the obvious portents of those catastrophic futures and were thus, according to the backshadower, needlessly victimized by them. Such claims, which a surprising number of Holocaust historians have made about European Jews in the 1930s, treat the future as a foregone conclusion and thereby deny the freedom of historical actors to have envisioned or helped produce a different outcome, effectively limiting their choice to acceptance or vain rejection of the foreordained. Against such apocalyptic histories, Bernstein summons the practice of sideshadowing, a "gesturing to the side, to a present dense with multiple, and mutually exclusive, possibilities for what is to come" (1).[4] Historical sideshadowing wants to map, or at least gesture toward, roads no less possible for having been untaken by events, and the ethical stakes of such a project are not low for Bernstein. The foreclosure of futures-past does nothing less than impede collective mourning, insofar as that mourning must be able to count as possible a future in which the victims survived and flourished if it is to begin taking the measure of their loss.

David Scott's *Conscripts of Modernity* serves as my second reference point in the critical futurities problem-space. Like Bernstein, Scott explores how our capacity to imagine more habitable political futures relies on how we narrate not just the past generally but futures-past specifically. But where Bernstein wants to repopulate the past with counterfactual possibilities in order to aid the griefwork of the living, Scott urges the living to re-narrate futures-past so as not to be constrained by the now-obsolete emplotments of those futures by earlier generations. Genre is the key category here: it is time, says Scott, to retire the romance plot fashioned by the Caribbean anticolonial generation in the wake of that plot's failure to yield the emancipation it prophesied. Anticolonial romance, he argues, should be superseded by tragedy as the narrative frame through which to understand that past future. One may not agree that tragedy is the most explanatory or productive genre through which to reemplot that anticolonial experience with an eye to a future less haunted by its failure.[5] But Scott's focus on the present political consequences of futures-past, their variable emplotments, and their intergenerational transmission is extremely powerful. It reminds us both that past narratives about the future are crucial historical artifacts and that those artifacts need not be permitted to dictate the conditions of their reception and interpretation.

So far I have been talking about scholarly work in the last two decades. But if, as Bernstein and Scott have variously suggested, rhetoric, genre, and plot are core questions for critical futurities, then the novel too may be a site where the genres and plots of futures-past get archived or operationalized. Here we might be particularly interested in novels that abstain from conventional plotting in order to make plot an object of scrutiny—in order to mount an exhibition of plots and plotting that includes varieties of narrative forestructuring. Novels, too, in which multiple generic and rhetorical registers are in rotation and therefore denaturalized and held up to the light. Probably a capacious modernist novel written out of the experience of geopolitical crisis but backdated to a prewar moment, so as to meditate on one moment's particular structure of expectation and to model a later moment's relation to that structure. For Bernstein, this novel is Robert Musil's *Der Mann ohne Eigenschaften* (*The Man without Qualities*) (1930–42), whose refusal to backshadow despite its 1913 setting Bernstein celebrates alongside its practice of dense sideshadowing. I wish to take up a slightly earlier work of encyclopedic modernist narrative, Joyce's *Ulysses*, which was written during the paroxysmal years 1914 to 1921 but set in 1904 (so, as with Musil, we have a gap between a prewar horizon of expectation and a postwar space of experience). Both set and published in moments charged with imminence, *Ulysses* is a meditation on how forestructured narratives interface with spasmodic, often traumatic change.

There has been one influential attempt to link long modernist narratives such as Joyce's and Musil's through their prognostic gestures. This is Edward Mendelson's "Gravity's Encyclopedia" (1976), which, as its title announced, aimed to canonize Pynchon's then-recently-published *Gravity's Rainbow* by installing it in a sparse genealogy of "encyclopedic narratives" that included the *Divine Comedy, Don Quixote, Moby Dick,* and *Ulysses*. According to Mendelson, these texts share a number of traits, including prolixity, capacious accounts of at least one science and one art, and the conspicuous accommodation of multiple literary styles. They were also slightly out of joint with their time—that is, they were set neither in the moment of their publication nor in the remote, mythic past of epic. Mendelson reads this modest belatedness as a means to the end of prophecy-making: an encyclopedic novel, he says, lags just far enough behind its moment of publication—by the eighteen years separating 1904 and 1922, or by the twenty-eight years between the main action of Pynchon's novel and its publication date—to install itself as the harbinger of that present.

But Mendelson goes farther, arguing that such a text's trompe l'œil auguries confer a real prophetic authority:

> The main action occurs about twenty years before the time of writing, allowing the book to maintain a mimetic (or, more precisely, satiric) relation to the world of its readers, while permitting it to include prophecies that are accurate, having been fulfilled between the time of the action and the time of the writing. These "accurate" prophecies then claim implicitly to confer authority on other prophecies in the book [that] have not yet been fulfilled. (163)

It's not clear why a text's having conspicuously repackaged hindsight as prevision should confer credibility on its prophecies about a future that is still to come. Still, for Mendelson the genre's oracular quality is neither accidental nor merely rhetorical: "An encyclopedic narrative," he writes, "prophesies the modes of human action and perception that its culture will later discover to be its own central concerns" (178). The strangeness of these texts, according to his argument, is partly the strangeness of the future, which reveals itself first to the encyclopedic novelist and only later to its culture. That culture Mendelson specifically identifies as belonging to the emerging *nation*—the industrial United States anticipated by *Moby Dick*, the Irish Free State by *Ulysses*, and the postwar U.S. empire by *Gravity's Rainbow*—to which the encyclopedic text stands in a singular, even messianic relation. Partly by giving rise to exegetical industries, these big books announce the coming of an autonomous, self-sustaining national culture.

Ulysses would seem to play right into Mendelson's hands. As one of the Anglo-Irish litterateurs in "Scylla and Charybdis" says, "Our national epic has yet to be written" (*U* 9.309), and in this formulation the text appears at once to predict Irish nationhood and to nominate itself as that emerging nation's epic. Certainly the prospect of an Irish nation-state attracts a good deal of *Ulysses'* premonitory energy.[6] But the nature and import of the book's political forecasts are more ambivalent than in Mendelson's narrative of triumphant state formation and literary messianism. Joyce's book never makes or alludes to a prophecy of national becoming without in some way delimiting or annulling it. Sometimes this happens through carnivalesque interruption, as when the final words of Robert Emmet's speech from the dock—"When my country takes her place among the nations of the earth, then and not till then let my epitaph be written. I have done"—are broken up by the sounds of passing tram and passing gas (see *U* 11.1284–94)

(Sullivan, Sullivan, and Sullivan 60). That syntax—"x will not happen until y transpires"—should be familiar to us from literary modes that consecrate prophecy at moments of regime-change: the tragic ("Macbeth shall never vanquished be until / Great Birnam Wood to high Dunsinane Hill / Shall come against him") and the epic ("Troy will not fall until Philoctetes brings his bow from Lemnos"). "*Fuit Ilium!* The sack of windy Troy. . . . The masters of the Mediterranean are fellaheen today," says Professor MacHugh in "Aeolus," just after claiming that John F. Taylor's speech about the youthful Moses and the Egyptian high priest has "the prophetic vision" (*U* 7.909–11). Yet whether we think Taylor's speech eloquent or merely a sack of wind, its "prophetic" qualities have more to do with vatic tone than with any accurate prediction of the Irish-language revival's having achieved the fullness of Moses—a fullness curbed, in any event, by the latter's having died without entering the land of promise, as J. J. O'Molloy regretfully points out (*U* 7.872). And this is true again and again in *Ulysses*: the *making* of political prophecy is an occasion for *checking*, and often for *mocking*, political prophecy.

But you can mock prophecy without dimming its glamour—without detracting from its claim to be sacred, privileged speech. The surest way to *deconsecrate* prophecy is not to mock it but to insist on its historicity—on its lack of untimely vantage, its being an artifact perfectly synchronous with its moment. If *Ulysses* is a veritable museum of prognostication, it curates its exhibits with care, ensuring that we may track prophecy to its historical ground. Sometimes this ground is closer to the present than it seems. Bloom, toward the end of "Nausicaa," recalls "Mother Shipton's prophecy that is about ships around they fly in the twinkling" (*U* 13.1065–66). He is thinking here about famous lines in which the Tudor prophetess from Yorkshire was thought to have predicted the steam engine, the railway, the diving suit, the submarine, the dreadnought, the air balloon, the telegraph, the gold rush, and the end of the world in 1881.

ANCIENT PREDICTION
(Entitled by popular tradition "Mother Shipton's Prophecy")
Published in 1448, republished in 1641

Carriages without horses shall go,
And accidents fill the world with woe.
Around the world thoughts shall fly
In the twinkling of an eye.

The world upside down shall be
And gold be found at the root of a tree.
Through hills man shall ride,
And no horse be at his side.
Under water men shall walk,
Shall ride, shall sleep, shall talk.
In the air men shall be seen,
In white, in black, in green;
Iron in the water shall float,
As easily as a wooden boat.
Gold shall be found and shown
In a land that's now not known.
Fire and water shall wonders do,
England shall at last admit a foe.
The world to an end shall come,
In eighteen hundred and eighty one.[7]

But this wasn't, in fact, a Tudor-era prediction: by 1904, the passage Bloom recalls was widely known to have been introduced into an 1862 edition of Richard Head's *The Life and Death of Mother Shipton* by a bookseller named Charles Hindley, whose admission of the hoax nine years later did not prevent hysteria from breaking out in rural parts of England as the year 1881 drew near.[8] Hindley's misattribution of backdated prophecies to a long-dead prophet—his faked "revival" of a Renaissance text—is a classic example of something called *vaticinationes ex eventu,* the disfigurement of the archive to make the past appear to predict an already-realized future.[9] By including this example of *ex eventu* prophecy, then, *Ulysses* fortifies its readers against the very technique by which Mendelson says encyclopedic novels secure their prophetic authority, exhibiting the production of false apocalyptic prophecy as itself a legibly historical act.

If we turn to the *avant-texte* of Joyce's novel, we find not just an archiving but also a refusal of *ex eventu* prophecy at the compositional level. (Here I look to the genetic archive not as a means of reconstructing Joyce's intentions but as a map of both the roads leading to the published text and the roads not taken—that is, as a counterfactual space of literary possibility.) Among the foregone textual futures of *Ulysses,* in a 1919 draft of the "Cyclops" episode, there is a backdated prophecy of the Great War. In the draft, a pubgoer named O'Madden Burke tells his fellow drinkers that "there's a war coming on for the Sassenachs and the Germans will give them a hell of a gate of going. What the imperial yeomanry got from the boers is only what you might call a hors d'oeuvre. . . . But win or lose, . . . they'll be up against a conundrum, . . . a fellow that'll kill his man for every man they kill. Wait till you see."[10] Had this prophecy remained in the published text, it would have exemplified just the sort of authority grab that Mendelson ascribes to premonitory encyclopedic narratives. But the passage was deleted from the episode prior to the Rosenbach Manuscript, as if to stage in the longitudinal flow of revision the same rejection of prophecy that the published text performs at the level of theme and rhetoric. The remaining adumbrations of the Great War and of the prospect of the peace of nations in the published *Ulysses* are much more oblique ones, and they are often cheek-by-jowl with language about the future's resistance to divination (Epstein; Spoo; Fairhall; Stead).

What is true of forged prophecy is also true of good-faith prediction: both acts are historically intelligible ways of being in a particular present—of being, after all, the contemporaries of our contemporaries. In "Ithaca" we learn that a drawer in the Blooms' walnut sideboard contains "a sealed prophecy (never unsealed) written by Leopold Bloom in 1886 concerning the consequences of passing into law of William Ewart Gladstone's Home Rule bill of 1886 (never passed into law)" (*U* 17.1787–90). Here we find prophecy—again, pointedly failed—where *Ulysses* has taught us to expect it: filed away in the archive, among dirty postcards and pennibs and a toddler's drawings. A form of utterance in which the knowledge, fears, and desires of a particular moment can be read with special clarity, prophecy, for all its yearning to part the curtains of the future, may be the historical artifact par excellence.

I want to pause, though, over Bloom's prophecy to observe that the "Ithaca" narrators, who can cross even the boundary between factual and counterfactual—telling us, for example, to what purpose Bloom *could have* applied the boiled water (*U* 11.275–76), what careers he *could have* pursued (11.787–94), or why he *would have* smiled if he had smiled (11.2126–31)—these narrators decline to unseal the envelope and expose the verbatim contents of Bloom's prophecy. Why? At the very least, this act of narratorial reticence bespeaks a deep sympathy with Bloom, a choice to leave unread what he has either forgotten about or decided not to open. If Bloom has made a decision—the likelier reading, given that he has taken pains to conserve the envelope among other important documents that he has occasion to revisit—it seems to be the decision to preserve his forecast unopened until the prospect that inspired its writing may be fulfilled. That is, as long as Irish Home Rule remains unachieved, the prophecy will remain unread by both Bloom and the narrators.

This would seem to resurrect the syntax of "not until . . . only then" that *Ulysses* has elsewhere mocked, there as here in respect to future-conditional political change. But there's a difference: whereas the delimiting clauses in my earlier examples—Emmet's "*When* my country takes its place" and the weird sisters' "*Until* / Great Birnam Wood to high Dunsinane Hill / Shall come against him" and the prophet Helenos's "*until* Philoctetes brings his bow"—camouflage prophecy in the language of contingency, Bloom saves his sealed forecast in the truly contingent hope that the conditions for opening it might arrive. For starker contrast, set Bloom's gesture beside the eschatological couplet Charles Hindley ascribed to Mother Shipton: "The world to an end *shall* come / In eighteen-hundred and eighty-one." A simple future utterance like this one radiates certainty until it fails to transpire, whereupon its prophetic authority is discredited and dispelled. But to leave unopened your eighteen-year-old forecasts about the consequences of a still-unrealized political condition: such an act may be susceptible to disappointment, but not to discrediting. Unlike the brittle prophetic utterance, Bloom's reserve (which is also the text's) has the resilient, ongoing quality of an act of vigilance, the result of not one but a series of decisions to keep on waiting, keep on hoping. Ernst Bloch, the great theorist of political hope, had this to say of prophecy that manipulates the present through false guarantees about the future:

> There was a man who exchanged paper money of his own making for cash, imprinted with the words "Payable in the Currency of God's Kingdom on Judgment Day." Which sounds like a model for the enormous swindle perpetrated by the Thousand-year Reich. . . . It was the vilest caricature of Adventism, of the false Messiah, of the expectation of Christ's Second Coming on the day after tomorrow—and nothing came of it, except blood. "God arrives next Tuesday at 11:25 a.m. at the Illinois Central, hurry there to welcome him!" In this way a religious or (so to speak) utopian psychosis was started once in Chicago. (*Literary Essays* 339–40)[11]

As the ever-imminent Dr. John Alexander Dowie, aka Elijah III, who "Is coming! Is coming!! Is coming!!!" in *Ulysses* (8.15), reminds us, "The Deity ain't no nickel dime bumshow" but "a corking fine business proposition"

(14.1585–87). The "swindle" of the confident short-term divination always charges a heavy up-front fee in worldly currencies while promising hundred-fold profits in the world-just-to-come. In contrast to this swindle of certitude, Bloch describes a *"well-founded"* hope that

> must be unconditionally disappointable ... because it is open in a forward direction, in a future-oriented direction; it does not address itself to that which already exists. For this reason, hope—while actually in a state of suspension—is committed to change rather than repetition, and what is more, incorporates the element of chance, without which there can be nothing new. Through this portion of chance, however sufficiently determined it may be, openness is at the same time also *kept open*. At least to the extent that hope, whose field of action this is, pays in the coin of hazard so as not to be indebted to the past. (*Literary Essays* 341)

The kind of disappointment entailed in well-founded hope, Bloch adds, is its "creative 'minus' . . . as distinguished form the false 'plus'" of overconfident prophecy (*Literary Essays* 340). I have already suggested, in effect, that *Ulysses* is an encyclopedia of the "false 'plus,'" seeking through its inventory of accidental and falsified and commodified prophecies to fortify its readers against such confident swindles. Where it would leave us, I conjecture, is in a space of the "creative 'minus'": a space of potential, even ongoing disappointment that we have nevertheless come to understand as indissociable from a rigorous hope.

That's a rather fine description, in fact, of the book's three "nostos" episodes, and particularly of "Ithaca." No passage in that episode better captures the fusion of disappointment and hope, of hazard and openness, than the excursus on clown and coin in Bloom's musings. Stephen has declined Bloom's proposal of asylum, and the two men discuss counterproposals—scenarios in which Italian lessons, vocal coaching, and intellectual dialogue could be exchanged for the benefit of Stephen and both Blooms. But then the question comes: "What rendered problematic for Bloom the realization of these mutually selfexcluding propositions?" And the answer is one of those moments where the bottom drops out of polite conversation, exposing a fund of loss. Bloom doubts things will work out with Stephen for two reasons: first, "the irreparability of the past"—because dead sons do not come back to life and the intuitive particolored clown is not his child; and second,

The imprevidibility of the future: once in the summer of 1889 he (Bloom) had marked a florin (2/-) with three notches on the milled edge and tendered it in payment of an account due to and received by J. and T. Davy, family grocers, 1 Charlemont Mall, Grand Canal, for circulation on the waters of civic finance, for possible, circuitous or direct, return.

Was the clown Bloom's son?
No.

Had Bloom's coin returned?
Never. (*U* 17.973–88)

That "Never" has an undeniable affective truth for a man whose dead son and dead father are never coming back, who has made many unrewarded donations to various goodwill economies, and who has even been punished for those donations. And it is grammatically true that the coin has *never*—that is, *not ever*—returned. But in a temporal sense, that "never" is hyperbolic, is not strictly true; it would be more accurate to say "not yet." (Which raises the question: under what conditions and for what reasons is *not yet* misrecognized here for *never*?)[12] What's more, even were the marked coin to return it would not demonstrate the *previdibility,* or foreseeability, of the future; its return, no less than its failure to return, would demonstrate the *imprevidibility* of the future.[13] The future's resistance to divination and its attendant capacity (or even tendency) to disappoint our hopes—these are the positive conditions rather than the costly outcome of paying in the coin of hazard for the chance that something unforeseen will happen. That more is at stake here than coin or clown or even a new friendship becomes apparent in the next exchange:

Why would a recurrent frustration the more depress him?
Because at the critical turningpoint of human existence he desired to amend many social conditions, the product of inequality and avarice and international animosity. (*U* 17.989–92)

Tied up in the question of Bloom's future-conditional disappointments is nothing less than utopian political hope, a hope whose referent seems to supersede the political form of the nation-state while memorializing some of its sorrows in the phrase "international animosity." This isn't to suggest that *Ulysses* is only awaiting some cosmopolitan post-national order; only that the political futures it takes the trouble to conjure are not limited to Irish nationhood—that it keeps vigil over more than one unopened envelope.

In "Aeolus," Lenehan says of the prophet Moses that he died "with a great future behind him" (U 7.875–76). Preposterous truth, as we've already seen, often thrives in the patter of clowns, and Lenehan is one of Joyce's favorites. Here, Lenehan's jest reminds us that the future is always the-future-as-seen-from-somewhere, whether from Egypt or Pisgah, and that past hopes and preparations for the future, although they recede, may be recovered and rehabilitated as resources in the present. History, that is, may be a repository of foregone possibilities, unrealized desiderata, utopias that keep informing our plans. Paul Ricœur could almost be glossing Lenehan when he laments that "we have so many unfulfilled plans behind us, so many promises that have still not been held, that we have the means of rebuilding the future through reviving our heritage in its multiple forms" (Ricœur 58; Bindé 112–13). Or Ernst Bloch again:

> [Hu]mankind is not yet finished; therefore, neither is its past. It continues to affect us under a different sign, in the drive of its questions, in the experiment of its answers; we are all in the same boat. The dead return transformed: those whose actions were too bold to have come to an end (like Thomas Münzer); those whose work is too all-encompassing to have coincided with the locality of their times (like Aeschylus, Dante, Shakespeare, Bach, Goethe). The discovery of the future in the past, that is the philosophy of history, hence of philosophical history as well. ("Dialectics" 8)[14]

And, we might add, of a philosophy of literature as an archive of not-yet-completed futures, one that seeks ways of changing literature into a literature of changing the world. Reviving mothballed forms and dormant emplotments; checking for a pulse among left-for-dead texts: now *that* would be a renaissance—and a rereading very different from striving to catch up to a work deemed ahead of its time. We have a great future behind us, and one of its names is *Ulysses*.

I would like to conclude with a provocation informed by my reading in critical futurities. In the first chapter of *Conscripts of Modernity*, Scott asks what it would mean to continue to think not just about but through a book (in his case, C. L. R. James's *Black Jacobins*) whose own political futurity seems to have been superseded. How, then, could Joyce's book, with its apparent fixation on the emergent postcolonial nation speak to us, as the nation-state seems less and less adequate to the problem of our own political futures?[15] Although Irish nationhood is the most proximate political future on which *Ulysses* trains its hopes, it is neither the only one nor the anointed one; the populous futurities of the text, happily, enable it to accommodate our shifting attention as regards the text's hopefulness, our move to questions that are more salient to our own moment—questions about non-state actors, about paths between late-imperial ennui and violent extremism, about scarcity's intimate links to conflict, about global flows of capital and culture and war and work. Becoming our own contemporaries in relation to *Ulysses* may involve an end to reading Joyce's book as if its outermost hopes, premises, and inquiries were our own—that is, an end to striving to become *its* contemporaries. Without committing violence to its historicity, we must continue to make Joyce's book *our* contemporary—to highlight those more latent futurities within it that can speak to the questions that press most urgently on our moment. With apologies, but also thanks, to Stephen Dedalus: if *Ulysses* is to be important, it must be because it belongs to us.

Notes

1. Yet in "Ireland: Island of Saints and Sages" (1907), Joyce had barred the way specifically to prophecies about Ireland's political future, writing, "Alas, we amateur sociologists are only second-rate soothsayers; we look into and rummage around in the intestines of the human animal, and in the end, we confess that we see nothing there! Only our supermen can write the history of the future" (*OCPW* 125). The opening line of Ellmann's biography essentially nominates Joyce as one of those supermen.

2. Here I follow Arthur Danto in understanding prophecy to be a historical statement about the future: "The prophet is one who speaks about the future in a manner which is appropriate only to the past, or who speaks of the present in the light of a future treated as a fait accompli. A prophet treats the present in a perspective ordinarily available only to future historians, to whom present events are past, and for whom the meaning of present events is discernible" (9).

3. Critical futurities scholarship draws heavily on discussions of political temporality in the work of Walter Benjamin, Theodor Adorno, and Ernst Bloch. David Scott's work draws, additionally, on Reinhart Koselleck's *Futures Past: On the Semantics of Historical Time*. In postcolonial history and theory, Scott's work is both joined and resisted by that of Gary Wilder (see note 5 below) and others. Queer theory has produced vital work in critical futurities, particularly in Lee Edelman's critique of "reproductive futurism" and Heather K. Love's retreat from triumphalist narratives of queer emancipation; see, respectively, Lee Edelman, *No Future: Queer Theory and the Death Drive*, and Heather K. Love, *Feeling Backward: Loss and the Politics of Queer*

History. Michael André Bernstein's *Foregone Conclusions* has helped stimulate new work in literary studies on counterfactual plotting in both fiction and law; see Gallagher, "Undoing"; and Gallagher, Maslan, and Saint-Amour.

4. Bernstein takes the term *sideshadowing* from Morson's *Narrative and Freedom*. *Foregone Conclusions* and *Narrative and Freedom* were originally to have been a single coauthored volume until the authors decided to publish their work separately; see Morson 283 n. 4.

5. Gary Wilder offers just such a response to *Conscripts of Modernity*, arguing that "it is possible to accept [Scott's] critique of revolutionary anticolonialism without concluding, as he does, that all stories of colonial emancipation must be replaced with stories of impossible alternatives and tragic dilemmas." Wilder looks not at obsolete emplotments of the political future but at "futures that were once imagined but never came to be, alternative futures that might have been and whose not yet realized emancipatory possibilities may now be recognized and reawakened as durable and vital legacies" (102–3).

6. Indeed, Enda Duffy has argued that *Ulysses* is "*the* book of Irish postcolonial independence," both because it registers those (diegetically future) events that were concurrent with its composition and that led to the foundation of the Irish Free State and because it attempts to model subaltern subjectivities and communities that might come into being after independence. Duffy 1, emphasis in original.

7. Qtd. in Harrison 12–13. The claim that the prophecy was first published in 1448 seems to be an instance of spectacular carelessness, as the year of publication antedates the traditionally held year of Mother Shipton's birth by forty years.

8. The April 26, 1873, issue of *Notes and Queries* reported that "Mr. Charles Hindley, of Brighton, in a letter to us, has made a clean breast of having fabricated the Prophecy quoted at page 450 of our last volume, with some ten others included in his reprint of a chap-book version, published in 1862" (qtd. in Harrison 43). The 11th edition of the *Encyclopaedia Britannica* records, "The suggestion that Mother Shipton had foretold the end of the world in 1881 was the cause of the most poignant alarm throughout rural England in that year, the people deserting their houses, and spending the night in prayer in the fields, churches and chapels."

9. Hindley's choice of Mother Shipton as the vehicle for his hoax testifies, in a roundabout way, to the cultural authority attributed to the early modern period by the Victorians. Literary forgery may be the sincerest form of flattery, insofar as the forger seeks to camouflage an original work, and with it her proprietary claim upon it, beneath the greater glamour of another author or epoch. Oscar Wilde's "The Portrait of Mr. W. H." (1889) is, among other things, a meditation on forgery as erotic self-immolation; like Hindley, Wilde's protagonist performs this act at the altar of a Renaissance text—in his case, Shakespeare's *Sonnets*—and takes advantage of nineteenth-century scholarship on the period to bolster his credibility.

10. Buffalo MS V.A.6, p. 3; *Archive* 13:134c; *Buffalo* 180–81. I am grateful to Michael Groden for pointing me to this passage in the pre-publication material.

11. The piece, titled "Can Hope Be Disappointed?" was Bloch's inaugural lecture at the University of Tübingen, delivered on November 17, 1961.

12. The same question and observations apply to those two instances of *never* in the description of Bloom's "sealed prophecy (*never* unsealed)" concerning "Gladstone's Home Rule bill of 1886 (*never* passed into law)" discussed above (*U* 11.1788–90; emphasis added). Although it is true that the particular Home Rule bill in question was *not ever* passed into law, the general political condition of Home Rule is one that has simply *not yet* come to pass by June 1904. In relation to that future-conditional Home Rule, Bloom's prophecy has *not yet* been unsealed.

13. The *OED* records a use of *imprevisibility* in 1887. But Joyce's use of *imprevidibility* in "Ithaca" is the first appearance of the word in English and thus, in a term appropriate to the passage, a coinage. Like the florin (a British two-shilling coin named after a thirteenth-century Florentine coin) with which it is thereby linked, the word *imprevidibility* is marked by an Italian origin, in *imprevedibilità*, "unforeseeability," "unpredictability," or "capriciousness."

14. "Dialectics and Hope" was originally a chapter in Bloch's *Subjekt-Objekt, Erläuterungen zu Hegel* (1951). Thomas Münzer was a radical theologian in early-sixteenth-century Germany about whom Bloch elsewhere wrote, "Above all, Münzer is history in a fruitful sense; he and his cause and all things past that are worth recording are made to obligate us, to enthuse us, to support more and more that which is always meant to be for us" (*Thomas Münzer* 129).

15. Some of Joyce's earlier work is even less willing than is *Ulysses* to nominate the nation-state as Ireland's future-conditional political form. As I have argued elsewhere, this unwillingness has less to do with raw pessimism about Ireland's intractable "paralysis" than with a receptivity to a future political form that might be far stranger than the nation-state. See Saint-Amour.

Works Cited

Bernstein, Michael André. *Foregone Conclusions: Against Apocalyptic History*. Berkeley: U of California P, 1994.

Bindé, Jérôme. "Toward an Ethics of the Future." *Globalization*. Ed. Arjun Appadurai. Durham: Duke UP, 2003. 90–113.

Bloch, Ernst. "Dialectics and Hope." Trans. Mark Ritter. *New German Critique* 9 (Autumn 1976): 8.

———. *Literary Essays*. Trans. Andrew Joron et al. Stanford: Stanford UP, 1998.

———. *Thomas Münzer als Theologe der Revolution*. 1921. Qtd. and trans. in Bloch, *Literary Essays* 129.

Danto, Arthur C. *Analytical Philosophy of History*. Cambridge: Cambridge UP, 1968.

Duffy, Enda. *The Subaltern "Ulysses."* Minneapolis: U of Minnesota P, 1994.

Edelman, Lee. *No Future: Queer Theory and the Death Drive*. Durham: Duke UP, 2004.

Encyclopaedia Britannica. Cambridge: UP, 1911.

Epstein, E. L. "Nestor." *James Joyce's "Ulysses": Critical Essays.* Ed. Clive Hart and David Hayman. Berkeley: U of California P, 1974. 17–28.

Fairhall, James. *James Joyce and the Question of History.* Cambridge: Cambridge UP, 1993.

Gallagher, Catherine. "Undoing." *Time and the Literary.* Ed. Karen Newman, Jay Clayton, and Marianne Hirsch. New York: Routledge, 2002. 11–29.

Gallagher, Catherine, Mark Maslan, and Paul K. Saint-Amour, eds. Forum on Counterfactual Realities, in *Representations* 98 (2007).

Harrison, William H. *Mother Shipton Investigated: The Result of Critical Examination in the British Museum Library, of the Literature Related to the Yorkshire Sibyl.* London: W. H. Harrison, 1881.

Koselleck, Reinhart. *Futures Past: On the Semantics of Historical Time.* Trans. Keith Tribe. Cambridge: MIT P, 1985.

Love, Heather K. *Feeling Backward: Loss and the Politics of Queer History.* Cambridge: Harvard UP, 2007.

Mendelson, Edward. "Gravity's Encyclopedia." *Mindful Pleasures: Essays on Thomas Pynchon.* Ed. George Levine and David Leverenz. Boston: Little, Brown, 1976. 161–95.

Morson, Saul. *Narrative and Freedom: The Shadows of Time.* New Haven: Yale UP, 1994.

Ricœur, Paul. *Amour et justice.* Tübingen: J.C.B. Nohr, 1990.

Saint-Amour, Paul K. "'Christmas Yet to Come': Hospitality, Futurity, the *Carol,* and 'The Dead.'" *Representations* 98 (2007): 93–117.

Scott, David. *Conscripts of Modernity: The Tragedy of Colonial Enlightenment.* Durham: Duke UP, 2004.

Spoo, Robert. "'Nestor' and the Nightmare: The Presence of the Great War in *Ulysses.*" *Twentieth Century Literature* 32 (1986): 137–54.

Stead, Alistair. "Great War *Ulysses.*" *James Joyce Broadsheet* 71 (2005): 4.

Sullivan, T. D., A. M. Sullivan, and D. B. Sullivan, eds. *Speeches from the Dock.* Rev. ed. by Seán Ua Ceallaigh. 1968. Dublin: Gill and MacMillan, 1882.

Wilder, Gary. "Untimely Vision: Aimé Césaire, Decolonization, Utopia." *Public Culture* 21 (2009): 102–3.

9

Scribbling into Eternity

Paris, Proust, "Proteus"

> Did Shakespeare know what he was creating when he wrote *Hamlet*; or
> Leonardo when he painted the *Last Supper*? After all, the original genius
> of a man lies in his scribblings. . . . [I]f the minute scribblings that compose
> the big work are not significant, the big work goes for nothing no matter
> how grandly conceived. Which of us can control our scribblings?
> They are the script of one's personality like your voice or your walk.
>
> James Joyce in conversation as reported by Arthur Power

```
  /   -  /   -  /   -  /   /  - /   -  /
```
"Won't | you come | to San- | dymount, | Ma | deline | the mare?" (*U*
3.21–22). These catalectic "iambs marching" sound in poet Stephen Dedalus's mind as his own jambs march the strand in "Proteus."[1] Gifford and
Seidman gloss this floating apostrophe, this idle-seeming invitation qua
prosodic example, as a possible echo of Madeleine Lemaire, the Parisian
society painter whose fashionable salon in the rue de Monceau mingled
belle époque aristocrats with artists, poets, and composers. Doubtless
young Joyce was not among her guests, nor, probably, did he see Marcel
Proust's homage, "La cour aux lilas et l'atelier des roses: Le salon de Madame Lemaire," published over the pseudonym Dominique in *Le Figaro*
on May 11, 1903. That was a month almost to the day after John Joyce's tele-
gram summoned his son home from Paris to his dying mother's bedside—
too late for the impoverished Irish student ostensibly reading medicine
in the capital of the world republic of letters to have perused it there, nor

likely noticed by the aspiring Irish-European writer in the Latin quarter hat once home.[2]

Yet Joyce had lost no time getting hold of work by French contemporaries to fuel his single-handed Irish renaissance. On a 1903 side trip from Paris to Tours with his Siamese friend from the Bibliothèque Sainte-Geneviève, he had acquired Edouard Dujardin's *Les lauriers sont coupés* (1887–88), a technical inspiration for Stephen's streaming thoughts in "Proteus"—that most Parisian of episodes—when Joyce, fourteen years later, wrestled shapes strewn over his native provincial shores into avant-garde narrative form.[3] In the rather less likely event that Joyce chanced upon Proust's rare, self-published first book, *Les plaisirs et les jours* (1896), before drafting "Proteus" around 1917,[4] he would have found it lavishly adorned by Lemaire's still lifes and dramatic illustrations, which Proust hoped would entice the Faubourg grandees to acquire it for their libraries.[5] Although Stephen's Madeleine Lemaire echo carries no necessary Proustian aura—with or without Proust, her name floated on the air in 1903 Paris—his preoccupation in "Proteus" with audience, posterity, and legacy evokes Joyce's parallel course from obscurity to world fame. Stephen's doggerel conjuring a salonnière for Sandymount, his juvenile fantasy that his epiphanies might be discovered in the world's great libraries "after a few thousand years," his wistful "Who ever anywhere will read these written words?" (*U* 3.143, 3.414–15) all evoke the young Joyce who composed fifteen epiphanies during his short stay in Paris, and who, in October of the year Stephen walks Sandymount strand in mourning clothes, again flew to Dublin on a wing and prayer that as yet lacked an Ovidian imprimatur. "Am I walking into eternity along Sandymount Strand?" (*U* 3.18–19). Insofar as Stephen recaptures his creator's youth, his catalectic march *is* taking him "into eternity"—into the *Ulysses* "he" will write "in ten years," although he cannot know it—by way of Paris, where an obscure provincial genius might catch the eye, if not of a society painter or duchess, then of a Sylvia Beach, an Ezra Pound, a Harriet Weaver to back his dream of a place in the world's great libraries.[6]

If "Proteus" would not be "Proteus" without the Paris that published and lauded its Irish guest along with its native Proust, its 1917 composition date would seem too early for "Madeline the mare" to resonate with Proust or *Plaisirs*. Only in 1920, while worrying that he had "made a bad impression" in Paris, did Joyce acknowledge having read "some pages" of "a certain Mr. Marcel Proust," which seemed to him to confirm his own superiority.[7] Not until May 1922 were Joyce and Proust brought face to face, at the Schiffs' celebratory dinner at the Hotel Majestic for the premiere of Stravinsky and Diaghilev's ballet *Le renard*; a month before Proust died, Joyce may still have only browsed the early volumes of *À la recherche du temps perdu*.[8] While preparing *Ulysses*' third edition, he wrote Beach, he had perused "the first two volumes . . . of A la Recherche des Ombrelles Perdues par Plusieurs Jeunes Filles en Fleurs du Côté de chez Swann et Gomorrhée et Co., par Marcelle Proyce et James Joust."[9]

By a commodious vicus of recirculation whereby what is unconscious and what deliberate become shadowy and incalculable, these whimsical lost umbrellas and blossoming girls of Proyce and Joust draw us back toward *Ulysses*' earliest extant draft: the "Proteus" manuscript of summer 1917, acquired by the National Library of Ireland (NLI) in 2002 and published online by the Library in April 2012;[10] as well as the quasi-epiphanic *Giacomo Joyce* (not necessarily its real name), its last image of "a woman's hat, red-flowered, and umbrella, furled," trailing an enigmatic "Envoy: Love me, love my umbrella" (*GJ* 16). In his preliminary description of the NLI "Proteus" manuscript, Daniel Ferrer correlates the sixteen discrete fragments that comprise it with the published text and remarks its formal affinity with the 1914 *Giacomo Joyce*.[11] Sam Slote links the early draft's fragmentary form to Joyce's concept of the epiphany and notes that its last vignette recasts the "Paris epiphany" of prostitutes passing on the boulevards in "garments soft as" the adulterer's voice.[12] That epiphany in turn recalls the "narrow Parisian room" of *Giacomo Joyce*, where a revenant silently urges a "Voice of wisdom" to "say on" and then resolves to "go": "Adultery of wisdom" (*GJ* 15). Echoing "Giacomo Joyce"'s not un-Proustian search for love among the umbrellas, Joyce's 1922 Proust spoof, tossed up from the oceanic punnery that was already becoming the spawning grounds of the *Wake,* bodies forth the protean nature of things—figured in "Proteus" as the nature of words, time, language in time—that both artists' works explore and, as genetic texts unfolding in perpetual renascence, embody.

To these formal and thematic resonances of *Giacomo Joyce*'s still life "Umbrella with Red-Flowered Hat" with Paris, Proust, and early "Proteus," we may add a striking remark that Joyce scribbled into his *Scribbledehobble* notebook circa summer 1923: "Proust, analytic still life: finest prose he read for a long time."[13] Surely any evocation of *Les plaisirs et les jours,* wherein Lemaire's literal still lifes counterpoint Proust's "analytic" ones, must be fortuitous, for who reading Proust in 1922–23 would bother with *Plaisirs*? Yet if Arthur Power's memory of his conversations with Joyce is reliable, not only did Joyce somewhere, sometime encounter Proust's first book but he claimed to prefer it to *A la recherche*. As Power reconstructs their exchange, Joyce judged Proust the "most important" and "best of the modern French writers":

> no one has taken modern psychology so far, or to such a fine point. I myself think, however, that he would have done better if he had continued to write in his earlier style, for I remember reading once some early sketches in a book of his entitled *Les plaisirs et les jours*, studies of Parisian society in the '90s, and there was one in it, "Mélancolique Vil-légiature de Mme de Breyves" which impressed me greatly. If he had continued in that early style, . . . he would have written the best novels of our generation. But instead he launched into *À la recherche du temps perdu*, which suffers from over-elaboration. (78)[14]

Power was not a tape recorder, and this remembered voice of Joyce may gloss over vagaries of perception, the acid rain of time, and conscious or unconscious embellishment. That said, Joyce's "I remember reading *once*" and his impression of the "early style" of Proust's Phèdre-like Madame de Breyves locate his reading of *Plaisirs* at some retrospective distance from this conversation. So does his recollection of *Plaisirs* as a work of promise that *Recherche* fails to fulfill, for it suggests an idealized memory of the former as much as a slight acquaintance with the latter. This reconstructed conversation, then, does not foreclose the possibility that Joyce read *Plaisirs* early enough that his Madeline could echo Proust's.

Power's Joyce says more on the subject of Proust. He rebuts Power's charge that Proust is a snob, ranking him with Balzac and Thackeray despite his interest in "decaying aristocrats."[15] And he rejects Power's complaint of his stylistic experimentation:[16]

> It was not experimentation. . . . [H]is innovations were necessary to express modern life as he saw it. . . . A living style should be like a river which takes the colour and texture of the different regions through which it flows. The so-called classical style has a fixed rhythm and a fixed mood which make it to my mind an almost mechanical device. Proust's style conveys that almost imperceptible but relentless erosion of time which . . . is the motive of his work. (79)

This description of Proust's "necessary" modern style also fits Joyce's, none better than that of "Proteus."[17] The turn from a "fixed," "mechanical" "classical style" to a contemporary "living style" suggests the Dujardin-inspired current of Stephen's perceptions, thoughts, and feelings, flowing "like a river" along the boundary where mind meets world, transparent to the changing features of the "regions through which it flows." Thus Sandymount strand strewn with signifying "seaspawn and seawrack" (U 3.2–3) becomes Elsinore as Stephen taps his way blind; the fields of Mananaan's champing steeds; Uncle Richie's bedroom, revisited in imagination while Stephen's feet walk past; the Paris café where, drinking absinthe while his soldier son drinks milk, wild goose Kevin Egan would "yoke me as his yokefellow, our crimes our common cause" (U 3.228–29); a landing for Lochlanns' galleys; a sandtrap for turlehide whales set on by ancient starving people whose blood flows in Stephen's veins; a watery floor bearing up a relic of a lost Armada, a dog's carcass, a drowned man's corpse; an ever-changing backdrop as Stephen holds colloquy with philosophers, poets, and heretics, confesses fear of drowning, and scribbles a protean proto-poem, "Signs on a white field" (U 3.415).

So, too, the "imperceptible but relentless erosion of time" that drives Proust's work describes Joyce's long labor to still rushing, drifting, eddying, eventful time into a new narrative form in "Proteus." In later drafts, Joyce rearranged and augmented the NLI draft's discontinuous fragments, floating them on a fictional space-time continuum, a trompe l'œil river of words where grammatical tense and person (Stephen's "I," his self-arraigning "you," the über-narrator's third person) glint and shift like light on water. On another analytic plane, this river of words carries the flow of Stephen's thoughts, memories, and perceptions into that peculiar futurity embodied in the work of art that is "Proteus": time, life, wrestled to the ground, stilled into form, captured in narrative eternally present, a simulacrum of Stephen's waking, walking life to be read in time, any time, "there all the time without you" as the world borne away in time is not. Like Proust's Marcel, the Stephen who sees himself "walking into eternity along Sandymount strand" (U 3.18–19), moving through raining atoms of fictional "real" time "into" an eternity—theological, cosmological, and, of course, literary—that holds and stills all time, *already* walks in and (insofar as "he" is a portrait of Joyce, "his" future art the book in which he walks, the book just beginning in "Proteus") "into" another eternity: the illusion of stilled time, the still "modern *life*" that is the work of art. Amid landscapes, streetscapes, sandscapes of perspectively shifting church spires, Marcel and Stephen, virtual images of their creators as young men, walk *in* and *into* the books "they" will write: works of memory, imagination, art, in which they eternally walk.

Each, too, walks a secular pathway in and into eternity through their creators' modern arts of immanence, whereby sleights of the scribbling hand do not copy nature's shouts in the street but make of them "another nature."[18] "Proteus" zooms in on this *work* of wrestling modern time into "a living style" as Stephen scribbles phrases for his vampire poem via Douglas Hyde onto a scrap torn from Mr. Deasy's letter. As Stephen puts a pin in or pencil on words to keep them from drifting away on the river of time, the scribbling Joyce depicts *Ulysses*'s genesis in a grain of sand. Even the greatest work of art, says Power's Joyce, begins in nascent "scribblings," infused from the first with a natural signature—unconscious, singular, ineluctable, inimitable; their destination unforeknown and unforeclosed. "Though people may read more into *Ulysses* than I ever intended, who's to say that they are wrong: do any of us know what we are creating?" he remarks; "the original genius of a man lies in his scribblings. Later he may develop that talent until he produces a *Hamlet* or a *Last Supper*, but if the minute scribblings which compose the big work are not significant, the big work goes for nothing."[19] By this logic, Stephen's "scribbled note" (*U* 3.438) stands in fractal relation to the aesthetic forms that surround it: the epiphanies, *Giacomo Joyce*, "Proteus," the vampire poem of "Aeolus," *Ulysses*, those late last first scribblings "A way a lone a last a loved a long the" "riverrun"; all Joyce's works. And by this logic, the creator cannot foreknow the creation. Does the fictional Stephen who will write something "in ten years" know whether—or rather *that*—he is (already) scribbling *Ulysses*? Did Joyce know it as he scribbled this scribbler into the NLI draft, Stephen's writing hand a virtual extension of his own?

Not yet, not quite, for this scene evolves in the Buffalo draft, written some months later.[20] In NLI fragment 15, Stephen bends over a rock with his back to the sun and scribbles not yet the vampire lines (adumbrated in NLI section 13 and inserted as Stephen's text in the margin of Buffalo V.A.3–15); rather: "<*margin*: something he has twice forgotten in a dream>." While writing he contemplates his shadow, imagines it endless, sees himself throw it "<till the farthest star>" and call it back; he ponders whether, endless, it would still be his shape and links it to his writing and its reception: "I throw and call it back, writing these words. Who will read them? Who sees me? . . ." He then imagines telling an unnamed "her" in his "nicest" voice of

Berkeley's world perceived as colored figures on a plane and of the suffering and "grey breath" of Dante's dead souls, in hope that she will "lick [his] ear."

In the Buffalo draft, the NLI draft's sixteenth and last vignette of Paris prostitutes is moved to its final position earlier in the episode: "In [Polidor's] <Rodot's> Yvonne and Madeleine, belated, newmake their tumbled beauties."[21] This "Madeleine" appeared late in NLI section 16: Joyce first wrote "Yvonne," added "and Esther," then canceled "Esther" and substituted "Madeleine."[22] As Joyce develops the material of section 15, "her" projected caress in Stephen's fantasy becomes, after much scribbling, his pure longing:

> [Touch me. . . . I am lonely here. O touch me soon. What is that word that all [the world knew] others know? [say?] [will you not?] Touch, touch me.]
>
>   Touch me. Soft eye, soft soft soft hand. I am lonely here [alone]. O, touch me soon [or] <touch> now! What is that word [all others know] <*margin* <known to <all> men[?]; to their hearts.> I [will be] <am> quiet [to] here alone. Sad too. Touch, O touch me. [now]![23]

Stephen pockets his "scribbled note" and stretches back on the rocks watching "through [twittering] peacock[<twinkling>]twittering lashes the southing sun. I am caught in this burning scene. Pan's hour, the faunal noon. Among gumheavy serpent plants, milk-oozing fruits, where leaves lie wide on <tawny> waters. Pain is far. And no more turn aside and brood" (V.A.3–16, cf. U 3.441–45).

In this mid-June "faunal noon" after Mallarmé and Henri Rousseau, Stephen's synaesthetic mingling of French with Irish influences renders erotic longing as a pagan sublime. Yeats—who probably introduced Joyce to Mallarmé's work[24]—resounds in Fergus's song, and Joyce also echoes an earlier passage of his own: Stephen's "peacocktwittering" gaze makes new the dark regard of *Portrait*'s sexually "fallen" Stephen as he doodles "a widening tail, eyed and starred like a peacock's," onto a mathematical equation in his "scribbler" to the street cries of prostitutes outside his Belvedere schoolroom.[25] *Portrait*'s peacock-tail eyes open and close like "stars being born and quenched," crumbling to falling dust, and this "vast cycle of starry life" whirls his "weary mind" "outward to its verge and inward to its centre." As "distant music" summons Shelley's pale, weary moon wandering companionless, the "widening tail" becomes Stephen's "own soul going forth to experience, unfolding itself sin by sin, spreading abroad the bale-fire of its burning stars" until "cold darkness fill[s] chaos" (P 110–11).

In the NLI and Buffalo drafts of "Proteus," *Portrait*'s raging, cooling, crumbling peacock-tail stars, symbols of a soul consumed by lust in the temporal realm and doomed to eternal darkness, are extinct. New, invisible stars come out, symbols of aesthetic eternity. In the Mallarméan tropic sublime of Stephen's pagan reverie, "Pain is far." Erotic desire escapes sin, damnation, and fallen temporality and enters the eternal time of art and ritual evoked by Mulligan's satyr "foot that beat the ground in tripudium," added in the margin of the Buffalo draft (V.A.3–16, cf. *U* 3.448). His foot in Buck's castoff boot, Stephen dreams—and Joyce writes—the pagan priest's exultant triple-meter dance into the "faunal noon" of this "hellenised" island shore. Here "Esther," deleted in NLI section 16, returns, inserted after Buck's "foot I dislove": Stephen remembers "A girl I knew in Paris," the possibly German, Jewish, or German Jewish Esther Osvalt, whose boot fit him: "*Tiens, quel petit pied!*" (V.A.3–16). Through poem, dream, dance, memory, and imagination in this Dionysiac Greek-French-Irish-German-Jewish moment, Mallarmé's "L'après-midi d'un faune," Debussy's "Prélude à l'après-midi d'un faune," Nijinsky's dazzling, scandalous choreography, Mulligan, Oscar Wilde, and Esther Osvalt all come to Sandymount.[26]

When Joyce, revising the Buffalo draft, came upon Stephen wondering, "Who watches me here? Who ever anywhere will read these written words?" did he glimpse his own shape in Stephen's shadow endless till the farthest star (V.A.3–15)? For he turned to a new page and scribbled more: "They are there darkly behind this light, darkness shining in the brightness, worlds. Me sits there, with his [ash thyrsus lituus] augur's [ash] rod of ash, in borrowed sandals, by day beside an unbeheld sea, [by night walking] in violet night walking beneath <a reign of>uncouth stars."[27] In a still later typescript these unknown stars, invisible at noon, radiate the ineluctable *natural* signature evoked by Power's Joyce: "Darkly they are there behind this light, darkness shining in the brightness, delta of Cassiopeia, worlds."[28] Stephen's mind's eye gradually perceives, shining darkly behind bright noon, his Greek D(edalus) in the delta star of Shakespeare's W—the constellation Cassiopeia, near Pegasus, "his eyeballs stars" (*U* 3.111). As a painter signs a finished canvas, Joyce "watches" his autobiographical projection "frozen in stereoscope" (V.A.3–16) and, by a grammatical sleight of hand, fixes sand-drifting memory in his book's eternity: "*Me* sits *there* with *his* augur's rod of ash . . . I throw this ended manshape from me, manshape ineluctable, call it back." Projecting himself eternally watching his scribbling shadow-self eternally wondering "who watches me," entwined with his creation like

a Möbius strip or a noon shadow endless to the farthest star, did the artist scribbling signs on the Buffalo draft's last white page see the end that
"Proteus"'s godlike über-narrator seems to know?[29] Scribbling his way from
Portrait's dying stars to "Proteus"'s eternal faunal noon, Joyce arduously
wrestled phenomenological spacetime into a darkly shining heaventree,
"there" all the time in Stephen's day as in Joyce's book.

Again our vicus is commodious, for Stephen's Pan's-hour reverie evokes
less Proust than Mallarmé, whose endless shadow brushes both Proust and
"Proteus."[30] The invisible shadows cast by noon's dark starlight figure poetic genius as a natural power, inborn like one's voice or walk, the stars its
signature. The timeless noon of "Proteus" furthers Stephen's hope that his
writing will be read in a few thousand years, for if this dark horse's slender
epiphanies cast no such endless shadow, the book that contains him writes
his scribblings large. At the same time, these noon stars, invisible yet darkly
shining in Stephen's mind's eye, evoke Mallarmé's *l'absente*, that flower absent from all bouquets which poetry makes appear—the pure image of modern aesthetics, of that "other nature" that art brings from beyond nature's
veil.[31]

No more than Stephen scribbling his vampire poem or Joyce his early
drafts could Proust foresee what he was creating when, in 1908, he described
a "snowy evening, not long ago," when he "came in half frozen" and his

> old cook offered to make me a cup of tea, a thing I never drink. And
> as chance would have it, she brought me some slices of dry toast. I
> dipped the toast [*pain grillé*] in the cup of tea and as soon as I . . . felt
> its softened texture, all flavoured with tea, against my palate, some-
> thing came over me—the smell of geraniums and orange-blossoms, a
> sensation of extraordinary radiance and happiness; . . . [T]he shaken
> partitions in my memory gave way, and into my conscious mind there
> rushed the summers I had spent in the aforesaid house in the coun-
> try. . . . And then I remembered. Every morning . . . I went down to
> my grandfather in his bedroom, where he had just woken up and was
> drinking his tea. He soaked a rusk [*biscotte*] in it, and gave me the rusk
> to eat. (*Contre Sainte-Beuve*, 19–20)

In 1908 Proust was not sure what he was scribbling: an essay perhaps?
an imaginary conversation with his (dead) mother attacking Sainte-Beuve
for reducing art's value to its creator's biography?[32] He did not yet foresee
that refutation writ large in his great novel about the "work" of art: here, as

in "Proteus," nothing so simple as to capture and still protean time; rather, to wrest from mundane experience and make visible something more than time ever was or is or could be without the artist's labor: *l'absente*.

So Proust's 1908 memory of his grandfather's tea, fragrant with geranium and orange-blossom, unfurls through slow years into Tante Léonie's boiling infusion of lime-blossom, concocted of dry stems "twisted . . . into a fantastic trellis, in the interlacings of which the pale flowers opened, as though a painter had arranged them there"; lime leaves like "the transparent wings of a fly, the blank side of a label, the petal of a rose," which reveal to the narrator—as if nature were a book where one reads "with astonished delight the name of a person one knows"—what they once were and still are, only aged, so that "in these little grey balls I recognised green buds plucked before their time" and "the rosy, lunar, tender gleam that lit up the blossoms among the frail forest of stems from which they hung like little golden roses"—the very petals that "had perfumed the evening air," though "half-extinguished . . . in the diminished life which was now theirs."[33] Insofar as Marcel's memory of his grandfather's tea, revived by a bit of tea-soaked toast, is a remnant of biography, of actually lived time, it belongs to Woolf's category of "the creative fact, the fertile fact, the fact that suggests and engenders" (Woolf 197)—in this case, a Mallarméan art that Proust already in 1908 described (contre Sainte-Beuve) as "too superior to life . . . to be content to copy it" (*Selected Letters* 2: 374). (Indeed, could any tea convey the intricate delicacy and sublime fragrance of Proust's language?) An art, then, in search not of *lost* time, nor of time arrested—as by the deft still lifes of Madeleine Lemaire, than whom, Proust remarked, only God had created more roses[34]—but of time as absent from time *actually lived* as Proust's lime-blossoms are from all tisanes; time not regained but transfigured, by scribbling, into the eternal time of reading, the timeless noon of art; time that belongs not to contingent nature, to the "heavy sands" of "language tide and wind have silted here" (*U* 3.288–89), or to *Portrait*'s dying stars—but to that *other nature* art conjures, as when Proust's eternal childhood wafts from a cup of lime-blossom tea he never sipped, or Joyce refracts a walk on Sandymount strand through his Irish Stéphane's prismatic gaze.

This modern art that does not copy nature yet is born of nature's ineluctable contingency, this art that brings forth from mundane time "worlds" otherwise invisible (*U* 3.410), engenders fascination with the creative process: with such actual scribblings as track the emergence of Joyce's and Proust's great works and such scenes as that of Stephen's protean scribbling, so drawn as to evoke the ineffable signatures that shine darkly in all scribblings, however absent (in the documentary sense) from all manuscripts. As the rushing rivers of modern time erode the idea that all history moves toward one theologically ordained goal, genetic texts capture marks of that *natural* history implied by Kant's designation of geniuses as "nature's favorites," whose power to create that other nature makes us "feel our freedom" from ineluctable contingency—a history only retroactively visible as scribbling into eternity.

I began by asking whether Joyce's Madeline echoes Proust's Madeleine. That limited question opened onto a broader reach: the natural history of scribbling, legible in genetic hieroglyphs as writers forge paths from "modern life" to "a living style," "another nature"—for Joyce, inseparable from an Irish renaissance that gives new life to earlier art, including his own. Only in Mallarmé's ideal silence could art escape contingency, yet these commodious modern faubourgs where scribblers reborn as characters walk into eternity on Sandymount strand, or conjure from a tea-soaked rusk a Combray that never was, offer parallactic sightings of another *madeleine*, absent from all pâtisseries, yet quite as potent in "Proteus" as in Proust.

Notes

1. Joyce's marginal addition in Buffalo draft V.A.3–1 (cited from *JJA* 6 series 1: 239 throughout this paper) reads "A catalectic tetrameter of iambs marching"; the first line is tetrameter, the second trimeter. The catalectic (lacking the first, unstressed syllable) iambic feet are "Won't" and "Ma." Although some argue for "Acatalectic," negation makes nonsense of the passage.

2. I have found no evidence in Ireland's major libraries that *Le Figaro* circulated in Ireland in 1903, though a period publicity document offered foreign subscriptions and noted, "Le Figaro est lu dans le monde entier. Il est pour les Français à l'étranger ce que le Times est pour les Anglais" (reproduced in Avenel 238). Joyce might have seen a copy brought by some George Moore–like traveler.

3. See Joyce's letter of November 10, 1917 to Dujardin from Locarno (where he was working on "Proteus") seeking a copy of *Les lauriers sont coupés*, having left his first edition copy in Austria whence it was difficult to retrieve in wartime. Joyce introduces himself as an admirer of Dujardin's work, "si personnelle et si indépendante," and a humble toiler in the same literary vineyard (*SL* 229).

4. As Luca Crispi notes, Joyce, drawing on his 1910 Alphabetical Notebook (Cornell MS 25), "developed certain scenes, using the exact wording he would later incorporate in 'Proteus,'" while visiting Galway in summer 1912. During 1912–14 he drafted several episodes, including "Proteus." On June 16, 1915, he wrote Stanislaus that he

had drafted "Telemachus," the first episode of a three-part *Ulysses* then envisioned as twenty-two episodes (not eighteen). On July 24, 1917, he wrote Ezra Pound: "I write and think and write and think all day and part of the night"; his work on *Ulysses* "goes on as it has been going these five or six years. But the ingredients will not fuse until they have reached a certain temperature" (qtd. in Ellmann 416). That summer in Zürich he drafted the earliest surviving manuscript of "Proteus" (and *Ulysses*), now in the National Library of Ireland (NLI 36,369); a fresh reading of Dujardin (see note 3 above) may have fueled the fires that began to fuse the elements of "Proteus."

As Daniel Ferrer notes in his correlation table, this NLI "Proteus" draft begins with Stephen's brooding vision of Mulligan and Haines awaiting him that evening in the tower (*U* 3.271–81). The "Madeline the mare" lines appear only in the next extant "Proteus" draft (Buffalo V.A.3–1), a state "fairly close" to the 1918 *Little Review* text. Slote posits a lost draft between the NLI and Buffalo drafts ("Epiphanic 'Proteus'"). Owen posits a lost draft between the Buffalo and Rosenbach manuscripts (109). See also Groden; and Van Mierlo.

5. Gallimard/*La Nouvelle Revue française* did not reprint *Les plaisirs et les jours* until 1924. The Bibliothèque Sainte-Geneviève does not hold the 1896 edition; its online catalogue shows a "1920" imprint, evidently an error.

6. *U* 3.18, 10.1090. Joyce wrote Stanislaus from Paris on March 9, 1903, that he had composed "fifteen epiphanies—of which twelve are insertions and three additions" for the series begun in 1900 (*SL* 17).

7. Joyce to Frank Budgen, October 24, 1920 (*SL* 273).

8. Arthur Power relates Joyce's account: "all he said to me was 'Do you like truffles?' 'Yes,' I replied, 'I am very fond of truffles.' And that was the only conversation which took place between the two most famous writers of their time" (79). By October 1922 six volumes had appeared, from *Du côté de chez Swann* (1913) and *A l'ombre des jeunes filles en fleur* (1916) through *Sodome et Gomorrhe I* (1921) and *Sodome et Gomorrhe II* (1922).

9. Joyce to Beach, late October 1922, quoted in Ellmann 508n. Ellmann notes that Joyce substituted *gâteau au cumin* for the French translator's *madeleine* to denote the seedcake that consummated Leopold and Molly's love among the rhododendrons.

10. See http://catalogue.nli.ie/Record/vtls000194606 (accessed 12 Apr. 2012). The NLI published the manuscripts online when Danis Rose's print edition appeared; as of this writing copyright is in dispute. As Groden, Ferrer, Slote, and Van Mierlo note, the NLI draft, probably composed in summer 1917, records an early state of "Proteus" as a series of quasi-epiphanic fragments (related to earlier epiphanies and the 1903–10 Pola and Trieste/Alphabetical notebooks) which were only that fall rearranged and fleshed out for the episode's May 1918 *Little Review* publication. As Ferrer notes, fragment 15 of the NLI "Proteus" draft correlates with *U* 3.406–35, and fragment 16 (the revised Paris epiphany) with 3.209–15.

11. See note 4 above where Ferrer is discussed.

12. Slote, "Epiphanic 'Proteus'"; see epiphany 33 in Scholes and Kain 43; and Owen.

13. "Proust, analytic still life: finest prose he read for a long time (A. E. on J. S.)" (George Russell on James Stephens?) in the "Scylla and Charybdis" section of Connolly's *James Joyce's Scribbledehobble* (104); transcription of Buffalo notebook VI.A, p. 571. See Jorn Barger, "A Preliminary Stratigraphy of 'Scribbledehobble'" (www. robotwisdom.com/jaj/fwake/stratig.html). Later entries on the same page raise the possibility that Joyce linked Proustian involuntary memory to collective human memory on the way to the *Wake*: "dream thoughts are wake thoughts of centuries ago: unconscious memory: great recurrence: race memorial"; although, as Geert Lernout cautions, such elliptical notes permit everything, thus prove nothing.

Ellmann's transcription—"Proust, analytic still life. Reader ends sentence before him" (Ellmann 509)—omits "finest prose he read for a long time" and leaps, sans ellipsis, from *Scribbledehobble* p. 104/Notebook 571 ("Proust, analytic still life") to *Scribbledehobble* p. 118/Notebook 721 in the "Oxen of the Sun" section: "Proust reader ends sentence before him." Barger notes "Connolly's many transcription errors."

14. These conversations occurred from 1921 to February 1932, ending, Power says, when he slighted Joyce's grandson's birth. That Power's Joyce recounts the 1922 dinner, and that they speak of Proust in the past tense, place this conversation after Proust's death in November 1922. Thus Power's Joyce could have read the 1924 reprint of *Les plaisirs* rather than the first edition with Lemaire's illustrations.

15. Power's Joyce distinguishes Proust's "adoration—for 'blood'" from Saint-Simon's "entirely political" description of Louis XIV's court (79). By contrast with Saint-Simon's "hard, dry, incisive manner without imagination or psychology even," Proust imbued blood with "an almost mystic significance. Do you remember his description of the first time he met a duchess: an Irish prelate meeting the Pope could not have made a greater occasion of it, a wizened old dame, if I remember rightly [he doesn't], but whose tread sanctified the ground" (80–81).

16. Proust, Power complains, "sees everything through a veil, and his characters get lost in a sea of words. There is no sharpness about him. . . . [A]ll those well-fed leisured people irritate me . . . people isolated out of life to whom love seems more like a disease than a passion. Though you say that his purpose was to give as full an impression as he could, I feel that he lacks the necessary restraint that every artist should have. . . . What did he gain by this experimentation in style?" (78–79).

17. Cf. Joyce's reported comments on the handling of time in his own and Proust's works in Potts 129, and, indirectly, on their class difference, 227.

18. Kant proposes that "we feel our freedom" (the only transcendental idea that admits of empirical experience) in contemplating the power of genius ("nature's favorite") not merely to copy nature but to create "another nature"; this aesthetic theory is also a defense of art (§46–49, 86, 91).

19. Power 89, cf. this article's epigraph. "Joyce" adds that in "the new aesthetic . . . 'only that which is ugly is beautiful.'"

20. See Buffalo V.A.3–16. Slote, "Epiphanic 'Proteus,'" describes Joyce's "theoretically endless" composition process as a "silt[ing] over" of the NLI fragments with new language in successive drafts, each epiphany both a linguistic record and a "linguistic event" that attracts more sand-drifting words.

21. Buffalo V.A.3–8, cf. *U* 3.212.

22. Joyce added other Paris touches in the margins and between the lines: "That is Kevin Egan's [gesture] movement . . . Hlo! *Bonjour*" and the Esther Osvalt memory, discussed below. Thanks to Daniel Ferrer for indispensable help.

23. Buffalo V.A.3–16, cf. *U* 3.434–36.

24. As Carpenter notes, Joyce would have read Yeats's 1898 essay quoting Arthur Symons's quotations of Mallarmé in *The Symbolist Movement in Literature* (1896); Dujardin knew Mallarmé, who, Carpenter argues, "furnish[ed] the design and inspiration" for *Ulysses* (187).

25. Hurley links this moment in "Proteus" with the *Portrait* passage (144).

26. Vaslav Nijinsky choreographed and danced Debussy's "Prelude," inspired by Mallarmé's poem, for the Ballets russes. First performed at the Théâtre du Châtelet in Paris on May 29, 1912, the ballet ended in a simulated masturbation gesture that caused a furor, including an indignant campaign in *Le Figaro*.

27. This scribble appears, as an insertion for page 15, on the last page (19) of Buffalo V.A.3 [*Joyce's numbers indicate revised syntax*]:

    2   3   4   1

"They are there darkly behind this light, . . . uncouth stars. *insert:* bilgewater of Centaur" (Buffalo V.A.3–19)—the last phrase inserted where centaur Stephen relieves himself in the "fourworded wavespeech" scribbled in the margin (Buffalo V.A.3–17).

28. TS, Buffalo V.B.2, *JJA* 6 1:259.

29. Van Mierlo observes that Joyce drew "some of his stellar vocabulary" from his extensive notes on Alan Leo's "The Soul of Astronomy" (8), e.g., "the universal handwriting, written in plainly decipherable hieroglyphics, upon the wall of heaven. (Leo 1019)" (9). This evidence suggests that this part of the NLI Subject Notebook may postdate the NLI "Proteus" draft and the first state (prior to Joyce's marginal revisions) of the Buffalo draft (V.A.3).

30. See Carpenter; Hayman; Slote, *Silence*; Tadié 249–51 and passim; Goodkin, chap. 2; Ergal.

31. Stéphane Mallarmé, "Crise de vers": "Je dis: une fleur! et, hors de l'oubli où ma voix relègue aucun contour, en tant que quelque chose d'autre que les calices sus, musicalement se lève, idée même et suave, l'absente de tous bouquets" ("I say: a flower! And, out of the oblivion where my voice casts every contour, insofar as it is something other than the known bloom, there arises, musically, the very idea in its mellowness; in other words, what is absent from every bouquet") (Mallarmé 210). Echoes of this essay pervade "Proteus," e.g., books in a glass case casting "lights across the sky," the crisis of verse as "a trembling of the veil in the temple," the Laforguian "charms" of

slightly off-meter lines, the "dissolution of the official verse form," each soul "a mel-ody" seeking renewal, each its "own flute or viola" (201, 204–5), cf. Stephen: "Some-where to someone in your [nicest] <flutiest> voice (V.A.3–15, V.B.2).

32. On the early genetic history of *À la recherche* see Pugh, *Birth* and *Growth*.

33. Proust, *In Search of Lost Time* 1: 69–70.

34. "[J]e ne sais plus quel écrivain a dit que c'était elle 'qui avait créé le plus de roses après Dieu'" ("La cour aux lilas . . .," *Le Figaro* 11 May 1903: 3).

Works Cited

Avenel, Henri. *La presse française au vingtième siècle.* Paris: Flammarion, 1901.

Carpenter, William. "'Le Livre' of Mallarmé and James Joyce's *Ulysses.*" *Mallarmé in the Twentieth Century.* Ed. Robert Greer Cohn with Gerald E. P. Gillespie. Madison, NJ: Fairleigh Dickinson UP, 1998. 187–202.

Connolly, Thomas E., ed. *James Joyce's Scribbledehobble: The Ur-Workbook for "Finnegans Wake."* Evanston: Northwestern UP, 1961.

Crispi, Luca. "Manuscript Timeline 1905–1922." *Genetic Joyce Studies,* no. 4, 2004. On-line at www.antwerpjamesjoycecenter.com/GJS/GJS4.

Ellmann, Richard. *James Joyce.* New and rev. ed. New York: Oxford UP, 1982.

Ergal, Yves-Michel. *"Je" devient écrivain: Essai sur Joyce et Proust.* Mont-de-Marsan, France: Editions InterUniversitaires, 1996.

Ferrer, Daniel. "What Song the Sirens Sang . . . Is No Longer Beyond All Conjecture: A Preliminary Description of the New 'Proteus' and 'Sirens' Manuscripts." *James Joyce Quarterly* 39.1 (2001): 53–67.

Gifford, Don, with Robert J. Seidman. *"Ulysses" Annotated: Notes for Joyce's "Ulysses."* Berkeley: U of California P, 1988.

Goodkin, Richard E. *Around Proust.* Princeton: Princeton UP, 1991.

Groden, Michael. "The National Library of Ireland's New Manuscripts: An Outline and Archive Comparisons." *Joyce Studies Annual* 14 (2003): 5–17.

Hayman, David. *Joyce et Mallarmé.* 2 vols. Paris: Lettres Modernes, 1956.

Hurley, Robert Edward. "The Proteus Episode of James Joyce's *Ulysses.*" Unpublished Ph.D. diss., Columbia University, 1963.

Kant, Immanuel. *Critique of Judgment.* Trans. J. H. Bernard. New York: Hafner, 1951.

Lernout, Geert. "The *Finnegans Wake* Notebooks and Radical Philology." *Probes: Genetic Studies in Joyce.* Ed. David Hayman and Sam Slote. Amsterdam: Rodopi, 1995. 19–48.

Mallarmé, Stéphane. *Divagations.* Trans. Barbara Johnson. Cambridge: Harvard UP, 2007.

Owen, Rodney Wilson. *James Joyce and the Beginnings of "Ulysses."* Ann Arbor: UMI Research Press, 1983.

Potts, Willard, ed. *Portraits of the Artist in Exile: Recollections of James Joyce by Europeans.* New York: Harcourt Brace Jovanovich, 1979.

Power, Arthur. *Conversations with James Joyce.* Ed. Clive Hart. Chicago: U of Chicago P, 1974.

Proust, Marcel. *Contre Sainte-Beuve. Marcel Proust on Art and Literature 1896–1919.* Trans. Sylvia Townsend Warner. New York: Carroll & Graf, 1984.

———. "La cour aux lilas et l'atelier des roses: Le salon de Madame Lemaire." *Le Figaro* 11 May 1903: 3.

———. *In Search of Lost Time.* Trans. C. K. Scott Moncrieff and Terence Kilmartin. Rev. D. J. Enright. 6 vols. New York: Modern Library, 1992.

———. *Selected Letters.* Ed. Philip Kolb. Trans. Terence Kilmartin. 3 vols. London: Collins, 1983–2000.

Pugh, Anthony R. *The Birth of "À la Recherche du temps perdu."* Lexington: French Forum, 1987.

———. *The Growth of "À la Recherche du Temps Perdu": A Chronological Examination of Proust's Manuscripts from 1909 to 1914,* 2 vols. Toronto: University of Toronto Press, 2004.

Scholes, Robert E., and Richard M. Kain, eds. *The Workshop of Daedalus.* Evanston: Northwestern UP, 1965.

Slote, Sam. "Epiphanic 'Proteus.'" *Genetic Joyce Studies,* no. 5, 2005. Online at www.antwerpjamesjoycecenter.com/GJS/GJS5.

———. *The Silence in Progress of Dante, Mallarmé and Joyce.* New York: Peter Lang, 1999.

Tadié, Jean-Yves. *Marcel Proust: A Life.* Trans. Euan Cameron. New York: Penguin, 2000.

Van Mierlo, Wim. "The Subject Notebook: A Nexus in the Composition History of *Ulysses*—A Preliminary Analysis." *Genetic Joyce Studies,* no. 7, 2007. Online at www.antwerpjamesjoycecenter.com/GJS/GJS7.

Woolf, Virginia. "The Art of Biography." *The Death of the Moth and Other Essays.* San Diego: Harcourt Brace Jovanovich, 1942. 187–97.

10

Joyce's Hand in the First
French Translation of *Ulysses*

LILIANE RODRIGUEZ

Since it was published in 1929, seven years after the launch of the famous original, French readers of *Ulysse* have been familiar with credits on the cover of the first French translation: "Traduit de l'anglais par M. Auguste Morel, assisté par M. Stuart Gilbert. Traduction entièrement revue par M. Valery Larbaud avec la collaboration de l'auteur [Translated from the English by Auguste Morel, assisted by Stuart Gilbert. Translation entirely revised by Valery Larbaud with the collaboration of the author]."[1]

Yet several critics have questioned the extent of Joyce's collaboration, since in the 1920s Joyce was already writing *Finnegans Wake* and was busy with Lucia's illness and his eye problems. How could he possibly have spent any significant time on the French translation of his novel? Others have noticed that "Joyce himself was regularly approached on matters of detail and interpretation" (O'Neill 40).

But his collaboration has never been clearly defined. To assess it, I collected a corpus of quotes, dispersed in a number of libraries, all referring to Joyce's collaboration, articles and books, letters published and unpublished, correspondence crisscrossing between Joyce, Larbaud, Morel, Jean-Aubry, Marcel Ray, Monnier, Weaver, Beach, Gide, Fargue, Gallimard, and so forth, and other documents, such as the early translated excerpts of *Ulysses* and the final two complete typescripts of the French *Ulysse*, annotated by Larbaud, Morel, Gilbert, and Monnier.[2]

While reading letters we seldom pay close attention to short comments like "I have sent you the manuscript" or "Have you received my suggestions?" But when one starts collecting such incidental remarks, a corpus builds up.

Although incomplete, it is substantial enough, with over six hundred quotes, to investigate Joyce's participation in the French *Ulysse*. The question is, Was he casually involved or fully committed? And why would he care at all, when he had so many other pressing issues to deal with? He cared because Morel's French too often slid into outdated naturalism and symbolism, tendencies that Joyce could not allow in the translation of his groundbreaking masterpiece. This article examines evidence of Joyce's consistent role in the French translation of *Ulysses*. It demonstrates that his involvement and commitment were driven by his innovative aesthetic program.

The 1929 French translation can be seen as the English original reborn. Its rebirth was a difficult one, spanning seven years of intense collective labor, quite similar to the double birth of Mortimer Edward Purefoy and of the English language in the "Oxen of the Sun" episode of the novel. Its "renascence" is also related to the Renaissance in that Joyce, the translator and reviewer, perpetuates the great tradition of sixteenth-century humanists, like Estienne Dolet,[3] who believed in the artistic and philosophical importance of translation, and who worked in earnest and anxiety, just like Joyce and his team did. Their steady collaboration during the 1922–29 adventure of the first French translation bears testimony to the survival of a Renaissance ideal: the resilient belief in the necessity of disseminating groundbreaking texts through translation and their view of translation as an art, a craft, and a vector of enlightenment in the face of censorship. The legal tornado whipped up by the original *Ulysses* in 1922 also draws Joyce closer to Dolet and the legal torments he endured all of his life (Alary). Four centuries apart, and through different degrees of adversity, both had to confront dogmatism, whether religious or artistic, and still, both contributed tremendously to European humanism. The following pages will demonstrate the author's active participation in the first translation of *Ulysses* and will point out the five translation principles that Joyce and his translators shared with Dolet, who defines them in *La manière de bien traduire d'une langue en aultre* (1540).[4]

First we will look at the team of translators that Joyce assembled, and his interaction with them.

A Chronology of Joyce's Contact with His Translators

Documents show that Joyce became involved in the translation from the start, in 1921. He participated in the first translation attempts of three excerpts, from "Telemachus," "Sirens," and "Penelope," intended for the December 7, 1921, Reading Event, held in Paris, at Adrienne Monnier's Maison des amis des livres. Valery Larbaud gave a lecture on Joyce and read these excerpts in French. The latter had been "selected" by Larbaud, as related by Joyce (*LIII* 53). Monnier had asked Jacques Benoist-Méchin to translate the excerpts when Larbaud said he was too busy to do it himself (Monnier, *Les gazettes* 23; Monnier, *Rue de l'Odéon* 154–55). Joyce revised the "Telemachus" and "Sirens" excerpts: "I went over them with Benoist-Méchin" (*LIII* 53). The "Penelope" excerpt was reworked by Joyce and Léon-Paul Fargue. Larbaud received it only a few hours before the event, and read it as such.[5]

Documents also attest that Joyce stayed involved all along, from 1921 to 1928. He remained close to his translators, as evidenced by records of frequent meetings with them over the years. He met them relentlessly, and in a variety of configurations: separately, or in groups of two, three, or all together.

Regular contact with Larbaud started in 1921, as attested in published and unpublished correspondence. The tone of Joyce's invitations is always keen, if not insistent. In February 1921 he invites Larbaud for dinner.[6] On May 19, 1923, he writes: "Can you come on Monday instead at same hour 4?"[7] On April 1, 1924, he writes: "call at 8 instead of 7:30."[8] On November 4, 1924, dinner is offered: "can you . . . dine with us on Saturday next at 8 p.m. here? We hope so" (*LIII* 108). On November 20, 1924, another "translation tea" is organized by Joyce, proof of ongoing discussion on the translation: "Thanks for the typescript. It almost finishes the question but there are just two points I would like to discuss. . . . We could discuss it then" (*LIII* 111). In early June 1925 the request is pressing: "Can you put off your journey for a day and dine with us on Monday I hope so" (*LIII* 121). On October 3, 1925, Joyce extends another invitation for tea.[9] On May 2, 1925, it is for dinner: "I wanted to ask you all last week but heard you were indisposed."[10] On January 26, 1927, he asks Larbaud again: "dine with us and a small party at Langer's on February 21" (*LIII* 151). On February 10, 1927, Joyce reminds Larbaud that "we ought to dine together one of these nights" (*LIII* 154). And so on.

Contact with Auguste Morel, the main translator of *Ulysses*, is well established by 1924. Joyce reports having had "an interesting conversation with Morel in Carnac and Vannes" (*LIII* 107). He stayed with him in Brittany and talked with him on a number of occasions. From 1927 on, other meetings took place, now with Morel and Stuart Gilbert, the third main party in the French *Ulysse*. Sometimes, Joyce convened meetings with Larbaud, Morel, and Gilbert, such as dinner at the Trianon restaurant in Paris (*LIII* 173).

Contact with Gilbert produced a large number of documents concerning the translation. It started on May 9, 1927, with Gilbert's letter to Joyce. Gilbert tells Joyce about the mistakes he noticed in the 1926 published excerpt of Calypso (*LIII* 159).[11] The number of meetings with Gilbert quickly multiplied, to answer "enquiries as to the exact meaning of innumerable passages" (*LI* 29). A sometimes-piqued Larbaud was witnessing the Joyce-Gilbert increasing dialogue. On October 4, 1927, Larbaud complains to Monnier that "les remarques de Gilbert, sans ordre, souvent énigmatiques, sont bien agaçantes [Gilbert's notes, muddled, often enigmatic, are irritating]" (Larbaud, *Lettres à Monnier* 316). In a footnote, Monnier adds that two months later Larbaud felt very frustrated when trying to work with "les notes encore plus nombreuses et disparates prises par Stuart Gilbert au cours de ses conversations avec Joyce sur le dernier épisode d'*Ulysse* [the even larger number of ill-assorted notes taken by Gilbert during his conversations with Joyce on the last episode of *Ulysses*]" (316). Gilbert was trying hard to keep up with his many encounters with Joyce. Later, Larbaud informs Monnier that he has received "Penelope," with "son volumineux commentaire [its voluminous commentary]" (326) by Gilbert.

Larbaud completed the revision in 1928, alone in Italy for several weeks: "Il est donc entendu que je reprendrai . . . et terminerai seul la traduction de *Ulysses* [It was agreed that I would revise . . . and complete the translation of *Ulysses* alone]."[12] During all this time, he remained in touch with Joyce. Unfortunately, most of their correspondence is lost, but we hear echoes of their ongoing dialogue in peripheral letters to others. On August 18, 1928, Larbaud writes to Monnier: "vous trouverez, à la place des pages manquantes, ma version (manuscrite) des passages omis dans la copie: S. Gilbert et A. Morel unifieront nos deux versions et la traduction ainsi obtenue sera soumise à James Joyce [To replace the missing pages, you will find my (manuscript) version of excerpts omitted in the copy: S. Gilbert and A. Morel will integrate our two versions and the resulting translation will be submitted to James Joyce]" (Larbaud, *Lettres à Monnier* 326). In October 1928, Joyce relates sending more of his suggestions to Monnier, and adds: "I hope you will soon be in Paris so that we can have a chat" (*LIII* 182).

In the 1928–29 Berg Typescript,[13] two notes by Larbaud to the printer are meticulously repeated at the start of each episode:

Lorsqu'une des mes corrections semblera discutable ou inadmissible aux traducteurs, la question sera soumise à James Joyce et résolue d'après sa décision [In case any of my revisions seems questionable or unacceptable, it shall be submitted to James Joyce, and the matter will be resolved according to his decision].

Les corrections proposées par les traducteurs après que j'aurai rendu la copie de l'imprimeur à Mademoiselle Monnier seront soumises à l'approbation de James Joyce [Revisions proposed by the translators after I have returned the printer's copy to Miss Monnier shall be submitted to James Joyce for his approval].

To summarize Joyce's involvement with the French translation so far, one can assert that Joyce was very active at the beginning, as a translator himself of the first excerpts. From 1924 to 1927, Morel began anew the translation of the whole novel, supervised by Larbaud. Joyce kept contact with both of them, as attested by the frequency of their meetings. After the inclusion of Gilbert in 1927, Joyce's involvement with the translation intensified, until publication in February 1929. Joyce's unfailing and energetic involvement is mirrored in their correspondence. Larbaud and Gilbert's letters often echo Joyce's and vice versa, with continuing discussion taking place between letters.

The above quotations are only some examples of the continuing conversation between the author and the translators. Now, having outlined the chronology of Joyce's contact with his translators, we need to look at his involvement in the translation.

Joyce and His Team

If Joyce had never been interested in translation, his "hand" in any translation would not even be an issue. He always felt extremely "delighted" to read translations of *Ulysses* in other languages.[14] But the French translation brought him more than mere delight. He interacted with his French translators and organized them into a team with a plan and a mission.

Several collaborators witnessed his method: "Il a une méthode de travail extraordinaire [He has an extraordinary method in his work]."[15] According to Philippe Soupault, *Ulysses* is "ce livre où jamais rien n'est laissé au hasard [this book where nothing was done at random]" (Soupault 48). And again: "Je pus suivre son étonnante méthode et admirer sa mémoire [I noticed his extraordinary method and admired his amazing memory]" (22). Joyce applied the same method to translation: as Soupault testified later: "M. Joyce nous exposait les difficultés. . . . Ces séances duraient trois heures. . . . James Joyce nous enseigne qu'on ne travaille pas à la petite semaine [Mr. Joyce would outline the difficult points. . . . These sessions lasted three hours. . . . James Joyce is teaching us that one does not work without an overall plan]."[16]

Among other criteria, the Joycean perfect team has a leader. Joyce selected Larbaud as ultimate reviser: "Of course you are to have the casting vote in all discussions" (*LIII* 164). Larbaud's supreme authority was sealed in 1928 at the famous Trianon dinner. Team members had to abide by the "Trianon Treaty as the best way to avoid friction" (*LIII* 173). Later in 1928, when Larbaud suggested André Maurois to replace himself as reviser, Joyce was "utterly opposed to any such change" (*LIII* 176) and managed to keep Larbaud until publication.

Joyce's trust in Larbaud as main reviewer, and in Larbaud's choice of Morel as main translator, illustrates Dolet's second translation principle: it is necessary "que le traducteur ait parfaicte congnoissance de la langue de l'autheur, qu'il traduict: & soit pareillement excellent en la langue, en laquelle il se mect a traduire [that the translator have a perfect knowledge of the author's language, and that he be equally excellent in the language in which he sets out to translate]" (Dolet 12). Here Dolet introduces the linguistic distinction between competence and performance, and states that competence in the source language must be perfect, and performance in the target language, excellent. Joyce knew of Morel and Larbaud's commendable competence in their understanding of English, based on their many previous translations, and Larbaud's stylistic excellence was visible in his poetry and prose.

The team organized by Joyce included one more member: the author himself. Joyce enjoyed being part of a translation group, as Monnier recalls about *Finnegans Wake*: "atteler sous sa direction une équipe de sept personnes . . . pour se donner le plaisir de dire mes 'Septante' [to harness under his leadership a team of seven . . . to have the pleasure of saying my 'Seventy'" (Monnier, *Dernières gazettes* 19).[17] After helping Savitsky with her translation of *Portrait* ("I helped the translator a good deal" [*LIII* 29]), Joyce extended his assistance to his *Ulysses* translators: "J'ai reçu, à Paris, un mot de Joyce lui-même dans le sens que vous m'aviez fait prévoir. C'est très encourageant. Il y aura donc les 2 listes dont je vous ai parlé: choses à discuter à trois, et choses à demander à Joyce [I confirm that I have received in Paris a note by Joyce himself, in the direction you prepared me to expect. It is very encouraging. Therefore, there will be the 2 lists I mentioned to you: questions to answer among the three of us, and questions to Joyce]."[18] Joyce also helped translators as a group (e.g., "le conseil des trois").[19] Occasionally, he sent them primary documentation, like the original *Martha* record to Morel (*LIII* 120).

As team member, Joyce had other responsibilities, such as steadfastly resolving conflict between revisers: "I know from Miss Monnier that you are undergoing the torture of acting as umpire between the translators and me," Larbaud wrote Joyce in 1928.[20] And of course, he helped translate many difficult points and revised scores of others.

Joyce's Strategic Involvement with the French Text

The October 1928 letter from Joyce to Larbaud is a key document concerning his revision of the typescript. In the first paragraph of that letter, Joyce describes another "collapse" of his sight, and the injections he needs to regain his ability to read. He concludes the paragraph with the following remark: "Apparently I have completely overworked myself and if I don't get back sight to read it is all U-P up" (*LIII* 182 and 182 n. 3).[21] As it stands, literally, "U-P" means "underproof"[22] for distilled spirits having less than the standard amount of alcohol. In *Ulysses,* as we know, "U-P up" is used metaphorically to depict Denis Breen as having less than the standard amount of something (sanity, mental abilities).[23] In this letter to Larbaud, Joyce puns again on "U-P" to say that, should his lessened vision persist, the manuscript might be "U-P" (underproofed) rather than fully proofread. Joyce's pun in the letter highlights the fact that he considers his own proofreading essential. And, in the next paragraph, he summarizes his revision so far: "I passed on all your corrections with my suggestions to Miss Monnier. Morel I have not seen this long time but I shall write to him if and when I feel a little stronger" (*LIII* 182).

So, Joyce was not just maintaining casual conversation with the translators. He revised the French typescript hands-on, and on a regular basis. In November 1924 he writes to Larbaud: "Thanks for the typescript. . . . Morel has done, it seems, 100 pages of *Ulysse*" (*LIII* 111). In the following years, more revision is reported: "The [French] translation is now finished. VL [Valery Larbaud] sent me a list of difficulties which I solved for him" (*SL* 334).

Joyce sometimes contributed directly to the French text: "I am glad you liked my name for the little priest" (*LIII* 182). Examples of authorial collaboration are attested in his correspondence. In 1927, for example, Larbaud consulted Joyce on Morel's "sapré" (for sacré) and "jujupes"[24] in "Proteus," which he disliked: "Qui nous départagera? [Who will decide?]." In a footnote, Monnier answers: "C'est Joyce lui-même qui tiendra ce rôle d'arbitre, le plus souvent par le truchement de Stuart Gilbert qui le consultait chaque fois qu'il en était besoin [Joyce himself acted as the arbiter, most often through the intervention of Stuart Gilbert, who consulted him as often as necessary]."[25] In 1928, Larbaud presents Joyce with his translation of *mutton kidneys*. Joyce answers: "both your versions of 'rognons, etc.' are better" (*LIII* 178–79). In a 1928 letter, Larbaud seeks Joyce's approval on the translation of "two shafts of soft daylight."[26] And after asking Joyce the meaning of "she bumps,"[27] Larbaud opted for "[Hop] sauti-sautant la vieille,"[28] from a popular song of Napoleon III's time. Numerous other examples bear Joyce's hand. Joyce's revisions were not merely punctual. In his own series of manuscript notes, Morel quotes a long paragraph Joyce himself translated from "Oxen," and he marvels at Joyce's translation, "la leçon fournie par Joyce about Oxen."[29]

In fact, the range of questions Joyce was asked form a vast denotative and connotative array. In his answers, whether directly addressed to his translators or indirectly carried through Gilbert's intervention, Joyce was always quick to steer the text in one direction or the other.

Joyce insisted on closeness to original denotation. In his letters he repeatedly expresses his concern over mistranslation. In 1927, now with Gilbert's help, he continued to keep his eye on the denotative level of the translation, clarifying the English meaning when consulted by Gilbert, who was "noting everything, that in my [Gilbert's] sense, didn't render the exact sense of the original."[30] Joyce comes across as inexhaustibly accessible to discuss (mis) translations, as attested by his correspondence. "I passed on all your corrections with my suggestions to Miss Monnier. Morel . . . has misunderstood here and there but it would be unfair to lay too much stress upon that in a work of such length and difficulty" (*LIII* 182). Gilbert adds: "I consulted Joyce about some dubious passages . . . notes [were] sent month by month to Morel. Larbaud . . . put an immense amount of work on the text."[31] In fact, by the end of 1927 the consultation between Joyce and Gilbert was so frequent that it resulted in numerous notes, including the 161-page document on "Penelope" sent by Gilbert to Larbaud. Gilbert met with Joyce so often that some of his rushed notetaking was perceived as overabundant and sketchy by a frustrated Larbaud (as quoted above). Joyce utterly trusted Larbaud's keen eye for semantic accuracy: "it was absolutely necessary to have V. L.'s final revision, as he is accurate, slow, fastidious and rather timid" (*SL* 335). Just like Joyce, Larbaud searched for errors: "hier encore j'ai trouvé un contre-sens considérable dû à une distraction de Morel et que Stuart n'avait pas aperçu [again yesterday I found a major mistranslation due to a lapse of concentration on Morel's part, a mistake Gilbert had failed to notice]."[32] In the Berg manuscripts, ten pages in Larbaud's handwriting feature subtle denotative questions on "Circe," and Joyce's answers in Gilbert's hand, after consultation with Joyce. Here is an example: "'disorderly houses.' I propose to translate 'maisons de tolérance' [instead of Morel's] 'infâmes turnes.' Am I right? A[nswer]: Yes."

In the typescript itself,[33] most episodes also carry several "Ask Joyce" annotations in the margins. These questions to the author, the very last ones, conclude years of exchange over textual cruces. Here are some examples of denotative precision: "side-value" becomes "ristourne";[34] "tarbarrels, and not singly but in their thousands," becomes "une affaire de barils de goudron, pas d'un mais de mille";[35] and so on.[36]

Joyce's availability to clarify meaning supports Dolet's first translation principle: "En premier lieu, il fault que le traducteur entende parfaictement le sens, & matiere de l'autheur, qu'il traduict [First of all, the translator has to grasp perfectly well the meaning, and the subject matter, of the author he is translating]" (Dolet 11). By remaining available, Joyce contributed to the clarification of meaning. And he trusted his translators' understanding of the subject matter because they were literary translators and writers themselves.

Joyce wanted the translated text to be close to the original's denotation and to its various connotations. He was consulted on the full spectrum of linguistic variation: diachronic, diastratic, aspectual, idiolectal, and so forth. The French text was to be faithful to the original on all strata of language and style. A few examples will show the tight connotative control orchestrated by Joyce, particularly with the help of Larbaud's questions. Let's look at one case of aspectual variation. When Larbaud asked Joyce, "I propose to insert *deux fois*. Am I right?," Joyce provided an aspectually correct translation: "twi*c*st: *par* deux fois."[37] Joyce was right because the lexical aspect of *deux fois* is only iterative, while the English "twict" has a double aspect, iterative and augmentative. "Twict" emphasizes the fact that the action repeated twice was clearly intentional, rather than occasional or simply quantitative. The French preposition *par* in front of *deux fois* translates this emphasis perfectly.

Now, idiolectal variation gives a different voice to each character. Joyce did not want variation simplified, reduced to a "coarseness" (*SL* 335). Exchanges between Joyce, Larbaud, and Gilbert aimed at this type of character variation: "je tâche de rendre le *ton*. Stuart Gilbert le demande, l'a fait observer plusieurs fois. Il ne s'agit pas de semer un peu partout des mots argotiques ou vulgaires, des grossièretés et des cochonneries. Non: chaque personnage a son ton, ses tics, ses exclamations propres (ou sales, mais pas toujours),—et c'est cela qu'il faut *traduire* [I try hard to render the *tone*. Stuart Gilbert is asking for that, and several times has reminded me about it. The point is not to pepper the text with slang, coarse or dirty words. No: each character has a specific tone, verbal tics, a proper (or dirty, but not always) exclamatory style. And *that* is to be translated]."[38] Joyce was aware of options between source- versus target-oriented translation, and his advice to translators proves it. We have seen how he insisted on accuracy (source-oriented translation). For balance, he sometimes favored a target-oriented practice, aiming at a very fluent, reader-friendly French text. This was first possible because Joyce was part of the team, and a bilingual member too, perfectly knowledgeable in the target language (French) and the target culture (French society), since he lived in Paris, his "elected Ithaca" (Rabaté 49). Subsequently, his revision of the text was "désirable [desirable]" (Monnier, *Les dernières gazettes* 19). The target-oriented approach was also possible because of the linguistic level of his French team members, their outstanding vocabulary and grammar. Morel had an "amazing vocabulary."[39] Larbaud was a refined idiomatic speaker, an outstanding stylist, an experienced translator, and an innovative writer with a reputation for avant-garde work since his 1913 version of *Barnabooth*.[40]

Gallicizing the translation was part of the approach. It included, for example, translating proper names: Father Coffey became le père Serqueux; Nosey Flynn became Blair Flynn, and so forth, an exercise greatly enjoyed by Larbaud and Joyce, as attested in their correspondence. After all, this was a time when opera was sung in translation, in the language of the country hosting the performance. An avid operagoer, Joyce subscribed to this tradition and applied it to translation.

The above documents and quotes show that Joyce was steadily involved with the first French *Ulysse*. But more than involved, he was committed to it.

Joyce's Aesthetic Commitment: Translating Innovation

Actually, Joyce reached beyond the traditional distinction between tar-
get- versus source-oriented strategies by making the translators focus on
the innovative scope of the novel. The question of style was paramount for
him: this is where art dwells, when style stops being decoration to become
meaning. He paid the utmost attention to his contemporaries' styles. He
admired particularly Larbaud's, Fargue's, and Gide's styles. Elsewhere, he
commented on Giraudoux, a boring "rhetorician" (Parandovski 156).

Now, a first translation in any foreign language of an avant-garde novel
raises the question of its "reception" by foreign readers.[41] Would the translated *Ulysse* be as groundbreaking as the original novel, where nothing is
predictable? Style became paramount in the translation, too. That meant
focusing not exclusively on the structure of the text but also on its texture,
with all its channels for refined nuance and innovation. As we have seen,
Joyce gave his team plenty of specific instructions concerning connotation.
The same focus on style shaped the German translation: among the 6,306
changes in the second authorized German translation, 4,463 were stylistic
(Mitchell 202–3).

Aware that most French readers would read his novel only in French,
never to perceive the level of innovation of the original, Joyce intended to
avoid attracting lukewarm reviews. He sadly knew that Julien Green had
dubbed the language of the French *Portrait* "inert" (Savitsky) and did not
want the original *Ulysses* to be underappreciated through a mediocre French
version. A lot was at stake—enough for Joyce to be committed, rather than
just involved. The French *Ulysse* had to sound as new as the original, as
crafted a text, where "pas une fausse note, pas une erreur, pas un remords
n'est discernable [not a single wrong note, error or regret is discernible]"
(Soupault 27). Translating innovation became the mission statement of
Joyce's team, and the author's own commitment. To be groundbreaking, the
French version needed to be close to the original in an essential way: to be as
innovative. We saw earlier how Joyce insisted on accuracy in the translation
of denotation and connotation. Additionally, Gilbert, instructed by Joyce,
gave repeated instructions to Larbaud to avoid clichés (unless intended by
the author) and to focus on innovation.

Tracking down clichés or drab expressions became essential. Larbaud
corrected Morel's unwarranted clichés[42] when he spotted them. And translating Joyce's extreme innovations was a challenge: nothing close in existing

French literature could help the translators. Joycean neologisms and compounded words were among the difficulties. Larbaud had to be willing to
take risks, and he was: "j'*ose* autant que possible: néologismes; mots agglu-
tinés (odeurdemusc) [I *dare* as much as possible: neologisms, portmanteau
words, such as *odeurdemusc*]."[43] Larbaud's practice, encouraged by Joyce, is
in line with Dolet's third translation principle, which warns against "mot
pour mot" (word-for-word) translation, as it is a sign of "pauvreté, & deffault
d'esprit" [intellectual thinness and paucity] (Dolet 13).

Gilbert and Joyce were watching the results, sending regular reminders
to Larbaud: Gilbert proposes to "underline phrases and words whose edges
have been *abraded*[44] in the translation . . . neologisms, inversions, unortho-
dox combinations of words, etc."[45] Just three days later, Larbaud complies:
"Ce qu'il me dit de l'interprétation à superposer à celle de Morel va m'être
très utile. Je vais oser, en fait de néologismes et de déformations, jusqu'à
l'extrême gauche [What he tells me about the interpretation to be added to
Morel's interpretation will be very useful to me. In terms of neologisms and
distortion, I will go to any extreme]."[46]

Author, translators, and revisers converged in their effort: the French
Ulysse had to be stunning, all the more so that the 1920s literary scene was
artistically booming. In Paris, Joyce lived in the midst of drastic change
shaping a new decade: a page in literature was being turned, a new aesthetic
mode was emerging. Dada and surrealism made news. "Modernity" was the
obsession of the time. Larbaud describes how the exuberance of the 1920s
emerged from a postwar French collective feeling: "après quatre années
d'état de siège, de bombardement [after four years of siege, bombardment]"
(Larbaud and Laborde 9). In another instance he depicts Chas Laborde's
twenty-five etchings of Paris, capital of modern art, with its bustling department stores, subway stations, boxing matches, dance halls, horse races, and
so forth.[47] On the aesthetic front, two major styles were to be avoided: traditional naturalism and symbolism. In a decade when style and art were serious matters, and in a capital city where aesthetic quarrels raged, the French
Ulysse had to disconnect itself from passé literary schools.

Naturalism in *Ulysse* simply could not be of the 1900s type. Yet Morel remained influenced by it in his translation. In 1927, Larbaud describes Morel's
touche générale (overall touch) as "rude et grosse [rough and coarse]."[48] Joyce
had opportunities to discuss Morel's tendency with Larbaud, since one year
later he mentions it again to Weaver in similar terms: "like many other people by dint of brooding on it he sees one aspect to the exclusion of another.

In his [Morel's] case it is the coarseness" (*JJ* 616). Joyce was not concerned about Morel's translation sounding impolite, but outdated in tone. Unfortunately, Morel's sometimes out-of-place informality produced errors that had an impact on the nuanced aesthetics of the novel. In one case, Martha's language, in her letter to Bloom, was undereducated as rendered by Morel, with the "spelling of a maid." In another example, from the Berg typescript, Larbaud substitutes "un coup de pied quelque part" with "un coup de pied en traître"; "Il lui promène les doigts sur la figure" with "touche la figure avec les doigts"; "capable de tomber sur elle" with "pourrais me trouver nez à nez avec elle"; and so forth.[49] Joyce's and Larbaud's perception on Morel's "coarseness" is corroborated by the Berg *Ulysse* typescript, with Larbaud obliterating Morel's naturalistic touches in hundreds of places.

Avoiding an old naturalistic manner went hand in hand with observing the full stylistic spectrum of the original. As a singer and pianist, Joyce knew about tone and dynamic range in music. And an author is like the conductor of an orchestra, coordinating the various voices of the instruments. One thing a conductor tries *not* to do is level the dynamics of the different instruments.

Another passé literary style was the symbolist-decadent. In a sweeping movement, writers of the time were breaking away from lingering traces of that kind of symbolism. In a significant discussion on the topic, Larbaud sent to Monnier an article by Léon Delamarche, praising the novelty of Dujardin's *Lauriers*, in spite of some symbolist "stains."[50] To avoid turn-of-the century symbolism, Joyce did not even want to dwell on Homeric parallels in *Ulysses*. He made sure that the explicit Odyssean titles that he himself had given to the episodes in the first published excerpts[51] be removed from the publication.

But this is where the shoe pinches: Morel's tendency for naturalistic touches was not his only tendency. He had a deeper and more annoying preference: he was a symbolist poet, in theme and manner, writing precious, decadent verse. His symbolist taste surfaced in the translation, through a *style artiste* totally passé, a (by now) literary cliché of the worst kind.[52] As a symbolist, he was quite fond, for example, of archaisms. Larbaud systematically remedied this archaizing tendency for example substituting "escalier en caracole" with "escalier en colimaçon." The word *caracole* sounded discordant to him ("me choque").[53]

As a symbolist, Morel was also fond of rare words and precious metaphors. In his own long 1921 poem "Flores" he describes, in suave style, a profusion of exotic flowers from his native Réunion, such as the longanys "à l'essence ambroisée" (with an essence of ambrosia). Really, Robert de Montesquiou is not too far behind, lengthily describing blue hydrangea (also in a book of poems "tout entier consacré aux fleurs") and collecting rare epithets, like the "flot rosoyant de la pièce" (the rosying flow of the room) and the "chevelure blanche, vraiment argentée, presque candie" (Montesquiou 2: 146, 1: 14) (white head of hair, really silver, almost candied).[54] A lingering symbolist, Morel still subscribed to Montesquiou's preciosity, a style Larbaud had to curb. Larbaud examined with Joyce Morel's symbolist touches, just as he did the naturalistic. In one example, Morel's "d'un rien d'urine" (for "a fine tang of scented urine") is described to Joyce as "both *recherché* and facile." His expression "papilles gustatives" (taste buds, or *lingual papillae*) for Joyce's word "palate" is deemed "a little *précieuse*" but acceptable.[55] Similarly, in his fourth translation principle, Dolet condemns the affectation conveyed by "mots peu frequentés" (rarely used words) too far from the vernacular (Dolet 14).

Based on their correspondence, we can say that Larbaud and Joyce discussed Morel's naturalistic and precious styles, and during his very final revision of the manuscript in Italy, Larbaud, by then in contact only with Joyce, kept a tight check on these two aspects of Morel's translation. In the same way Morel's "coarse" naturalistic tendency appears in high relief based on the large number of revisions by Larbaud, scores of examples reveal Morel's symbolist tendency in the Berg typescript.[56] Here are a handful of decadent relics caught by Larbaud: "je suis environné . . . de difficultés, de chausse-trappes" was modernized into "d'obstacles, d'intrigues"; "les barbacanes se meuvent lentement" became more prosaic with "se déplacent sans cesse"; the Homeric "mouette au vol patineur" lowered its flight to "rasant-bas"; "couleur sang-de-boeuf" was toned down to "rouge-vif"; and the pseudo-Mallarméan "lit jaune aux ors assombris" was poetically transformed into "lit boueux et fauve"; and so forth.[57]

The semantic and stylistic checks and balances practiced by Larbaud and Joyce, in their effort toward a French rendition inspired by the uniqueness of the original, rests on Dolet's fifth translation principle: the observance of the "nombres oratoires" (the need to create linguistic harmony between meaning and rhythm) in the target text (Dolet 15). The French *Ulysse* was meant to be satisfying to the mind and a delight to the ear.

For Soupault, *Ulysses* was a new beginning in literature ("*Ulysses* marque, il faut le répéter, un commencement dans la littérature" [Soupault 45]). For Joyce, the French translation had to be just as new. Beyond involvement, he was aesthetically committed to supervising closely the French text, steering it away from traditional naturalism or symbolism, while carrying naturalism and symbolism into a new age.

Conclusion

To avoid dissatisfaction with the French translation, Joyce remained involved and committed during the seven years it took to complete the 1929 French translation of *Ulysses*. He maintained contact with translators and revisers to clarify meaning, denotation, and connotation. He responded with unabated energy to their questions, supplying primary documentation, reading manuscripts and typescripts, suggesting solutions, resolving disagreements, sending countless letters and dinner invitations, spending hours with translators, supervising them, year after year. Now that's involvement.

Yet, beyond such involvement, he was committed. In person or through Gilbert as his spokesperson and Larbaud as his right hand, he cast a wide net of control to ensure a satisfactory aesthetic rendition of his novel. He may not have revised every single word of the French text, but he carefully read the manuscript in progress until publication, advising translators on thousands of nuanced queries, each time giving the translation the orientation he wished, one significant touch at a time. In the inscription on the copy of *Ulysse* sent to Monnier, a pun summarizes his commitment in truly Joycean fashion: "A Adrienne Monnier cette traduction immaculée—blanche comme les nuits qu'elle lui a fait passer [To Adrienne Monnier, this immaculate translation, untouched, as were untouched by sleep the nights it gave her]."[58] It was an "immaculate" translation indeed, emerging from sleepless nights for translators, author, and publisher alike, a beautiful achievement: a French text freed from dated literary modes, immaculate, as in brand new, a new beginning, just like the original.

Tracking down Joyce's vigilant collaboration in the first French translation of *Ulysses* led us to an unexpected aspect of the author's activity: his commitment to the French text, overshadowed by his concurrent writing of *Finnegans Wake*. With a method and a vision congruent with the Renaissance translation principles of Estienne Dolet, Joyce spent precious time with the French translation, and it was time well spent: he met his goal. The French translation created such an impact, attracting both fascinated and adverse reactions, that it became, to quote Jacques Aubert, "a moment and a monument" in French literature (Joyce, *Ulysse*, 1995 ed., 1029). No wonder it took seventy-five years to have a second French translation: the first French *Ulysse* had received its aura from Joyce's hand.

Notes

1. *Ulysse* (Gallimard, 1929). Credits were regularly discussed by participants to reflect the actual participation of each translator or reviser. In his October 6, 1927, letter to Monnier, Larbaud writes: "Il me semble que l'ordre alphabétique s'impose: Gilbert, moi et Morel" ("It seems to me that the alphabetical order is obviously the best: Gilbert, me and Morel" (Larbaud, *Lettres à Monnier* 318). After much debating, the final formula was adopted in 1928 by Joyce and Monnier. See Larbaud's April 21 and May 9, 1928, letters to Monnier (336 and note 1; 337).

2. The *Ulysse* typescript revised by Morel, Larbaud, Monnier, and Joyce is housed at the New York Public Library, Berg Collection. The *Ulysse* typescript revised mainly by Stuart Gilbert is housed at the Henry Ransom Humanities Research Center at the University of Texas at Austin. See Bibliography for list of quoted documents. The complete list mentioning Joyce's participation is considerably longer than the one cited here.

3. Estienne Dolet (1509–46) was a French Renaissance Hellenist, poet, translation theorist, and publisher who translated into French many Latin and Greek works, in particular Cicero's, Plato's, and the Bible, and published Rabelais. Dolet was condemned for blasphemy, based on his translation of Plato's *Antiochus,* and burned at the stake in Paris.

4. This is the first essay on translation published in French.

5. Larbaud to Monnier, December 6, 1921, in Larbaud, *Lettres à Monnier* 73.

6. Letter in French, Vichy MS JJ64.

7. Vichy MS JJ45.

8. Vichy MS JJ46.

9. Vichy MS JJ53.

10. Vichy MS JJ48.

11. This was translated by Morel and appeared in *900: Cahiers d'Italie et d'Europe* (Florence-Rome) 1 (Autumn 1926): 107–31.

12. Larbaud to Monnier, April 21, 1928, in Larbaud, *Lettres à Monnier* 335.

13. Housed at the New York Public Library.

14. As reported by A. Hoffmeister about the Czech translation (Hoffmeister 120).

15. Larbaud to Marcel Ray, March 3, 1921, in Larbaud and Ray 11.

16. "Translating *Finnegans Wake* with Joyce and Léon" (Soupault 73–74, 78).

17. Monnier refers to the *Septante,* the oldest Greek translation of the Hebrew bible. Legend has it that, from 250 to 130 b.c., seventy translators, working independently, produced seventy identical translations of the original text.

18. Larbaud to Monnier, October 24, 1927, in Larbaud, *Lettres à Monnier* 325.

19. Larbaud to Monnier, November 29, 1927, in Larbaud, *Lettres à Monnier* 329 and 329 n. 1.

20. Larbaud to Joyce, October 2, 1928, Berg MS letter.

21. Ellmann's footnote refers to the postcard received by Denis Breen in *Ulysses*. However, Ellmann does not explain the meaning of the "U.p.: up" joke either in *Ulysses* or in this letter. See next note for meaning of joke.

22. As elucidated by Robert T. Byrnes in Byrnes 175–76; also quoted in Gifford and Seidman 163.

23. In other words, Breen is "cracked" or "nuts" in English slang, a meaning reflected in the first part of the French translation *Fou.*

24. Larbaud to Monnier, October 4, 1927, in Larbaud, *Lettres à Monnier* 314–15. The two words here contested by Larbaud did not appear in the *NRF* version revised by Larbaud.

25. Larbaud to Monnier, October 4, 1927, in Larbaud, *Lettres à Monnier* 314.

26. Larbaud to Joyce, October 2, 1928, in Larbaud, *Lettres à Monnier* 343–44.

27. Berg MS Folder 20.

28. Larbaud to Joyce, October 2, 1928, in Larbaud, *Lettres à Monnier* 344.

29. Berg documents: nineteen pages of text with Morel's MS corrections, and ten pages of notes by Morel. Berg *Ulysse* typescript: 367–435.

30. Gilbert, cited by Brown 30.

31. Volume of manuscript notes by Gilbert, HRC MS (quoted in Brown 30).

32. "pour 3 ou 4 fautes, il a 100 bonnes interprétations, et de vraies trouvailles [for 3 or 4 mistakes, there are 100 examples of accurate interpretation, and great finds]," Larbaud to Monnier, October 4, 1927 (Larbaud, *Lettres à Monnier* 314).

33. Berg *Ulysse* typescript.

34. Berg *Ulysse* typescript: 1057.

35. Berg *Ulysse* typescript: 1059.

36. All the examples quoted are in Larbaud's hand, since he was the last person to modify the typescript. Other corrections, albeit in Morel's hand or Gilbert's hand, may also have originated from Larbaud.

37. Berg document, ten pages of questions to Joyce by Larbaud, Folder 20. In the answer from Joyce, the letters "cst" in "twicst," as well as "par" in "par deux fois," are underlined in the MS. "Twict," pronounced [twaist], is a more modern spelling than "twicst"; and "twiceth" is archaic. Today, "twict" is only a regional word, still commonly heard in U.S. southern states (e.g., the Carolinas). In *Ulysses* it is used in "Circe" by Mary Driscoll: "And he interfered twict with my clothing" (*U* 15.376, lines 888–89).

38. Larbaud to Monnier, October 1, 1927, in Larbaud, *Lettres à Monnier* 312.

39. HRC note by Gilbert (quoted in Brown 30).

40. Larbaud's 1913 *A. O. Barnabooth, ses œuvres complètes* altered the boundary between genres and became a model of modernity for his generation.

41. For an account of the reception of *Ulysses* in France, see Slote 362–68.

42. In everyday life, Morel used the conventional language of the times, as in this letter to Larbaud: "A la réelle admiration que vous m'inspirez se joint un sentiment d'intime reconnaissance pour le précieux encouragement que vous voulez bien formuler" (Morel to Larbaud, January 22, 1920, Vichy MS).

43. Larbaud to Monnier, October 1, 1927, in Larbaud, *Lettres à Monnier* 312.

44. Underlined by author of letter.

45. Gilbert to Larbaud, August 5, 1927, Berg MS letter.

46. Larbaud to Monnier, August 8, 1927, in Larbaud, *Lettres à Monnier* 309. *Gauche* in French means "left" as well as "gauche" or "awkward." Larbaud is expressing his intention of transforming the French language to the limit of awkwardess, if need be, to accommodate Joyce's innovative English.

47. Respectively referring to etchings nos. 11, 10, 17, 18, and 13 in Larbaud and Laborde.

48. Larbaud to Monnier, October 6, 1927, in Larbaud, *Lettres à Monnier* 317.

49. The Berg *Ulysse* typescript, episodes 2:58, 5:124, and 5:124–25.

50. Larbaud to Monnier, August 13, 1923. Article by Léon Delamarche, *L'Éclair,* 13 Août 1923 (Larbaud, *Lettres à Monnier* 135–36 and n. 3).

51. Such as "Protée," which appeared in *Nouvelle Revue Française* on August 1, 1927, pp. 204–26.

52. Patrick O'Neill writes: "Morel's French Bloom, in short, has produced a by no means unaccomplished piece of writing," "he toys confidently in rococo fashion with . . . romantic conceits . . . 'You are mine. The world is mine.' 'Depuis que tu es mienne, ô mon nectar, ma lyre, / Y a-t-il un empire égal à mon empire?'" (118). O'Neill identifies this style as romantic, not suspecting that Morel was actually indulging in his favorite style of writing, the decadent (bearing in mind that the French word *décadent* and English word *decadent* are not exact synonyms).

53. Larbaud to Monnier, May 10, 1924, in Larbaud, *Lettres à Monnier* 159. *Escalier en colimaçon* is the compound noun that translates "spiral staircase." It means literally "stair shaped like a snail." For "snail," Morel used the archaic (and regional) *caracole* instead of *colimaçon*.

54. French "candi blanc" designates white candy sugar used in the coating of candied fruit.

55. Larbaud to Joyce, June 14, 1928 (*JJ* 614).

56. The Berg *Ulysse* typescript, episodes 2:57; 3:74; 3:77; 10:378; 17:1110.

57. Here again, I relied only on revisions in Larbaud's handwriting, since they were the last ones added to the typescript, and because revisions in Morel's, Gilbert's, or Monnier's hand may have been suggested by any of the translators, particularly Larbaud.

58. *Ulysse,* "Envoi" manuscript by Joyce, July 4, 1929. Bibliothèque littéraire Jacques Doucet, Paris.

Bibliography

Primary Sources, Manuscripts, and Typescripts

Correspondence (published and unpublished):

Larbaud, Valery: 100 letters and postcards (Vichy); others (Doucet, BNF).

Larbaud's correspondence with Gide, Jean-Aubry, Marcel Ray, Monnier, Beach.

Letters by Joyce, Morel, Gallimard, Monnier, Beach, Gide, Fargue.

The Berg *Ulysse* typescript, with manuscript corrections by Morel, Larbaud, Gilbert, Monnier, 1290 pages, 20 folders; 14 pages of questions to Joyce (4 from Morel, 10 from Larbaud), with answers by Joyce or after consultation with him; 19 pages of revisions by Morel, letters to and from Monnier. Larbaud's, Morel's, Gilbert's and Monnier's handwritings appear on the typescript. We need to remember that Morel's changes may have been dictated by Larbaud or Joyce, but Larbaud's corrections are only his, as he was the last person to revise the typescript.

The Austin *Ulysse* typescript, with corrections mainly by Stuart Gilbert; other documents, e.g., the 161-page commentary by Stuart Gilbert, established from conversations with Joyce.

Early Translations of Ulysses

"Calipso" excerpt, *900: Cahiers d'Italie et d'Europe* (Florence-Rome), I (Autumn 1926): 107–31. Translated by Morel.

"Protée" excerpt, *Nouvelle Revue Française* 1 Aug. 1927: 204–26.

"Ithaque" and "Penelope" excerpts. See below, Aubert.

Publications

Alary, Jacques. *L'imprimerie au XVIe siècle: Estienne Dolet et ses luttes avec la Sorbonne.* Genève: Slatkine Reprints, 1970.

Aubert, Jacques and Fritz Senn, eds. *James Joyce.* Paris: Editions de L'Herne. 1985, 101–11.

Attridge, Derek, ed. *The Cambridge Companion to James Joyce.* 2nd ed. Cambridge: Cambridge UP, 2004.

Byrnes, Robert. "U.P.: up Proofed." *James Joyce Quarterly* 21.2 (1984): 175–76.

Brown, John, L. "Ulysses into French." *Joyce at Texas, Essays on the James Joyce Materials at the Humanities Research Center.* Ed. Dave Oliphant and Thomas Ziga. Austin: Humanities Research Center, University of Texas at Austin, 1983. 28–59.

Dolet. *La manière de bien traduire d'une langue en aultre.* Lyon: Francoys & Claude Marchant Freres, 1540.

Fargue, Léon-Paul. *Portraits de famille.* Paris: Fata Morgana, 1897.

Gifford, Don, with Robert J. Seidman. *"Ulysses" Annotated.* 2nd ed. Berkeley: U of California P, 1989.

Gilbert, Stuart. *Reflections on James Joyce: Stuart Gilbert's Paris Journals.* Austin: U of Texas P, 1993.

Hoffmeister, Adolf. "James Joyce." Potts 119–36.

Joyce, James. *Ulysse*, in *Œuvres, II*. Sous la direction de Jacques Aubert. Paris: Gallimard, Bibliothèque de la Pléiade, 1995.

———. *Ulysse*. Traduction sous la direction de Jacques Aubert. Paris: Gallimard, 2004.

Larbaud, Valery. "A propos de James Joyce et de *Ulysses*." *Nouvelle Revue Française* 1 Jan. 1925: 8–17.

———. *Barnabooth. Ses œuvres complètes*. Paris: Nouvelle Revue Française, 1913.

———. *Lettres à Adrienne Monnier, 1919–1933*. Paris: IMEC, 1991.

———. *Lettres à André Gide*. Paris: A.A.M. Stols, 1948.

———. *Notes pour servir à ma biographie, An uneventful one*. Éditions Claire Paulhan, Collection "Tiré-à-part." Printed by Presses de l'Imprimerie Plein Chant, Bassac, Charente, 2006.

———. *Œuvres*. Paris: Gallimard, Bibliothèque de la Pléiade, 1958.

———. *Paris de France*. Maastricht: A.A.M. Stols, 1948.

Larbaud, Valery, and G. Jean-Aubry. *Correspondance, 1920–1935*. Paris: Gallimard, 1971.

Larbaud, Valery, and Chas Laborde. *Rues et visages de Paris*. Paris: Édition de la Roseraie, 1926.

Larbaud, Valery, and Marcel Ray. *Correspondance, 1899–1937*. 3 vols. Paris: Gallimard, 1980.

Lernout, Geert, and Wim Van Mierlo, eds. *The Reception of James Joyce in Europe*. Vol. 2, *France, Ireland and Mediterranean Europe*. London: Thoemms Continuum, 2004.

Mitchell, Breon. "A Note on the Status of the Authorized Translation." *James Joyce Quarterly* 4.4 (1967): 202–5.

Mogens, Boisen. "Translating *Ulysses*." *James Joyce Quarterly* 4.4 (1967): 165–70.

Monnier, Adrienne. *Les gazettes 1923–1945*. Paris: Gallimard, L'Imaginaire, 1961.

———. *Les dernières gazettes*. Paris: Mercure de France, 1961.

———. *Rue de l'Odéon*. Paris: Albin Michel, 1989.

Montesquiou, Robert de. *Les pas effacés*. 3 vols. Paris: Editions du Sandre, 2007.

Morel, Auguste. "Flores." *Les Ecrits Nouveaux* Mar. 1921: 42–47.

O'Neill, Patrick. *Polyglot Joyce: Fictions of Translation*. Toronto: U of Toronto P, 2005.

Parandovski, Jan. "Meeting with Joyce." Potts 153–62.

Potts, Willard, ed. *Portraits of the Artist in Exile: Recollections of James Joyce by Europeans*. Dublin: Wolfhound Press, 1979.

Rabaté, Jean-Michel. "Joyce the Parisian." Attridge 49–66.

Savitsky, L. Rev. of *Dedalus. Nouvelle Revue Française* 1 Dec. 1924: 246–49.

Senn, Fritz. *Joyce's Dislocutions: Essays on Reading as Translation*. Baltimore: Johns Hopkins UP, 1984.

Slote, Sam. "Après mot, le déluge! 1. Critical Response to Joyce in France." Lernout and Van Mierlo 362–81.

Soupault, Philippe. *Souvenirs de James Joyce: Traduction d'A. Livie Plurabelle de James Joyce*. Alger: Charlot, 1943.

Topia, André. "Retraduire *Ulysses*: Le troisième texte." *Palimpsestes* 15. Paris: Presses de la Sorbonne Nouvelle, 2004, vol. 1, 129–51, and vol. 2, 65–77.

11

Joyce's Dictionnaire des Idiotismes Reçus

Comparing the 1929 and 2004 Translations of "Eumaeus"

ROBERT BYRNES

It's a paradox well known in translation studies that translations date quickly, every generation or so, while originals only age, and very slowly, often becoming better with their years. André Topia asks why we have this "double standard." If the colloquial language in a translation of *Ulysses* irritates us with its eighty-year-old idioms, why don't the eighty-year-old idioms in the original bother us at all? Why is the original "unique" or "definitive," while successive translations never achieve a perfect "coincidence" with it, "sans jamais évidemment parvenir à la coïncidence idéale" (Topia 45). Why do translations have to be reborn, when originals last virtually forever? Perhaps great works introduce their colloquial idioms into each new generation, giving them life again, just as they keep "to be or not to be" alive, or "Ask not for whom the bell tolls." Perhaps, as Topia suggests, originals are part of a vast web of other great works in the canon, and evolve, in Eliotic manner, along with the literary tradition (Topia 46–47). But translations must be renewed, every thirty years or so, before they become rebarbative with fossilized locutions that aggravate the gentle reader. The original was perfectly contemporary when it first appeared, and the reader wants the translation to feel contemporary too—the original needs a new birth in every generation to retain the semblance of its ancient self.

This is all the more necessary for works with a great deal of monologue or dialogue, with their heavy burdens of ephemeral collocation and idiom. This is the register in which linguistic fashion revolves most rapidly, and where the out-of-date most quickly puts us out of countenance. It's all the more true of an episode that is written entirely in common parlance, like "Eumaeus," and surely no single episode, chapter, section, division, or fascicle in literary history (save the *Wake*) poses so many problems in translation as does this encyclopedia of Dublin cliché, nor is there any episode that must date a *Ulysses* translation more quickly. It's a supreme test of a translator's patience and scholarship, and it should be interesting to scrutinize the latest translation of "Eumaeus" against the first, of Auguste Morel, which, we remember, had Joyce's supervision and imprimatur to recommend it. And of course there's another reason a great piece of literature needs new translation every little while—literary criticism, in this case eighty-odd years of it since *Ulysses* was published. It elucidates artistic design that was invisible to the previous translator, and it cues a new one to look for patterns the earlier one didn't notice. In sum, we should see deeper into the real "Eumaeus" in a new version, and we should read it in our own idiom. As Jacques Aubert explains it in a "*Postface*" to the new translation, the new version should be "plus proche à la fois du texte de James Joyce et de nous" (972), closer both to Joyce's text and to us.

Why is "Eumaeus" so much fun in English, and so difficult to translate? The reason is that the real antagonists are the two completely different registers that collide here (the commonplace, the erudite) as Bloom-the-autodidact tries to impress Stephen the *Übermensch* Bachelor of Arts by pouring what he undoubtedly thinks is "educated" or even "literary" style into Stephen's ear (Bloom has threatened to write a squib for the tabloids titled "My Experiences in a Cabman's Shelter"). As Hugh Kenner long ago pointed out, "Eumaeus" reads as if Bloom were "in possession of the pen" ("*Ulysses*" 130), and as Karen Lawrence pointed out even longer ago, "the style has pretensions to elegance" (166). The first half of the fun is in Bloom's unwaveringly commonplace mind, even as he strives for an elevated discourse; the second is in his failures, his maladroitness as he struggles to produce strings of locution that are ceremonious, or formal, when not just neutral. He regularly falls out of his high style into informality and slang, producing comical effects that Catherine O'Neill calls "incongruities of register" (48). He also produces a number of "Bloomisms," my term for a congeries of malapropisms, botched idioms, blown quotations, grammatical solecisms, and awkward repetitions that make for repeated bathos, entirely confounding the impression he's trying to manage.

To scrutinize the language of this coruscating episode, and to provide a reference tool for translators, I've identified 2,923 clichés in "Eumaeus," and created a database with separate records for each of them. The database describes them, in searchable fields, according to their lexical type and subtype, transparency/opacity, style level, syntactic type, domain, and language. For the lexical types (e.g., complex units, collocations, adverbial units) and subtypes (e.g., verb nucleus idioms, binomials, similes), I've adapted phraseological typologies from linguists Rosemarie Gläser, Sylviane Granger, and Magali Paquot. In effect, the database analyzes and characterizes the episode's phraseological texture.

I went on to add parallel fields to every record to show the French translations of each Eumaean cliché, and then added more fields to analyze the translations themselves. The fields concerned with translation identify identical clichés, analogous clichés, and so forth (see table 11.1), and level of style. To compare the two French translations—Morel/Larbaud of 1929 and Bataillard/Aubert of 2004—I've entered all clichés of the first 10 percent of each, displayed directly underneath the English originals. With the parallel display, we see how many of Joyce's clichés the French versions translate and how much of Bloom's maladroit art they carry over. We'll see that the translations are dramatically different along some indices. Of course, there are a great many reasons to prefer one translation over another, and a few quantitative comparisons derived from a database are more in the nature of samplings than conclusive evidence for one or another preference. But they highlight some of the differences in *texture* between the two translations, and explain them as much as quantitative comparisons are able.

What must a translator do to succeed with this forbiddingly difficult episode? First, he or she must identify all clichés. The difficulty is that most of the clichés in "Eumaeus" aren't traditional opaque idioms like "cooked his goose" or "make ducks and drakes of," which appear in dictionaries. In fact, 40 percent are commonplace collocations like "highly advisable," "miraculous escape," and "blissfully unconscious," and another 25 percent are harmless-looking but clichéd adverbial phrases like "at all events," "once in a while," and "in the shape of," not all of which are lexicalized. Many of both kinds might look like ordinary language to a translator, whose first language usually wouldn't be English, and might not provoke him or her to find a similar cliché. How do the French translations compare? Table 11.1 shows some gross quantifications for the first 10 percent of the episode.

Both translations are impressive in identifying most clichés. Indeed, both have added clichés, as if to compensate for the ones they've missed. And both are resourceful in finding "analogous" or "work-around" clichés for

Table 11.1

	Morel	Bataillard
Identical clichés	50	59
Analogous clichés	114	115
Workaround clichés	50	51
Workaround (no cliché)	18	17
Word for word (no cliché)	5	5
Mistranslations	2	2
Omissions	13	10
Extra clichés	32	33

particularly sticky translation problems. For Joyce's "to swear a hole through a ten gallon pot" (*U* 16.79), for example, Morel offers the analogous "toujours prêts à jurer que le blanc c'est le noir" (540), and Bataillard the work-around "prêts à mentir comme des arracheurs de dents" (764). For Joyce's "foot it" (*U* 16.32–33), Morel supplies the work-around "en prenant le train 11" (539) and Bataillard the analogous "y aller *pedibus*" (762). On these gross quantitative indices, the translations are comparable.

Second, the translation must update colloquialisms that have fallen into desuetude. The first paragraph of "Eumaeus" supplies us with at least a dozen examples of Bataillard's handiwork, ranging from straight-ahead update into contemporary idiom, to more problematic conversions requiring some degree of work-around. "But how to get there was the rub," says Bloom. Morel's "c'était le chiendent" is very informal, unlike Bloom's ceremonious allusion to *Hamlet*, but consistent with his tendency to fall out of register. This expression faded out of use in the 1950s and 1960s, and only older speakers would resort to it now. Bataillard's "était le hic," also informal, is a good update, very contemporary, very frequently heard today. Again, Bloom's very informal or slang "e.d. ed," meaning fagged out, worn out, exhausted, drew from Morel "tous deux étant flapis," a phrase not really a cliché. It records fatigue in "flapi/e," a favorite adjective in the 1920s but long since superseded. Morel in effect substitutes an informal adjective for an informal idiom, and maintains the register. Bataillard's "tous deux étant à plat" is informal as well, but it's a true cliché, like "e.d. ed," and virtually everybody uses it these days. For one last example, in Bloom's "some fellows inside on the spree," we have in fact two pieces of clichéd diction, the slightly ceremonious or at least proper "fellows" and the informal "on the spree." Morel's "gaillards" for "fellows" is informal, and was still common through the 1940s and 1950s, but latterly its sexual connotations have prevailed over its basic valences of energy and robustness, so Bataillard has replaced it with the perfectly apt and equivalently informal "*types.*" Bloom's informal "on the spree" is still current in common parlance ("on *a* spree" in North America), while Morel's "faire la noce" is rarely heard among young people, though sixty-year-olds will employ it, and Bataillard's informal "faire la bombe," very current in the 1950s and 1960s, and already slightly dated, is well within contemporary horizons.

In a couple of examples we see Bataillard updating an idiom even if it costs him an inaccurate style level. Joyce's neutral "which he very badly needed" becomes in Morel "ce dont il avait fameusement besoin." Now "fameusement" is informal, but self-conscious and even campy in its placement here, so it cuts two ways, neither of them neutral, but somehow balancing out. It faded away after the 1950s, though seventy- and eighty-year-olds still use it today. Bataillard's "ce dont il avait gravement besoin" abandons neutrality altogether. He's using the adverb *gravement,* as it is largely used by people in their twenties today, to mean "extremely" in the informal register. (In neutral register, of course, it still means "solemnly," "seriously," "gravely.") Bataillard has introduced the vivid informality of the very young here, and the expression will likely date quickly in its turn, but at the moment it's entirely current. To borrow an example from the second paragraph, Joyce's "it is said," in "From Rourke's, the baker's, it is said," is ceremonious. Morel's *pardi,* meaning "of course" or "needless to say," is ceremonious as well. It's used today only by older people or as a self-conscious way of making a neutral statement suddenly ceremonial. Bataillard's "tout le monde le dit" is only neutral stylistically, but very common today, with Bataillard again plumping for an apposite contemporary idiom even if it costs him the register.

We need not multiply examples here unduly. Bataillard has renewed "Eumaeus" at the very heart of its franchise, with the contemporary idioms that a fluent phrase-monger would have on the tip of his tongue (let us say) and that would keep today's reader at a gallop from one cliché to the next, rather than pausing in irritation over the demoded, the precious, the passé, the outworn, or the unrecognizable.

Third, we can ask how the translators have done in handling some of the trickier problems I've lumped together under the category of "Bloomisms," and which eighty-two years of criticism have made more visible. We'll look at just a few kinds of Bloomism, and we'll notice that in this regard the Bataillard translation is more alert. Morel seems unaware of many of the difficulties, and translates *over* them, as one might say, rather than *through* them, as does Bataillard. Let's take one of Joyce's favorite grammatical solecisms, the use of "literally" as an intensifier when the meaning is clearly figurative rather than literal. (Joyce used it first in "The Dead," where the narrator, speaking in Lily's idiom, as Hugh Kenner has explained, says "Lily, the caretaker's daughter, was literally run off her feet" [Kenner, *Voices* 15].) Bloom makes this mistake several times in "Eumaeus," and Bataillard catches him every time, Morel noticing the problem only once. "A thrill went through the packed court, literally electrifying everybody" (*U* 16.1374), says Joyce. While Morel *corrects* Bloom, giving us "qui firent passer dans la salle bondée un long frémissement semblable à un courant électrique" (576), Bataillard translates the mistake as clearly as Bloom has made it, with "créant a frisson qui parcourut la cour bondée littéralement les électrisant" (808), preserving the fun. Again Bloom describes his last fourpence as "literally the last of the Mohicans" (*U* 16.1697–98), when they are figuratively so, and again Morel shies away from the solecism, amending to "exactement les derniers de ses Mohicans" (585). Bataillard's "littéralement les deniers du Mohican" (818) captures all of Joyce's fun, and adds some more of his own!

We see pretty much the same reflex in Morel to *correct* Bloom's malapropisms when he notices them. Bloom twice says "tender Achilles" when he means "Achilles tendon," as in "the most vulnerable point too of tender Achilles" (*U* 16.1640), and "in classical idiom, his tender Achilles" (16.1716). Perhaps Morel felt the mistake would be attributed to him rather than Bloom, if he translated it. Perhaps he didn't notice it at all. In any case, his "le point le plus vulnérable de ce tendon d'Achille" (584) and "en langage classique, son tendon Achille" (586) again *correct* Bloom (and Joyce) and flatten the fun. Bataillard's "le point hautement vulnérable aussi du tendre Achille" (816) and "pour parler comme les classiques, son tendre Achille" (819) sound as ridiculous in French as in English, and bravely square off against the insensitive reader.

It's harder to explain Morel's response to another of Bloom's malapropisms, "wrapped in the arms of Murphy" (*U* 16.1727). He clearly understands it's a malapropism for the clichéd "wrapped in the arms of Morpheus," and therefore part of Joyce's comedy, but he corrects it anyway, to the uninteresting "reposait encore entre les bras de Morphée" (586). Morel has given us a cliché. Joyce gives us a cliché and a malapropism, two for the price of one, as does Bataillard, with "reposait toujours de fait dans les bras de Murphy" (819). Indeed, Joyce goes to a great deal of trouble with some of his confections, and Morel's resistance to them is at times quite inexplicable, especially as they would be just as amusing in French. It's impossible to say "to sound the lie of the land" (*U* 16.1351) in English, as Bloom does, because only water can be sounded (with a "sounding line") to discover its depth. The cliché Bloom botches here is "to see the lay of the land." Morel tries to improve Bloom's usage again, giving us "était d'abord de tâter le terrain" (576), while Bataillard's "aurait consisté à sonder le terrain d'abord" (807) lets Bloom make the same mistake again in French.

Bataillard also succeeds better than Morel in emulating the most comical of Bloomisms, the inadvertent "awkward repetitions," first so-called by Fritz Senn (207–43), as in "a great field was *opened up* in *opening up* new routes" (*U* 16.531–32; my italics, here and throughout). A translator doesn't need a particularly fine ear to notice these chiming iterations, but they often require ingenuity to emulate in the target language. Here, Morel simply ignores the effect, producing the bland "un grand champ d'activité pouvait s'ouvrir avec la création de . . . routes" (552). Bataillard has found an ingenious work-around with "d'immenses *perspectives* s'offrait dans la *perspective* d'ouvrir de . . . lignes" (779), which mimes Bloom's maladeptness beautifully in its repetition of "perspective/s." Or take "he had never traveled *extensively* to any great *extent*" (*U* 16.501), which Morel renders flatly as "non pas qu'il eût jamais fait quelques lointains voyages au-delà des mers" (551). Bataillard's "ne signifie pas qu'il ait jamais été un *grand* voyageur sur une *grande* échelle" (778) finds another work-around in *grand(e),* producing the same feeling of awkward redundancy. Bloom's "the best plan *clearly* being *to clear out*" (*U* 16.1647) looks simple enough in English but presents several difficulties for the translator, since "to clear out" has no ready equivalent in French based on "clair" that might hark back to a previous "clairement." Morel actually *abbreviates* the phrase to "la meilleure solution étant de s'en aller" (584), leaving out some of Joyce's meaning and escaping the burden of translation thereby. Bataillard works back from his translation of "to clear out" with "dégager" to another inventive work-around, "le meilleur plan qui se *dégageait* étant de *dégager*" (816), which sounds as informal and inadvertent in French as in English.

Or let's look at a case where Bloom stumbles into an apparent paradox, with "she [Katherine O'Shea] also was Spanish or *half* so, types that wouldn't do things by *halves*" (*U* 16.1408–9). The English is ineluctably startling. "If she is only half Spanish, will she do things by quarters," the reader may wonder, then realize this clumsy conjunction can't actually be parsed. There's nothing to cause pause in Morel's rendering, which goes out of its way to obviate any such effect: "puisqu'elle aussi était Espagnole ou à peu près, des natures qui ne font pas les choses à moitié" (577). Bloom's awkwardness is simply translated away in the French. Compare this with Bataillard's "vu qu'elle aussi était Espagnole ou *à moitié,* des individus qui ne font pas les choses *à moitié*" (809), which flows as naturally in French as in English, to the same unhappy conjunction. My favorite of Bataillard's *trouvailles* is his handling of one of Murphy's ungrammatical repetitions, which seems to come as Murphy himself attempts to imitate Bloom's pseudo high style. In "Why, the sailor answered, *upon* reflection *upon* it" (*U* 16.458), Murphy amalgamates two English possibilities. He might have used the common adverbial locution "upon reflection." A third-person narrator might have said, "Murphy reflected upon it." But it's not correct English usage to conflate them. This kind of awkward repetition inside a usage mistake is at the very heart of "Eumaeus," where the struggle to speak above one's linguistic repertoire leads Bloom and even Murphy to innumerable stylistic improprieties, even at the microscopic level, as here. In Morel's translation, the funny infelicity simply disappears: "Ben, répondit le marin, pour dire le vrai de la chose" (550). Perhaps Morel missed the problem altogether. Perhaps he found it difficult to emulate in French and simply let it go. Bataillard tries harder, and his solution is a work-around via an anacoluthon (change of syntactic structure in mid-sentence, usually caused by an emotion). Let's recap the context. The barkeep had remarked to Murphy that he "must have seen a fair share of the world." Bataillard has Murphy begin his answer with an awkward repetition, "Eh ben, répondit le marin, *à la* réflexion *à la*" (776). He then has Murphy abandon this syntactic structure and begin again with another, "oui, j'ai circumnavigué un brin." As these two structures are run together typographically, they perhaps cause more confusion to the reader than was entirely necessary. Bataillard might well have punctuated them to make the anacoluthon clearly visible: "Eh ben, répondit le marin, à la réflexion à la—oui, j'ai circumnavigué un brin. . . ." In any case, we see here the lengths to which Bataillard is ready to go to reproduce even the tiniest piece of the episode's clumsiness. "Eumaeus" is a great episode because of ten thousand such effects, and Morel lets many of them get away.

I had thought at one point that Morel might simply have been working fast, missing some repetitions, and letting the more difficult ones go by the board. But he seems to be actively trying to *help* Bloom out of his infelicities. Even where Bloom's maladeptness is obvious, and translates easily into French, Morel intervenes to prevent the indecorum. At the very beginning of "Eumaeus" Bloom makes his first, and one of his most ostentatious, repetitions, with "*hit upon* an expedient . . . might *hit upon* some drinkables" (*U* 16.7–10), both appearing in the same sentence, the effect extraordinarily obvious. Bataillard translates this without strain as "*découvrant* un expédient . . . où ils *découvriraient* peut-être quelque chose de buvable" (761), and the awkwardness could easily enough have been emulated several other ways. Morel has in fact gone to a great deal of trouble to refuse the repetition; his "eut une inspiration . . . et qu'on y tomberait sur quelque chose de potable" (538) mischaracterizes Bloom, making him a competent conversationalist rather than a muddler struggling to sustain an urbane prattle in the midst of a thousand difficulties, and failing miserably, sometimes a dozen times a page. It's true that Morel has translated Bloom's informality with "eut une inspiration" and "tomber sur," but he has "fixed" the awkward repetition. Bataillard's "découvrant/découvriraient" is more formal than "hit upon," but its repetition retains the awkwardness.

Two final examples will highlight characteristic differences in these translations. In a certain number of cases, where the English repetitions don't lend themselves easily to translation, Bataillard is ready to *overtranslate* the meaning in order to preserve the effect—while Morel simply *undertranslates* and abandons it. "Very largely a *question* of the money *question*" (*U* 16.1114), says Bloom, and Morel abridges the meaning to "alors que c'était presque toujours la question d'argent" (568). Bataillard's "était très largement une *question* d'argent, *question* qui est le nerf de la guerre" (799) adds a common French cliché, "le nerf de la guerre." This is consistent with the meaning of Bloom's nearby effusion on "quarrels" but well beyond the English in its specificity. This overtranslation isn't, however, any kind of mistake. Joyce wrote the sentence to make Bloom look awkward more than for any other reason, say, for example, the consistency of this platitude with Bloom's nonviolence. Bataillard has followed Joyce where Morel feared to tread, as Bloom might say. He has translated the awkward *effect,* which is crucial, and let the meaning somewhat drift.

Let's take one last example. Bloom's idiom infuses the narrator's throughout the episode, via what Kenner has called the "Uncle Charles principle"

(*Voices* 15–38). The narrator is speaking of Bloom as Bloom would speak of himself when he describes him as "Being a levelheaded individual who could *give points to* not a few *in point of* shrewd observation" (*U* 16.218–20). The repetitions occur so closely together that they can't be missed, and they're so funny that they can't be ignored in an accurate translation. Morel's "qui pouvait rendre des points à plus d'un observateur sagace" (544) simply throws away the effect—perhaps because it's difficult to find a French semantic equivalent. But again Bataillard translates at the very heart of "Eumaeus," placing improprieties ahead of meaning. With "qui aurait pu *rendre des points en bien des points* à maint observateur avisé" (768), Bataillard translates the signifier rather than the signified—he makes sure that two idioms with "points" in them appear side by side in the sentence, inescapable in their clumsiness, even though the second idiom in French doesn't translate the second in English. This is very bold. In general it's a dangerous tendency to translate loosely, but this is a mistranslation with a mission—to preserve the coruscation of stylistic effect in "Eumaeus," and to translate all the fun in the episode; here Bataillard lets the meaning hitch a ride as best it can, probably what Joyce was doing himself.

Finally, what about the larger drama, Bloom's battle to maintain his high style against the entropic tendency of clichés toward informality? Here we see startling differences. In the English *Ulysses* about 20 percent of the clichés are formal or ceremonious, 20 percent are informal, and 60 percent are neutral; the balance is almost perfect between Bloom's high-flown language and his falls into informality, and occasional slang. In Morel the balance is lost, but to no great purpose: 24 percent high style, 13 percent informal or slang, and 63 percent neutral. The number for informality falls significantly, so Bloom's tone doesn't collapse as often—somewhat reducing the comedy. Bataillard's version, however, conveys a strikingly different balance, one that to my ear at least, actually highlights the linguistic drama in "Eumaeus." Fully 37 percent of the Bataillard clichés are ceremonious or formal, while 18 percent are informal, making for a vivid contrast (with 43 percent neutral). Is this more of a contrast than necessary, or true to Joyce? In every translation there's a kind of blurring that dampens literary effects as they cross from the source to the target language. Joyce's linguistic drama is so subtle in English that it's easily lost in translation. One might argue that the Bataillard translation highlights the drama of style levels, and compensates for the blurring effect of translation.

The database has established certain quantitative similarities between the two translations, has helped us inspect Bataillard's craftsmanship as he updated idioms, and has made it easy to assess renderings of several kinds of Bloomism. On this latter index, Bataillard comes out a little ahead. However, the database has many more categories of comparison, all of which would be necessary for a full assessment. And this study only looks at the first 10 percent of each translation. Any definitive comparison would await much more exhaustive investigation. But perhaps we may already allow ourselves a generalization. Over the last eighty-eight years of response to "Eumaeus," and especially with the work of Kenner, Senn, and O'Neill, we've come to realize that "Eumaeus" is one of the most energetic, scintillating, and purely *fun* style exercises in the novel. Joyce was a phraseologist *avant la lettre,* and it's Bloom's apparently inexhaustible repertoire of commonplace phrasemes, clumsily managed, wildly seesawing in register and tone, that makes up all the entertainment. At the end of our inquiries, I expect we'll prefer the translation carrying over the greater part of this pure stylistic fun.

Works Cited

Gläser, Rosemarie. "The Stylistic Potential of Phraseological Units in the Light of Genre Analysis." *Phraseology: Theory, Analysis, and Applications.* Ed. A. P. Cowie. Oxford: Clarendon Press, 1998. 125–44.

Granger, Sylviane, and Magali Paquot. "Disentangling the Phraseological Web." *Phraseology: An Interdisciplinary Perspective.* Ed. Sylviane Granger and Fanny Meunier. Amsterdam: John Benjamins Publishing Company, 1982. 27–49.

Joyce, James. *Ulysse.* Traduction Auguste Morel et al. Paris: Gallimard, 1936.

———. *Ulysse.* Nouvelle traduction sous la direction de Jacques Aubert. Paris: Gallimard, 2004.

Kenner, Hugh. *Joyce's Voices.* Berkeley: U of California P, 1978.

———. *"Ulysses."* London: George Allen and Unwin, 1982.

Lawrence, Karen. *The Odyssey of Style in "Ulysses."* Princeton: Princeton UP, 1981.

O'Neill, Christine. *Too Fine a Point: A Stylistic Analysis of the Eumaeus Episode in James Joyce's "Ulysses."* Trier: WVT Wissenschaftlicher Verlag Trier, 1996.

Senn, Fritz. *Nichts gegen Joyce: Joyce versus Nothing.* Ed. Franz Cavigelli. Zurich: Haffmans Verlag, 1983.

Topia, André. *"Finnegans Wake*: La traduction parasitée." *Palimpsestes,* no. 4, "Retraduire" (Publications de La Sorbonne Nouvelle, Octobre 1990), 45.

Contributors

Philippe Birgy is a professor with the university of Toulouse-Le-Mirail, France, where he teaches twentieth-century literature at the department of English. He is the author of *Une terrible beauté: Les modernistes anglais à l'épreuve de la critique girardienne*, an application of René Girard's anthropological method to the works of Eliot, Joyce, Pound, and Woolf, and the general editor of *Caliban*, a French journal of the humanities published by the Presses Universitaires du Mirail.

Robert Byrnes, Department of Rhetoric, Writing and Communication, teaches the Joyce Seminar at the University of Winnipeg, in Manitoba, Canada, as well as courses in media history, new journalism, and composition. His current research is on comparative literature, translation, phraseology, and computer-assisted textual analysis. He has published articles in the *James Joyce Quarterly*, the *Journal of Teaching Writing*, and *Jadt 2010: Statistical Analysis of Textual Data*.

Maria-Daniella Dick recently gained her Ph.D. from the University of Glasgow, where she is currently teaching. She has previously published on the work of Jacques Derrida and on Italian modernist poetry and is now preparing her thesis, titled *Dante. . . . Joyce. Derrida*, for publication. Another text, *The Derrida Wordbook*, coauthored with Julian Wolfreys, is forthcoming.

Daniel Ferrer is director of research at the Institut des Textes et Manuscrits Modernes in Paris.

Christine Froula, professor of English, comparative literary studies, and gender studies at Northwestern University, has published widely on interdisciplinary modernism, including *Virginia Woolf and the Bloomsbury Avant-Garde, Modernism's Body: Sex, Culture, and Joyce, Style and Error in Pound's Cantos,* and "Proust's China." Current projects include *Reading Joyce's "Ulysses": Poetics and Politics of the Everyday, Modern Time,* and *Acts of Imagination: Ethos, Ethics, Artmaking.*

François Laroque is professor of English literature at the University of Paris Cité Sorbonne. He is the author of *Shakespeare's Festive World* and *Court, Crowd and Playhouse* and is editor of several volumes published by Presses de la Sorbonne Nouvelle, Paris. He has published new editions and translations of Marlowe, Shakespeare, and their contemporaries as in his recent two-volume anthology of non-Shakespearean drama (1490–1642), *Théâtre Élisabéthain,* coedited with Jean-Marie Maguin and Line Cottegnies. But he has always had a particular interest in and personal enthusiasm for the works of James Joyce, on whom he has written several articles.

Jim LeBlanc is director of Library Technical Services at the Cornell University Library, where he has worked since completing his Ph.D. in French literature at Cornell in 1984. His research interests are varied and include metadata and library processing workflows, existential phenomenology, popular music, and Joyce studies. Jim has published several short essays on Joyce's *Dubliners* and on *Finnegans Wake,* and he has participated regularly in conferences and symposia devoted to Joyce's work over the past two decades. In 2005 he chaired the host committee for the North American James Joyce Conference, held at Cornell. In 2011 he served as the academic program coordinator for the 2011 North American James Joyce Conference in San Marino and Pasadena, California.

Jonathan Pollock is professor of English and comparative literature at the University of Perpignan, France. He is the author of *Qu'est-ce que l'humour?, Le moine (de Lewis) d'Antonin Artaud, Le rire du Mômo: Antonin Artaud et la littérature anglo-américaine,* and *Déclinaisons: Le naturalisme poétique de Lucrèce à Lacan.*

Liliane Rodriguez teaches linguistics, comparative stylistics, translation, and the Joyce Seminar at The University of Winnipeg, Canada (Department of Modern Languages and Literatures). Her main research is in lexicometry, dialectology, and bilingualism. She is the author of several books, including *La langue française au Manitoba (Canada): Histoire et évolution lexicométrique*, and of many articles in linguistics and translation studies.

Federico Sabatini is a postdoctoral fellow in comparative and English literature at Turin University. He has published the book *"Im-marginable" Lo spazio di Joyce, Beckett e Genet* (shortlisted for the Carver Prize 2008) and edited and translated *Scrivere pericolosamente*. He has coedited with Teresa Prudente the forthcoming volume *Cinematic Strategies in XXth Century Narratives and Beyond*. He has published articles on Joyce, Beckett, Pound, Woolf, and Giordano Bruno. His interests focus on modernism and intertextuality, philosophy, science, and the interrelation of the arts.

Paul K. Saint-Amour is associate professor of English at the University of Pennsylvania and has been a fellow at the Stanford Humanities Center, the Society for the Humanities at Cornell, and the National Humanities Center. His book *The Copywrights: Intellectual Property and the Literary Imagination* won the MLA prize for a first book. Saint-Amour is the editor of *Modernism & Copyright* and coedits, with Jessica Berman, the Modernist Latitudes series at Columbia University Press. He is currently at work on a book-length project titled *Archive, Bomb, Civilian: Modernism in the Shadow of Total War*.

Sam Slote is associate professor in the School of English at Trinity College Dublin. His most recent book is *Joyce's Nietzschean Ethics*.

André Topia was professor emeritus of English literature at the Sorbonne Nouvelle, Paris. This is his last book.

Tracey Eve Winton is an architect and scholar who holds a Ph.D. in the history and philosophy of architecture from the University of Cambridge, and an M. Arch. in the history and theory of architecture from McGill University. She teaches design, cultural history, and urban history at the University of Waterloo School of Architecture, Canada, and in Italy, where she is director of studies for the Waterloo Rome program in Architecture. She is currently completing a translation of the *Hypnerotomachia Poliphili* (1499) and a book based on her doctoral thesis, titled *A Skeleton Key to Poliphilo's Dream: The Architecture of the Imagination in the "Hypnerotomachia."*

Index

THE FLORIDA JAMES JOYCE SERIES

Edited by Sebastian D. G. Knowles

Wake Rites: The Ancient Irish Rituals of Finnegans Wake, by George Cinclair Gibson (2005)

Ulysses *in Critical Perspective*, edited by Michael Patrick Gillespie and A. Nicholas Fargnoli (2006)

Joyce and the Narrative Structure of Incest, by Jen Shelton (2006)

Joyce, Ireland, Britain, edited by Andrew Gibson and Len Platt (2006)

Joyce in Trieste: An Album of Risky Readings, edited by Sebastian D. G. Knowles, Geert Lernout, and John McCourt (2007)

Joyce's Rare View: The Nature of Things in Finnegans Wake, by Richard Beckman (2007)

Joyce's Misbelief, by Roy Gottfried (2007)

James Joyce's Painful Case, by Cóilín Owens (2008)

Cannibal Joyce, by Thomas Jackson Rice (2008)

Manuscript Genetics, Joyce's Know-How, Beckett's Nohow, by Dirk Van Hulle (2008)

Catholic Nostalgia in Joyce and Company, by Mary Lowe-Evans (2008)

A Guide through Finnegans Wake, by Edmund Lloyd Epstein (2009)

Bloomsday 100: Essays on Ulysses, edited by Morris Beja and Anne Fogarty (2009)

Joyce, Medicine, and Modernity, by Vike Martina Plock (2010; first paperback edition, 2012)

Who's Afraid of James Joyce?, by Karen R. Lawrence (2010; first paperback edition, 2012)

Ulysses *in Focus: Genetic, Textual, and Personal Views*, by Michael Groden (2010; first paperback edition, 2012)

Foundational Essays in James Joyce Studies, edited by Michael Patrick Gillespie (2011)

Empire and Pilgrimage in Conrad and Joyce, by Agata Szczeszak-Brewer (2011)

The Poetry of James Joyce Reconsidered, edited by Marc C. Conner (2012)

The German Joyce, by Robert K. Weninger (2012)

Joyce and Militarism, by Greg Winston (2012)

Renascent Joyce, edited by Daniel Ferrer, Sam Slote, and André Topia (2013; first paperback edition, 2014)

Before Daybreak: "After the Race" and the Origins of Joyce's Art, by Cóilín Owens (2013)

Modernists at Odds: Reconsidering Joyce and Lawrence, edited by Matthew J. Kochis and Heather L. Lusty (2015)

The Ecology of Finnegans Wake, by Alison Lacivita (2015)

James Joyce and the Exilic Imagination, by Michael Patrick Gillespie (2015)

www.ingramcontent.com/pod-product-compliance
Lightning Source LLC
Chambersburg PA
CBHW021403090426
42742CB00009B/983